J G Cruikshank
Dec 25th /89
given by Wartha

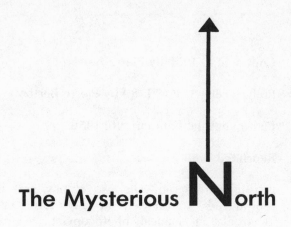

The Mysterious North

by Pierre Berton

M&S

First published February 20, 1956

Reprinted 1989

Canadian Cataloguing in Publication Data—

Berton, Pierre, 1920–
  The mysterious North

Includes index.
ISBN 0-7710-1211-x (bound) ISBN 0-7710-1210-1 (pbk.)

1. Northwest Territories—Description and travel.
2. Yukon Territory—Description and travel.
3. Northwest Territories—History. 4. Yukon
Territory—History. I. Title.

FC4167.B47 1989   917.19′2   C89-094468-7
F1090.5.B47 1989

Printed and bound in Canada by
T. H. Best Printing Company Limited

McClelland & Stewart Inc.
The Canadian Publishers
481 University Avenue
Toronto, Ontario
M5G 2E9

For Janet

MAPS

ACKNOWLEDGMENTS

The maps were drawn by William Parlane of Toronto. The author is grateful for the helpful advice of several northern experts who read the manuscript before publication: Mr. J. W. Anderson, of the Hudson's Bay Company; Dr. Svenn Orvig, of the Arctic Institute of North America; and three members of the Canadian Department of Northern Affairs and Natural Resources, Mr. G. W. Rowley, Mr. R. A. J. Phillips, and Mr. C. J. Marshall. Any mistakes or omissions that remain are, of course, the author's own responsibility.

CONTENTS

Books by Pierre Berton

The Royal Family
The Mysterious North
Klondike
Just Add Water and Stir
Adventures of a Columnist
Fast, Fast, Fast Relief
The Big Sell
The Comfortable Pew
The Cool, Crazy, Committed World of the Sixties
The Smug Minority
The National Dream
The Last Spike
Drifting Home
Hollywood's Canada
My Country
The Dionne Years
The Wild Frontier
The Invasion of Canada
Flames Across the Border
Why We Act Like Canadians
The Promised Land
Vimy
Starting Out
The Arctic Grail

PICTURE BOOKS
The New City (with Henri Rossier)
Remember Yesterday
The Great Railway
The Klondike Quest

ANTHOLOGIES
Great Canadians
Pierre and Janet Berton's Canadian Food Guide
Historic Headlines

FOR YOUNGER READERS
The Golden Trail
The Secret World of Og

FICTION
Masquerade (pseudonym Lisa Kroniuk)

Preface to the 1989 Edition

The Mysterious North was published in 1956, after I had completed the last of five journeys that extended over an eight-year period and took me from the Alaska-Yukon border to the northern tip of Baffin Island. It was my second published book, and it won me my first Governor General's Award.

It was written with an international audience in mind. In those days Canadian authors tended to seek out American publishers because the literary audience in Canada was so small. My prime publisher was Alfred A. Knopf of New York, who sold the sheets to McClelland and Stewart in Toronto. The book was later published in England. It has been out of print for nearly twenty years.

Essentially, this is a travelogue that moves through time as well as space – from the ice age to the immediate post-war era. My interest in the north sprang, of course, from my Yukon background, but I knew very little of the land beyond the Mackenzie Mountains. And so before setting out on these journeys I gave myself a course in the history, geology, and ecology of the Arctic and sub-Arctic. This stood me in good stead when, thirty years later, I began work on *The Arctic Grail*.

The Mysterious North is very much a book of its time. It was written during a yeasty period when we were all dazzled by the great Canadian boom. Journalists and politicians were fond of quoting Wilfrid Laurier's prediction that the twentieth century was ours. In those heady post-war days, with new discoveries being hailed almost weekly, the north was not only mysterious and romantic (my newspaper series on Headless Valley made front pages everywhere) but it was also seen as the undeveloped treasure house of the nation, ripe for exploitation and profit. When, in 1954, *Maclean's* magazine devoted an entire edition to the north, the magazine enjoyed its greatest newsstand sale in twenty years. My lead article in that issue served as the basis for part of this book. Three years later, John Diefenbaker swept into power with his "Vision" of the north. Nobody, including Diefenbaker himself, knew exactly what that meant, but it had a magnetic appeal for those who could not help but feel guilty about their ignorance of the empty realm beyond the frontier.

Guilt is the right word, I think. Nine out of ten Canadians were (and still are) huddled into a narrow two-hundred-mile deep strip hugging the American border. It didn't seem right that ninety per cent of the country

13

should be virtually empty. People thought of the north as they had once thought of the west in the days before the Pacific railway. Somebody should go up there – *do* something: dig, mine, cultivate, build cities, prosper – make use of all that waste space!

Well, the north is still largely empty, though perhaps not quite as mysterious as it was when this book was published. But that cannot be called a waste. Emptiness, after all, is one aspect of Canada that helps make us unique. In the three decades since *The Mysterious North* was published, wilderness has become a precious commodity, space a depleting resource.

In one sense, very little has changed since the fifties. It has taken only a few paragraphs at the end of each of the four major sections to bring the reader up to date on what has happened in the intervening years. But in another sense, everything has changed. Our attitudes have changed. We have begun to care about the northern environment and about the native peoples who are part of that environment. These concerns, which are only touched on in this book, are already having a profound effect on the way the north is governed and exploited.

"Ecology" was not a buzz-word in the fifties. I doubt that many people then had any idea what it meant. I know I didn't. Oddly, I first heard the word during the flight to Pond Inlet described in Part IV. The scientists heading for Bylot Island were planning, among other things, to study the ecology of the natives. The result was a best-selling book, *Spring on an Arctic Island*, by one of that number, Katherine Scherman, whose father had founded the Book-of-the-Month Club.

In those days, very few Canadians – very few northerners, in fact – were concerned about the Arctic environment, perhaps because there was so much of it. It is true that there were deposits of the white man's rubbish fouling small corners of the land from the upper Yukon (Whitehorse's garbage dump) to Coral Harbour. But these were mere pinpoints on a landscape that seemed to roll on forever, untouched and untrammelled. No one was concerned then about such things as oil spills or gas pipelines. I shudder now when I contemplate Thayer Lindsley's abortive plan to back up the Yukon River and flood the Trail of '98, but I did not shudder then. I called it "the north's most imaginative industrial scheme." How could I

14

have written that without a note of censure? Well, that was the way we thought about the north in those days – and that included those of us who were born and raised there.

The most remarkable and encouraging change has been the new attitude toward the native peoples. One can only hope that it has not come too late. More and more the aboriginal peoples are taking control. The government has been dragged kicking and screaming into a series of settlements with the Inuit, Dene, and Métis – settlements not made easier by differences between the separate cultures. But it will take more than a few signatures on a few documents to give these much-abused and exploited people back their pride.

Nonetheless, the change is startling. The young Indian activists I chatted with in Diamond Tooth Gertie's saloon in Dawson City a few years ago bore little resemblance to the sombre natives from whom we purchased moccasins and birchbark baskets in the old days. These eloquent and clear-headed young men knew exactly what they wanted, and in the end they got it. After fifteen years of negotiation, the Council of Yukon Indians (astonishingly, it is now made up entirely of native women) has agreed in principle to a final land claims settlement. The Council didn't exist when I wrote this book; neither did the Inuvialuit Development Corporation, the Nunavut Constitutional Forum, or all the other activist organizations that are giving the north back to the original peoples. It's significant that both the Commissioner of the Yukon and the government leader have Indian wives.

There's no doubt that television has made an impact, for better and for worse. The influence of the medium was brought home to me in the summer of 1972 when I took my family on a raft journey down the Yukon River. There we were, drifting across an empty land, the river coiling throughout the endless carpet of forested hills. The great terraced valley was virtually empty of humankind – we had seen no one for the best part of that day. At last, in the distance, we spotted a curl of blue smoke rising from the river bank. A few minutes later we came upon a group of Indians curing salmon in the age-old way – the wrinkled old women scraping the flesh from the bones, the young men smoking the fish and hanging it on racks in the sunshine, the children gambolling among the bushes. I was explaining to my offspring that we had actually moved backward in time – that this very scene could have been enacted centuries before – when I was interrupted by a young man who came to the water's edge, handed me a pen and paper, and asked me for my autograph. "My mother," he explained, indicating one of the old women working at the bench above, "is a great fan of 'Front Page Challenge.'"

Television has been the activists' tutor. Along with the soap operas and the sports and the shrill evangelism it has provided a primer for quiet revolution. Today the major land claims still outstanding are all in the process of being settled. The Inuvialuits of the Mackenzie Delta and the Beaufort Sea now have title to some fifty thousand square miles of Arctic real estate. The Dene and Métis to the south have agreed in principle to the largest land transfer in Canadian history – more than seventy thousand square miles of hunting and trapping territory. The Inuit of the eastern Arctic are close to a similar settlement. The aboriginal peoples are starting to run their own show: half of the governing NDP caucus in the Yukon is native; only nine of the twenty-four members of the Northwest Territorial Council are white.

Soon, if the natives themselves can come to an agreement, the Territories will be divided into two political divisions: Nunavut, controlled almost entirely by the Inuit of the eastern Arctic, and Denendeh to the west, controlled by Métis, Dene, Inuvialuit, and whites. The names – in two dialects – tell the story. Both mean the same thing: *Our Land*.

Has this development come too late to save the native culture? When I travelled through the north for this book, the Distant Early Warning line was under construction. I described the scene at Frobisher Bay (as it was then called) – the gigantic flying machines, tractors, and fork lifts, the American pilots and Canadian labourers, ". . . Coca-Cola, T-bone steaks, Irish stew, dumplings, grapefruit, pickles, ham and eggs, apple pie, and ketchup, ketchup, ketchup. . . ." This expensive and arguably unnecessary project was designed primarily to allow the United States enough lead time to fight an aerial war – presumably a nuclear one – over our Arctic wastes. It also played havoc with the native culture, as a perceptive new book, *Arctic Twilight*, by Kevin McMahon, makes clear.

The DEW line is already obsolete, but the idea of a Maginot Line of defence against the Soviet Union has not been discarded, even in the age of Gorbachev. Instead of twenty-two radar stations, the new line, known as the North Warning System, will have forty-seven. Designed to detect low-flying cruise-type missiles, they will be strung out along Canada's Arctic coast. The job will take until 1992 and cost a billion and a half dollars. Once again, in this most fragile of environments, where (as I have pointed out in this book) a birch tree can take a century to grow as thick as a finger and cart tracks aren't mossed over even after thirty years, a new and potentially devastating invasion of strange men and strange machines is taking place.

When *The Mysterious North* appeared in the fifties, ''the people of the north were living as close to a primitive existence as could be found on this planet'' (McMahon's words). But with the coming of the DEW line ''this world was instantly and radically transformed by the arrival of the American armed forces and Canadian bureaucracies that blew into the north like a wind of steel.'' Now history is being repeated.

No one who travels to Whitehorse, Yellowknife, or Inuvik can help but notice the effects of alcohol on the people of the north. Some years ago the Yukon government threw up its hands and scrapped all laws about drinking. Since the jails were already overcrowded, why bother to arrest anybody? Let them drink as they please! For a time in the Yukon, before the laws were tightened again, you could drink literally anywhere – even in your car. Walking down one of Dawson's plank sidewalks a few years ago, I was hailed by a group of Indians who proffered a half-empty bottle of vodka. I took one pull; they took several. It was not an uncommon experience.

In the Mackenzie Delta things are worse. Statistics on suicide, alcoholism, drug and sexual abuse among the Inuvialuit far exceed those for the rest of the country. In *The Mysterious North*, I had something to say about the welfare state and its effect on the Inuit. The free chest X-ray, the family allowance, and the old age pension have certainly given the natives a measure of security and increased the survival rate. But these people need more than handouts; they need to be given back their pride. They cannot achieve that under a colonial system.

The good news is that the Canadian north is emerging at last from its colonial status. The bad news is that it has taken so long. No government department can give the native peoples a sense of their own worth. That they must provide for themselves by running their own affairs and controlling their own destinies. It is their north and they know it in all its guises, achingly beautiful at times, fiercely menacing at others – alluring, forbidding, seductive, chilling. It is all of these things and more, but to these adaptable people, whose feeling for the land goes back to the era of the Bering land bridge, never really mysterious.

Part I

THE MYSTERIOUS NORTH

I suppose this book was really begun a quarter of a century ago when I was a boy living in the Yukon and the north was the only land I knew. I was brought up in a small frame cottage in Dawson City, where the walls were a foot thick and filled with sawdust to keep out the cold, where a pot of dog food—rice and caribou meat—bubbled perpetually over a wood fire, and where the water was brought around to the door in icicle-draped buckets at twenty-five cents a pail.

Our home lay nestled against the low benchland that skirts the swampy flats beside the gray Yukon River. Behind us rose the black bulk of the hills, clothed in spruce and birch and poplar. Behind those hills lay other hills, and when you climbed to the top of the farthest hills, there were yet more hills stretching endlessly into the north. If a man wanted to walk in a straight line due north he could cross those hills for four hundred miles until he reached the edge of the Arctic sea, and he would come upon no trace of human life.

I have never quite been able to escape the memory of those lonely hills. In the winter nights, when the roar of the river was hushed by a mantle of ice, when the frost-racked timbers cracked like pistol-shots in the cold, when the ghostly bars of the northern lights shifted across the black sky, we would sometimes hear the chill call of the wolf, drifting down from the wilderness behind us. It is an eerie sound, plaintive, mournful, mysterious. The wolf is like the husky and the malemute: his vocal cords are so constructed that he cannot bark, but only howl across the endless hills. If the north has a theme song, it is this haunting cry, which seems to echo all the loneliness and the wonder of the land at the top of the continent.

When I was a small boy, it used to fascinate and terrify me, perhaps because in all my years in the north I never actually saw a wolf alive. To me he was only a footprint in the snow and a sound in the night, an unseen creature who lurked in the shadow of the nameless hills.

For eleven childhood winters I heard the cry of the wolf, and then I left the country with no intention of returning. But the north has dogged my footsteps and I have never quite been quit of it. Within five years I was back again on the aspen-covered slopes of the Klondike, working with a pick and shovel in a gold camp. I spent three summers at it and then, when war broke out, I left it again, believing that this was the end. It was only the beginning: since those days in the Yukon I have crisscrossed the north from the Alaska border to the tip of Baffin Island, from Churchill on Hudson Bay to Coppermine on the Arctic coast. I have eaten moose steak on the Peace River, buffalo meat in Fort Smith, Arctic grayling in Whitehorse, and reindeerburgers in Aklavik. I have driven the Alaska Highway in a Ford, landed in Headless Valley in a Junkers, crossed Great Slave Lake in a tugboat, and chugged into the heart of Labrador on an ore train.

This book is the narrative of several trips made into various parts of the Canadian north in the days since the war. It is a personal account and does not attempt to be definitive. Indeed, no book on the north smaller than an encyclopedia could be that. The more I see of the country, the less I feel I know about it. There is a saying that after five years in the north every man is an expert; after ten years, a novice. No man can hope or expect to absorb it all in a lifetime, and fifteen generations of explorers, whalers, fur traders, missionaries, scientists, policemen, trappers, prospectors, adventurers, and tourists have failed to solve all its riddles. To me, as to most northerners, the country is still an unknown quantity, as elusive as the wolf, howling just beyond the rim of the hills. Perhaps that is why it holds its fascination.

I began to put some of these thoughts down on paper on

a warm August day in 1954, while sitting on the deck of a stubby little tugboat bobbing down the great water highway of the Mackenzie river system. I had just flown down from Coppermine and Great Bear Lake through Yellowknife and was relaxing on the river before heading out into the Barrens. It occurred to me that this was as good a place as any to begin to write about the north, for the north lay all around me.

Directly behind me lay the Athabasca country: tar sands that won't give up their oil, a two-hundred-foot layer of salt almost too expensive to mine, and three enormous uranium mines. Off to the west rose the crags of the Nahanni, where I had once gone to seek a tropical valley and where six companies were now searching for oil. Beyond these ramparts lay my familiar Yukon River, which in another generation will yield up twice as much hydro power as the St. Lawrence Seaway. Over to the east, perched on the rim of the great Precambrian shield, sat the gold country of Yellowknife, whose rolling ocean of rocks holds unnumbered mines yet undiscovered. Beyond that the tundra, stark, lonely, and treeless, stretched off for five hundred miles to the shores of Hudson Bay. And to the north, ahead of me, the broad, cold river rolled on a thousand miles and more to the Arctic sea.

Here was the heart of the north. Seeing it like this, from the deck of a river boat, unrolling day after day like a green rag rug, you begin to comprehend something of its size and emptiness. The country north of the sixtieth parallel encompasses more than a million and a half square miles, but it holds only a fraction of one per cent of Canada's population. This Mackenzie watershed is the most densely populated part of all. Yet for almost a day, as I scribbled the notes for this book, we had been chugging down-river seeing scarcely a sign of human habitation.

On Great Slave Lake a boat with two men hove briefly

into view and then was swallowed up again, a vanishing speck on the vast leaden sheet of lonely water. These men were part of a crew helping to salvage tractors lost in the storms during the wartime construction of the great Canol oil pipeline.

It was another half day before we saw any other evidence of humankind. Then off in the distance, drifting up from the desert of poplar and scrub spruce, a wisp of cabin smoke curled thinly into the haze—nothing more. It belonged to a trapper living all alone with his dogs. It had been his habit in the old days, so the story went, to write to lonely-hearts clubs for prospective wives. Each fall a middle-aged woman would come up to visit him and, because of the remoteness of the land, would find herself trapped in the cabin for the duration of the long winter.

As a boy I had known the Yukon and therefore thought I knew the north, but the Yukon is only a pocket in the vast frontier land that occupies half of Canada. The Canadian north is so big that you could drop the state of Texas or the British Isles here and never notice either of them. One single island in the Arctic, Ellesmere, is almost as big as England and Scotland combined. The highest mountain on the continent lies north of the sixtieth parallel, and so does the deepest canyon, yet only a comparative handful of men have seen them. Since the mid-1930's a whole new group of islands, previously unknown, has been charted in Foxe Basin, north of Hudson Bay. Their total area is six thousand square miles, and one of them is twice the size of Prince Edward Island, a Canadian province. These new islands are nine hundred miles south of territory that has been explored for fifty years; yet one of them wasn't discovered until 1948. Until very recently no one had known of it, just as no one had known of the great Chubb crater, with its mysterious lake of green, hidden away in the black heartland of Ungava.

Where else in the world could a river one hundred and ninety miles long be lost for almost a century? Yet this is exactly what happened to the Hornaday, with its steep canyons and its sixty-foot waterfall, draining the unexplored country between Great Bear Lake and the Arctic coastline. That resolute little black-robed missionary the Abbé Emile Petitot, whose restless moccasins patrolled this emptiest and most desolate of northern lands, ran across the river in 1868. He mapped most of its course, but never reached its mouth. Later explorers found no trace of it and concluded that it didn't exist. For eighty years it remained a legend. And then just recently it was found to exist after all, just about where the old French priest placed it on his map.

The land through which the Abbé Petitot's will-o'-the-wisp river flows is still one of the great bare spots on the map of northern Canada. It is only in the last decade that aerial photography has begun to fill in some of these blanks. Not long ago I saw, in the Arctic Institute of North America, in Montreal, a remarkable example of what this has meant to the north. Lieutenant Colonel Pat Baird, the bearded explorer who was the Institute's head at the time, showed me two maps of the country north of Chesterfield Inlet, off the northwest coast of Hudson Bay. They were hanging side by side on the wall, one of them drawn in 1943, the other ten years later.

The newer map looked like any other northern chart: the familiar maze of ragged lakes and veinlike rivers, all surveyed by aerial photography. But the 1943 map was almost entirely blank, save for a few wavering dotted lines.

"This area covers thirty thousand square miles," Baird said. "The mapping planes have been over it now, but I don't suppose there's been a single white man into most of it."

All over the north there is land like this, waiting to feel the tread of the white man's moccasins. And yet, as one historian has pointed out, no other comparable area of the earth's surface presents such an extraordinary record of sustained exploration. There is an articulate record that reaches back nearly four hundred years into the mists of the Elizabethan age, and that record is still far from complete.

Like the aurora glowing greenly in the August night, the north continues to elude us. It remains as it was in Leif Ericsson's time, a secret land of mystery, enigma, and legend. Canada has the largest percentage of the world's Arctic and sub-Arctic territories. But we have less scientific information about them than we have of any other northern lands.

Men have plied the northern seas for almost four centuries, yet they still aren't fully charted. Lord Tweedsmuir, the son of a Canadian Governor-General, likes to tell of the time when, as a Hudson's Bay Company employee, he made a trip in the company's famous old supply ship *Nascopie*. They were crossing Hudson Bay when Tweedsmuir went into the chart room with the captain.

"Will you show me where we are?" he asked.

The captain laughed dryly. "Take a look at the chart on the wall. It is the latest Admiralty chart and by that chart we are one hundred and fifty miles inland."

The maps are still a maze of dotted lines and guesswork. On the walls of Wardair Ltd.'s office in Yellowknife is a huge map of the tundra country north to Coppermine. The center of the map is blank and the Wardair pilots have had to fill in their own lakes and rivers in pencil as they remember them from the air.

In June 1954 I flew across the east coast of Baffin Island where the dark sea cliffs are listed between sixteen hundred and twenty-five hundred feet high. But when the altimeter read twenty-five hundred, the cliffs still towered a thousand feet above us.

The north remains a country of unanswered questions, of geological puzzles and scientific mysteries.

What is the purpose of the narwhal's tusk—that single, spiraling spear of ivory that gave us the legend of the unicorn?

Who were the mysterious race of people who came before the Eskimos and left behind nothing more than a handful of strange fluted arrow points?

What causes the lemmings to swarm across the tundra in vast companies, breasting lakes and rivers in an undeviating migration?

Why do fish survive in lakes in northern Labrador where the water is so cold their blood should freeze solid?

Why does the caribou leave the treeline? Where do the Athapascan Indians come from? Is there a mother lode in the Klondike? Why is the north getting warmer? Who was the Mad Trapper of Rat River?

The answers to these northern puzzles are as elusive as the bones of Sir John Franklin, the most famous of all Arctic explorers, who vanished seeking a Northwest Passage. It wasn't until 1948 that we were finally able to answer—in the affirmative—a question that had been asked in the north for three centuries: does Hudson Bay freeze solidly in the center? And we still have only a smattering of knowledge about the one great natural phenomenon common to the entire land: permafrost. The problem of permanently frozen ground affects almost every enterprise contemplated in the north, and yet the very name wasn't coined until 1943. Until a very few years ago the only map of Canada showing the limits of permafrost was published in Russia.

The Arctic Institute, which has already sponsored one

hundred and eighty separate investigations into the north, recently published a twenty-two-page pamphlet listing a few of the thousands of questions about the north which desperately require answers. They range all the way from the death rate of the Arctic char, that wonderful pink-fleshed fish which is a staple of the Arctic coast, to the mysterious presence of a thin layer of blue ice on the snow pack at Mould Bay. The scientific problems presented by the north, says the pamphlet, are "literally innumerable."

So are its legends. The Canadian north has a fabric of mythology all its own. Since Alexander Mackenzie, the great northern explorer, was warned by the Slavey Indians of "monsters of horrid shapes and destructive powers," it has been a land of folklore. Here, where the caribou drift like specters across the tundra, and the aurora sweeps magically across the dark sky, and the sleigh dogs howl in a melancholy choir to the cold moon, it is easy to believe many things. The north is bestrewn with the myths of lost gold mines and tropical valleys and ghostly tribes of devouring Indians. I once went seeking some of these myths myself and I can testify to their durability.

The legends have been with us since the days of that earlier legend, the Northwest Passage, and they are all indigenous to the land. The supernatural creatures who roam the tundra and the forests are all gargantuan, for the north is too immense to harbor fairy folk. The Mahoni, who flit through the Peel River country in the northern Yukon, are enormous hairy giants with red eyes, who eat human flesh and devour entire birch trees at a gulp. The predatory Sasquatches of British Columbia's mountain caves are eight feet tall and covered with black woolly hair from head to foot. There are others, all kin to these: the terrible Brush Man of the Loucheaux in the upper Mackenzie, with his black face and yellow eyes, preying on women and children; the Weetigo of the Barrens, that horrible, naked cannibal, his face black with frostbite, his lips eaten away to expose his fanglike teeth; the eight-foot head-hunting "Mountain Men" of the Nahanni; and those imaginary beings of Great Slave Lake whom the Dogrib Indians simply call "the Enemy" and fear so greatly that they must always build their homes on islands safe from the shoreline where the Enemy roam.

The tales of Lost Gold Mines, which are numberless, have similar overtones of violence, and they all sound curiously alike: the lonely stranger emerges from unknown terrain, bearing a specific amount of gold, then goes back for more, to a violent and puzzling death. There is the mysterious figure of a man named McHenry, coming out of the northern Rockies with a gunnysack full of rich samples and then disappearing into the mountains never to re-emerge. There is a strange recluse from the Klondike, Axel Gold, coming down out of the crags of central British Columbia with a Swift's lard pail full of coarse gold, and then returning to be murdered. There are two indefatigable halfbreed brothers, Willie and Charlie McLeod, breasting the canyons of the Flat and the Nahanni with an Eno's Fruit Salt bottle plugged with nuggets and then going back to mysterious death. All these tales have a certain kinship, but the coincidence of this has not prevented hundreds of men from seeking the phantom of the Lost Mine, with all the optimism of the northern breed.

The hardiest myth of all is the wistful tale of the Tropical Valley. Into this chronicle of a warm and verdant oasis hidden among the impassable snows is distilled all the yearnings of men who have been chilled to the marrow by the northern winter. Long before James Hilton spun his narrative of a Shangri-La behind the cold Tibetan mountains, stories of a tropical valley were rife in the north. In the 1920's and '30's they settled around the Toad River among the mountain hot springs of British Columbia, south of the Yukon border. Even twenty-five years ago this country was so remote that the adventure magazines and Sunday supplements could, for a decade, talk glibly of a valley full of oranges and banana trees with monkeys, parrots, and prehistoric animals. In 1935 Dr. Charles Camsell, the federal Deputy Minister of Mines and one of the great figures of the north, flew into the Valley of the Toad. He reported flatly that the hot springs there had no effect on the climate and that "tropical conditions do not exist at any time." But four years later the British magazine *Wide World* was still referring to this area as a "sub-Arctic Garden of Eden."

When they built the Alaska Highway directly across the Toad River, the legend simply drifted north to the land of the Nahanni in the shadow of the Mackenzie Mountains, a massive and virtually unexplored range that sprawls over seventy-five thousand miles of country. Many men have been into the Nahanni country and tried to disprove the legends surrounding it. I am one of them. But the legends still go on, and they will go on until every square inch of forest, mountain, and tundra has been crossed and re-crossed, mapped, photographed, prospected, settled, farmed, trapped, or mined.

In the meantime the north remains an enormous jigsaw puzzle with a myriad missing pieces. Small wonder, then, that our views of it are conditioned by a tangle of misconceptions. These run all the way from the romantic belief that the north is a frozen world of ice and snow to the naive assumption that it may soon become a booming civilized community of cities and farms.

The greatest misconception, of course, is that "the north" is all of a piece from Alaska to Ungava. You might as well lump Scotland and Serbia together because they both belong in Europe. (It is almost twice as far from Dawson City to Fort Chimo on Ungava Bay as it is from

Edinburgh to Sarajevo.) There is no single *north*, in fact,
but several, each quite distinct in climate, topography,
economic and social structure.

Politically, there are many "norths" in Canada. All the
land north of the sixtieth parallel except northern Quebec
comes under federal government supervision. It consists
of two territories: the Yukon on the west, and the Northwest Territories on the east. The Northwest Territories are
so huge that they are broken into three districts: Mackenzie, the most productive, through which the great river
of the same name flows; Keewatin, which lies between
Mackenzie and Hudson Bay and consists largely of unpopulated tundra and Precambrian rock; and Franklin,
which encompasses most of the islands of the Arctic
Archipelago. These lands cover more than one million and
a half square miles, but to most Canadians the north also
includes the tops of several provinces: British Columbia,
Alberta, Saskatchewan, Manitoba, Ontario, and Quebec,
as well as Labrador, which belongs to the new province of
Newfoundland. The fact is that nobody can say where
"the north" actually starts. To Torontonians, Moosonee,
the gaudy little settlement on James Bay, is part of the
north. But although Moosonee is almost six hundred miles
north of Toronto, it is on almost the same parallel of latitude as Calgary, Alberta, which Edmontonians think of
as the deep south. To an Edmonton citizen, the north
scarcely starts until you reach Great Slave Lake, in the
Territories. Part of the reason for this is that the north does
not follow a parallel of latitude, but dips and rises across
the map with the treeline and the permafrost line and the
lakeline and the edge of the Precambrian shield. It is, at
best, an arbitrary area, distinguished as much by its con-
tradictions as by its uniformities.

The high Arctic, which knows no real summer, bears
little relation to the Yukon Valley of my childhood, where

the temperature can rise to a hundred degrees. The tree-less tundra northwest of Churchill, Manitoba, where century-old trees grow no higher than three inches, has little in common with the Mackenzie farmlands, where a stem of wheat can sprout five feet in a month. The stark, Precambrian rock on which Port Radium is perched is a long way removed from the spongy delta in which Aklavik is mired.

For the north is a land of violent contrasts. It has some of the most breath-taking scenery in the world. There is the unforgettable picture of Baffin Island rearing out of the Arctic mists, with its black cliffs and its blue mountains and its long fiords and its enormous emerald glaciers. There is the sight of Kluane Lake in the Yukon as you first come upon it from the Alaska Highway, a slender finger of the purest absinthe green, lying lazily at the foot of the continent's tallest mountain range, whose peaks plunge in purple slabs straight out of the clouds to the water's edge. There is the breathless spectacle of the Nahanni Valley with its enormous waterfall locked away beyond a series of dizzy, precipitous canyons.

But the north also contains some of the most desolate and monotonous stretches in the world. Dismal Lake, "a sombre sheet of water between threatening hills" north of Great Bear, is truly named. "Anything more unspeakably dismal than the western end I never saw," the traveler George Douglas was moved to remark. Another explorer, Henry Youle Hind, stood on the tableland above the Moisie River in Labrador and wrote that "words fail to describe the appalling desolation." Hesketh Prichard wrote that the Ungava Peninsula was "sheer desolation—abysmal and chaotic."

Indeed, there is so much monotony in the north that its very vastness takes on a sort of grandeur, like the Barren Lands that stretch across the top of the continent for hundreds of miles, their starkness broken only by those geological oddities with the elfin names: the pingoes and the polygons, the drumlins and the eskers.

The Canadian north contains more lakes than all of the rest of the world put together, all the way from little green-eyed Muncho on the Alaska Highway, to Great Bear, the continent's fourth largest, so cold that it often stays frozen until July. But it also encompasses one of the world's great deserts, the Arctic tundra, where the precipitation runs between two and ten inches yearly. The fact that thousands of lakes happen to lie in this desert country makes it all the more confusing.

The north is full of such paradoxes. In fact, it is possible to prove just about any theory by the use of isolated examples and statistics.

Is it a frozen waste? There are plenty of places where Eskimos wear fur-lined parkas the year around, where planes land on skis in June and the temperature never goes higher than fifteen degrees above frost.

Is it a sunny paradise? At Fort Smith, on the Slave River, the thermometer has sometimes reached 103 degrees above zero. This is hotter than has ever been recorded in Canada's southernmost city, Windsor, Ontario. Spring comes to Norman Wells, nudging the Arctic Circle, just as soon as it does to the Gaspé Peninsula in Quebec. The average July temperatures in Dawson City are the same as those on the central prairies. And the radio station at Resolution Island, off the coast of Baffin, has an average temperature in January slightly higher than the average for Winnipeg, eight hundred miles to the south. In fact, slightly colder temperatures have been recorded in the northern prairie provinces than have ever been recorded in Arctic Canada.

The truth, of course, is that the north is neither paradise nor wasteland. It remains a frontier country, with only two

The MYSTERIOUS NORTH

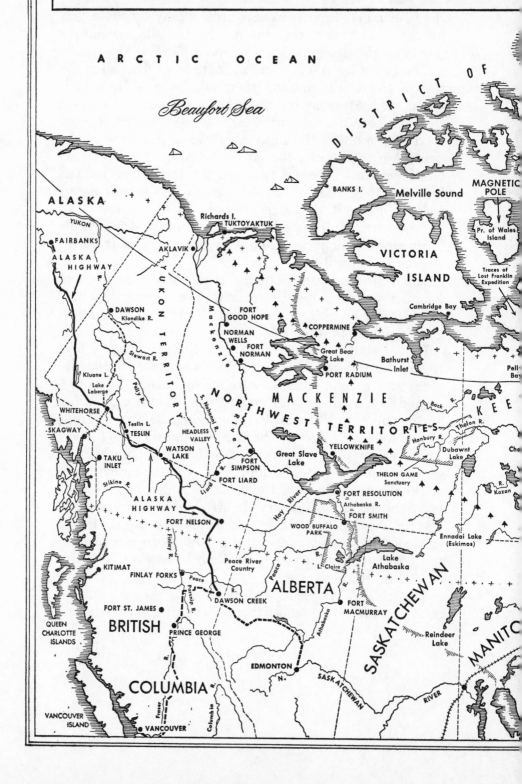

important resources, fur and minerals. (A third great resource, hydroelectric power, has yet to be developed.) It is still desperately remote and costly to reach and exploit, but it is capable of supporting if necessary (but only if necessary) a much larger population than it now enjoys.

It is popular to think of the north as booming. This is true only of certain areas. It is true, obviously, of that gnarled and ancient world of Ungava and Labrador, where the iron ore is already moving to the sea and where more is being found every year. Here, where the black spruce and larches rise like gaunt posts from the sphagnum mosses, lies an enormous waterfall, rarely visited by human beings. Its development will open up some of the bleakest and most productive country in the world. Already a railway has knifed its way across the Labrador tableland and sometime in the next decade perhaps this railway will continue north to the Arctic, to Ungava Bay, where new iron fields await a five-hundred-million-dollar investment.

At the other end of the north, in the southern Yukon, another boom is in the making, another staggering power project, which will flood the trail of '98, reverse the Yukon River in its tracks, and generate five million horsepower for a new smelter town on the Pacific coast.

These imaginative projects will mean mushrooming new communities. The north is used to boom towns. Unhappily, the booms so far have been followed by busts and the frontier is sprinkled with tragic monuments to these burst bubbles in the form of ghost towns, all the way from my home town of Dawson on the Klondike to the blueprint community of Cameron Bay on Great Bear Lake.

There remains one serious flaw in the northern economy: almost every community is built on a single resource. When the bottom falls out of gold, Yellowknife suffers a slump. When the bottom drops out of furs, the Mackenzie

River ports face a depression. John Hornby, a bizarre and mystic little Englishman who roamed the Barrens for a generation, called that stark country "the land of feast and famine." He wanted to write a book with that title, but he starved to death before he began it. The phrase remains an apt one and it could well apply to the north as a whole.

It is this boom-and-bust psychology that has given the north a certain feeling and look of impermanence. Nobody expects to stay very long in the north—or very long in one spot. There is no agriculture to tie people to a single site. Like the caribou and the lemmings and the nomadic Indians, northerners are apt to rove the land like gypsies. The Anglican missionaries, the Hudson's Bay traders, and the Mounted Policemen are switched from post to post like chessmen on a great board. The prospectors follow the big strikes, and the trappers follow the fur. This restless shifting gives the north a cohesion it otherwise would not have. Northerners know each other, even though a thousand miles separate their homes; men living in Whitehorse, Yukon, are bound to have acquaintances in Aklavik, Yellowknife, and Churchill. But it also contributes to the feeling, strong in every northern town, that everything is temporary. Many northern communities (Whitehorse is one example) are little better than shack towns for this reason. The homes are jerry-built and so are the buildings, and often enough they are sprinkled around the countryside without thought or plan as if tossed there by the passing winds.

The fact is that most people go north expecting to stay only a short while. And yet the country is populated by men and women (my parents were among them) who have stayed a lifetime. I can never forget the story of the young Scottish bride who came to Dawson City in the days before the First World War. She brought a trunk of wedding presents with her, but she didn't bother to unpack them, for she didn't expect to stay more than a few months. But the months grew into years, and the years grew into decades. She raised a family and watched it grow up. She learned to live with the north and to love it. The crisp feeling of the snow crust breaking under the moccasin in the winter, the bright tangle of kinnikinnick carpeting the forest floor in the summer, the exploding rumble of the ice breaking in the spring, the pungent odor of caribou rotting along the riverbank in the fall—all these sensations and impressions became a part of her life. Finally the time came for her to leave the north forever, and when she did, it was with that strange mixture of relief and reluctance that every northerner faces when the day of departure comes. She packed her trunks and went her way, but one trunk was already full. For here lay the still unopened wedding presents of thirty years before, the telltale symbols of her indecision about a land which, in all its mystery, both bewitches and repels—like the gossamer fog of winter clothing the dark valleys, or the chill call of the wolf drifting down from the unending hills.

Part II

THE REALM OF MYTH AND MIRAGE

1 | The Myth

There are certain moments in my memories of the north that stand out with peculiar clarity. I can never forget, for instance, a wild minute when I was five years old and my father took me through the black walls of Five Finger Rapids on the Yukon, in a poling boat. Nor can I forget the instant of utter silence that came after an aircraft's motors were stilled and I stood on the frozen Arctic Ocean at the very tip of Baffin Island. And there were the swift, hot moments when an army major, singing at the top of his voice, drove me through the heart of a forest fire on the Alaska Highway, with the spruce trees exploding on every side.

There is another scene that comes back to me, perhaps because of the cold: a bitter day in January 1947—the thermometer nudging forty below, the fangs of the northern Rockies hemming me in—when, in a tiny and ancient monoplane tossed by the eddying wind, I flew through a notch in the continental spine on a curious quest for a haunted valley.

Four of us—a pilot, a mechanic, a newspaper photographer and I—had reached the exact halfway point on a journey that was to take us one thousand miles due north of Vancouver into the region of the Mackenzie Mountains, near the border of the Yukon and Northwest Territories. I shall always remember how bitterly cold it was that day. It was so cold that the pilot had roasted the engine all morning with a plumber's blowtorch, and the mechanic had baked the battery in a trapper's oven, and the photographer's film-pack had gone brittle and snapped in his hands. The sky was quite clear, with that particular chill-blue quality which winter lends. Snows older than history lay on the slopes and the cirques of the mountains, and across this frozen backdrop the shadow of our little plane dipped and darted.

We were crossing some of the most dramatic country on the continent. Behind us, to the west, lay the great Rocky Mountain trench, an enormous natural ditch that cuts its way south from the Yukon to Montana. Ahead of us, on the eastern side of the mountain wall, lay the rich Peace River country, a twelve-thousand-square-mile tract of frontier, wrested from the wilderness by two generations of farmers. Beneath us, boring straight through the cordilleran backbone of the continent, defying all the laws of geography and common sense, was the Peace itself.

It is this scene that I remember so well: the mountains towering above us like immense vertebræ, the long shadows of the late afternoon drifting across the peaks, and the bitter, bone-chilling cold. We had been five days en route to our destination in the Northwest Territories, and we had reached only the halfway point. For four days the cold had held us prisoner in the historic and beautiful country of Simon Fraser and Alexander Mackenzie, the two great explorers who burst through these mountains a century and a half before on their pell-mell journeys to the Pacific. We did not know it then, but we had another six days of travel ahead of us before we would reach the hidden bowl in the mountains which we were seeking.

It is ironical that this journey should have been marked by the most intense cold I have known in the north, for our destination was supposed to be a tropical valley. We were headed for the land of the Nahanni, a name with a haunting lilt to it, and a haunting meaning: "people over there,

42

far away." We were seeking out a legend resurrected by
the newspapers in the doldrum days that followed World
War II—a familiar tale of a lost gold mine, a tribe of head-
hunting Indians, and a valley of palm trees hidden among
the snows. Our destination was the South Nahanni River,
a three-hundred-mile stream that wriggles through gloomy
canyons and sharp limestone crags to join the Liard some
seventy miles north of the British Columbia border. Here,
in an untraveled land, there was supposed to lie, as
one Sunday supplement writer phrased it, "a poisonous
Shangri-La, deep in the heart of the north." Here two halfbreed brothers named McLeod had vanished seeking gold,
a half century before, and thereby founded a myth. When
their headless skeletons were discovered, years later, on
the riverbank, there was talk of Mountain Men haunting
the canyon caves. The newspapers called the area Headless Valley and wrote of hot springs that kept it sheathed
in mists, of tropical foliage, prehistoric animals, strange
tribes, and, inevitably, a White Queen.

This was the northern never-never land toward which
we were winging as the brief winter sun dropped below
the mountains and the cold shadows deepened over the
Peace River. We were there because the legend had tantalized the nation all that winter until finally the *Vancouver
Sun* chartered plane and pilot and assigned me to fly to the
Nahanni.

Before this, all sorts of abortive expeditions had been
preparing to explore the valley, and as a result the press
had awakened to the realization that in the hearts of
thousands of sedentary office-workers there lay a latent
desire for adventure in the lonely corners of the hinterland.
A prospector who put a two-line ad in a Vancouver paper
asking for a partner to help him find the lost gold mine in
the Nahanni received one hundred and fifty-four replies
within a week. A motion-picture cameraman who asked

43

for help in making a movie of Headless Valley got five hundred enthusiastic responses in just three days. A fourteen-year-old boy in Albuquerque announced that the proposed expedition was "the most important thing that has happened in my life." A Scot on Vancouver Island offered to "mortgage everything including my bagpipes if I can go along." A man attempting to paddle a canoe from Victoria, B.C., to New York City wrote from the Peace River that he was ready to scrap the rest of the trip and go to Headless Valley instead.

Romantic stories about the valley made headlines. A prospector named Frank Henderson emerged from the Northwest Territories to announce that his partner had vanished in the Nahanni while searching for gold. The two men had been supposed to meet at the foot of an enormous waterfall, but one hadn't showed up. Henderson's remarks about the country sent small shivers down the spines of newspaper readers. "There is no denying the sinister atmosphere of the whole valley," he said. "The weird, continual wailing of the wind is something I won't soon forget." Another man came down from the Yukon and told of fighting his way through the Nahanni Mountains, down the paths of ice where strange carvings stood like guardian sentinels. The valley within these ramparts, he said, was virtually tropical, "or at least as warm as Vancouver."

Curiously, no newspaper printed a map of Headless Valley or identified it geographically, though the South Nahanni River is easily found and has been visited and explored intermittently by trappers and prospectors for a century. It lies in the heart of the Mackenzie Mountains, and a glance at the map would show it in the southwest corner of the Northwest Territories, just north of British Columbia, just east of the Yukon. But few bothered to search for facts about the Nahanni. It was more enticing to think of the Canadian north as an impassable frontier, empty of civilization—a magic and mysterious land where it would be perfectly plausible to imagine palm trees sprouting from the permafrost, where eight-foot head-hunters roam at will, and lost gold mines lie at the end of every rainbow.

To reach the Nahanni country, far off the scheduled air routes, I had to find a pilot, and a good one, for the journey led through northern British Columbia, where the terrain is rough as a hairbrush. It is beautiful to look upon, but dangerous to fly across—a technicolor land of purple valleys and blue forests, red canyons and bottle-green glaciers, wrinkled with mountains, creased with rivers, and almost empty of humankind.

Over these mountains and through these canyons for about a dozen years a pilot named Russ Baker had been bringing mail, beefsteaks, tinned beans, mining machinery, new brides, policemen, priests, prospectors, beaver pelts, gold samples, and almost anything else you can name, including upright pianos, in and out of the country. It was Baker I sought out, and it was Baker who took me to Headless Valley, along with Art Jones, the *Sun's* photographer.

I remember my first encounter with Baker. He happened to be in Vancouver on one of his rare holidays and I went over to his hotel to sound him out about landing me on the South Nahanni, a feat never before attempted in wintertime. He opened the door and waved me in, a thick thong of a man, tanned almost black by the sun. Spread out on the floor was a map of the Northwest Territories. He had circled a section of it, and I didn't have to look twice to see that it was the Nahanni. Like everybody else, he, too, very badly wanted to visit the legendary valley beyond the horizon's rim.

We made our decisions in a moment.

"I have a Junkers up at Fort St. James," Baker said. "We can catch Canadian Pacific Airlines out of here Saturday morning and be in Prince George in the afternoon. I'll have one of the boys bring the plane down and we'll fly up to the Fort and spend the night at my place. We can head out for the Nahanni the next day."

Fort St. James is almost in the exact center of British Columbia, a province half as big again as Texas. We planned to fly out from here northeast across the Rockies into the Peace River country and then north to the Liard River and the Nahanni.

Baker had ten thousand flying hours to his credit, but my first impression of him in an airplane was of a man unduly nervous. We were aboard the Canadian Pacific Airlines scheduled flight to Prince George and we had run into heavy snow and icing conditions. The beads of sweat stood out on Baker's brow as he stared out of the window into the blizzard, listening to the engines. He appeared to be certain that the plane would crash. It was simply that he himself was not flying the aircraft. Like many automobile-drivers, he made a nervous passenger.

The storm grew so heavy that the plane had to turn back to Vancouver, and thus it was Sunday afternoon before we reached Prince George. There, on the edge of the airstrip when we landed, was an old Junkers monoplane on skis. It was fifteen years old, with a single engine—the old-fashioned kind without the cowling.

"The Germans designed that plane back in 1918," Baker said. "She was a good plane then and she's a good plane now. She's been all over Canada, this one, for she used to belong to the old Canadian Airways.

"You know, in the old days, when I was really broke, all I had was a little red Fox Moth. Her performance was so poor I couldn't even carry a sleeping-bag, snowshoes, or emergency rations if I wanted to get a payload aboard. That didn't matter so much, because I was too poor to buy a sleeping-bag anyway. Hell, I didn't even have a radio or

an engine cover. She'd freeze up on me if I left her standing more than an hour. Then I'd have to borrow a couple
blankets, drape them over the engine, build a fire under
her, and stand inside to thaw us both out. These days it's
easier. I use a plumber's blowtorch."

As he spoke he began to turn over the engine of the
Junkers and soon we were flying over the white, rough
forestland that lies between Prince George and Fort St.
James, seventy-five miles to the northwest. We were now
in the very heart of British Columbia—familiar country to
Baker, who had no instruments to fly by and was his own
navigator and weather forecaster. His weather gauge had
always been a cabin's smoke, his barometer the sky at
dawn. His only landing strips were the choppy lakes or the
snow-choked rivers. He was accustomed to working like a
sailor and sleeping like an Indian, rolled up in his fur robe
in the snow. He was more than a pilot: he was cartog-
rapher, trapper, doctor, prospector, ambulance-driver,
mailman, fire-fighter, freighter, forest ranger, and chief
listener to the troubles of lonely men in log cabins. He had
long since learned to improvise in a country where you
can't always buy aircraft parts. When he blew the exhaust
stacks off a plane, he replaced them with stovepipes. When
he ripped the bottoms from his floats on a shallow river,
he pumped them out, stuffed them with rags, and flew on.

Baker had done just about everything that can be done
with a plane in mountain country. He had conducted a
search for two optimists trying to drive motorcycles from
Fairbanks, Alaska, to Seattle. He had flown Indian children, dying of meningitis, out to hospital. He had landed
on lakes ringed by fire to take out forest crews to safety.
He had flown posses into the hinterland to look for mur-
derers, and prospectors in to look for gold. He brought
news to men who seldom heard any. He was the first to
tell Charlie Frederickson, the lone white trapper in the

MacAuley Creek country, that a war had been going on for a year.

His responsibilities were heavy. When he flew a man in to a mountain lake, and left him standing alone on the shore, his season's grubstake piled about him, Baker knew he must return at the appointed time and bring him out again. For if he forgot a rendezvous, a man would starve to death with no way of escape.

It was Baker's practice to watch out for men who lived by themselves. One fall he dropped a trapper onto a little lake a hundred miles north of Fort St. James. Three months later, flying over the man's cabin, he felt something had gone wrong, for it looked strangely silent. On a hunch, he landed and there, tacked to a birch tree, was a slab of boxwood with the pathetic message: RUSS COME AND GET ME I AM BLIND. He snowshoed inland and brought out the sightless trapper, who had lain alone in darkness and pain for weeks with only a dog for company.

Now we were over Baker's headquarters, the tiny trapping settlement of Fort St. James. It straggled along the beach at the far end of Stuart Lake, a great inland body of water that was once the private ocean of the Hudson's Bay Company. It was hard to believe that this little town of five hundred souls—four hundred of them Indians—was once the fur emporium of the northwest, and that it is older than Vancouver, Victoria, Seattle, or any of the other cities of the Pacific Northwest.

Stuart Lake, a superb body of water ringed by sweeping mountains, has scarcely changed since that hot July day in 1806 when the first white men, Simon Fraser and his aide John Stuart, beached their birchbark canoes on its shores and astonished the Carrier Indians by blowing tobacco smoke through their nostrils—a phenomenon the natives were convinced involved the spirits of dead ancestors. Fraser was a partner in the North West Company, a homely man of towering resolve, lantern jaw, and bullet-head, and he and Stuart were so struck by the beauty of this lake and mountain country that they named it New Caledonia and erected the palisades of Fort St. James on the water's margin. Then Fraser plunged on to the Pacific down the black canyons and out into the broad delta of the great unknown river that now bears his name.

The fur traders and explorers had entered the country from the north and worked their way south. In 1806 Fort St. James and its neighbor, Fort McLeod, sixty miles to the northeast, were the only white settlements north of California. Lewis and Clark had only just crossed the Rockies, and British Columbia, Washington, and Oregon had yet to be carved out of the rolling mat of green that seems, from the air, to smother the country. In 1821, when the two companies merged, this immense empire of fur came under the absolute sway of the Hudson's Bay Company. The hub of this wilderness world was Fort St. James, and the Junkers was now skimming down onto the frozen surface of waters that once carried schooners bringing produce up the lake from portage points and returning with heavy bales of fur.

The beaver pelts and the foxskins are still trickling into Fort St. James. Fur still provides the lifeblood of a town that history has forgotten. The traplines that have radiated from the Fort since Fraser's time are still there. They run out from the bush country almost at the back doorsteps of the cottages, forming a great network that crisscrosses the northern half of the province. Even the six-year-old boys in the school have their own tiny traplines for catching squirrels.

But when we landed at Fort St. James, there was no doubt at all that, like so many other communities across the Canadian north, its fur days were numbered. The timber wolf, the forest fire, and the persistent trapper mining the fur like mineral ore had slowed the Niagara of pelts to a trickle.

As we walked up the trail toward Baker's home, we passed the old blockhouse built by Fraser's men and close by it the newer Hudson's Bay store, painted the familiar red and white. The white residences straggled along one side of the lake shore from the trading post. The shacks of the Indians were on the other side. This separation of native and white man in the north is more than physical. Canadians are apt to look down on Americans for their ostracism of the Negro, but the fact is that few if any Indians are accepted socially in the north. They attend segregated schools and they live in segregated communities. In Dawson City, where I was brought up, they were forbidden by the Mounted Police to attend white dances, and they invariably traveled below decks on the river boats. It is true that they receive many benefits and privileges from the federal government through its Department of Indian Affairs, and it may be argued that the separation is for the natives' own good, but I have never been able to see any great basic difference between our attitude to the brown man and the Dixie attitude to the black.

The Indians at Fort St. James are a primitive, nomadic people, wandering about the country in scattered groups and living just about as they always lived before the white man burst through the Peace Pass into their country. A few contemporary touches have been superimposed upon the early beliefs. In the graveyard at Fort St. James there are radio tubes placed on each mound, for the Indians believe that in this way the spirits of the dead can more easily communicate with those on earth. Static on the radio they believe to be the voices of the spirits talking through the tubes.

The Baker home, a low, white cedar-siding cottage, was perched on the top of a fifty-foot cliff, its enormous win-

dows peeping out from under a wind-blown fir and facing
the thirty-mile expanse of the lake. Thirty years before,
Baker told us, this house had been an old saloon and dance
hall across the road, sitting on foundations of peeled logs.
He had hauled it over to the cliff edge and rebuilt it.

The floor of the living-room had a curiously mottled
appearance and appeared to be of some rare hardwood. I
remarked on it and Baker's wife, Madge, laughed.

"Those are hobnail marks," she said. "They were made
by thousands and thousands of men in heavy boots dancing on the floor. We tried everything to get them out, but
luckily they wouldn't come. Everybody is always im-
pressed."

"There's thirteen layers of building material on those
walls," Baker said, and listed them all: a layer of stone
board, three layers of building paper, a layer of shiplap,
two layers of paper, a layer of two-by-four studs, more
shiplap, two more layers of building paper, a layer of tar
paper, and an outer layer of cedar. This may sound like a
man who wears eight suits of underwear under a coonskin
coat, but in January, when the houses creak and snap all
night with frost expansion, a thirteen-layer wall is good
insurance.

There was nothing primitive about this house. It was
heated by a central stone fireplace, with warm air vents
to every room, and a furnace in the basement. A little
power plant run on gasoline gave electric light. There was
a phone service, a single-party line of fifteen persons, so
that no matter where anybody was in town, he could always answer his own phone. The water was delivered in
buckets at a cost of fifty cents a barrel, but Baker had it
pumped into a pressure tank in the attic so that to all intents and purposes he had his own running-water system,
complete with flush toilet.

The back yard was a wild luxurious rock garden that

stretched for hundreds of miles to nowhere. The animals came almost to the door, grazing or prowling in their own unhurried fashion. One winter, Baker told us, a little skunk arrived, looking just like a tame cat, and scratched on the back door night after night, pleading to be taken in out of the cold. A porcupine slept in the woodshed, and deer browsed a few hundred yards away with the horses. You could hear the coyotes howling to the moon just beyond the trees, and when the skies turned frost-blue with cold, the northern lights danced across the sky.

Once again we got out the map of the north and spread it over the floor. Baker said we'd fly north the following morning to the juncture of the Finlay and Parsnip rivers, which come together to form the great Peace. We'd stay at Finlay Forks overnight, then fly through the Peace Pass in the Rockies to Fort St. John. From there we'd head north, along the Alaska Highway through Fort Nelson, and then move on up to Fort Liard in the Northwest Territories. Then we'd fly on to the mouth of the Nahanni River and into Headless Valley.

I asked him if he'd ever been in the Nahanni country, and he said vaguely that he'd never actually been on the spot but he thought he could find his way around all right.

"Suppose the ice on the river is rotten because of the hot springs?" Art Jones, the photographer, asked.

"I've got two empty oil drums and a heavy-duty jack tucked into the old Junkers," Baker said. "If we go through the ice, I think we can jack her up okay. One thing I want to pick up at Fort St. John, though, is a good stove. If we were stranded in there somewhere, we could set up the stove inside the plane, chop a hole through the roof for a smokestack, and we'd all be snug as bugs in a rug. Let's go to bed. We'll need an early start tomorrow."

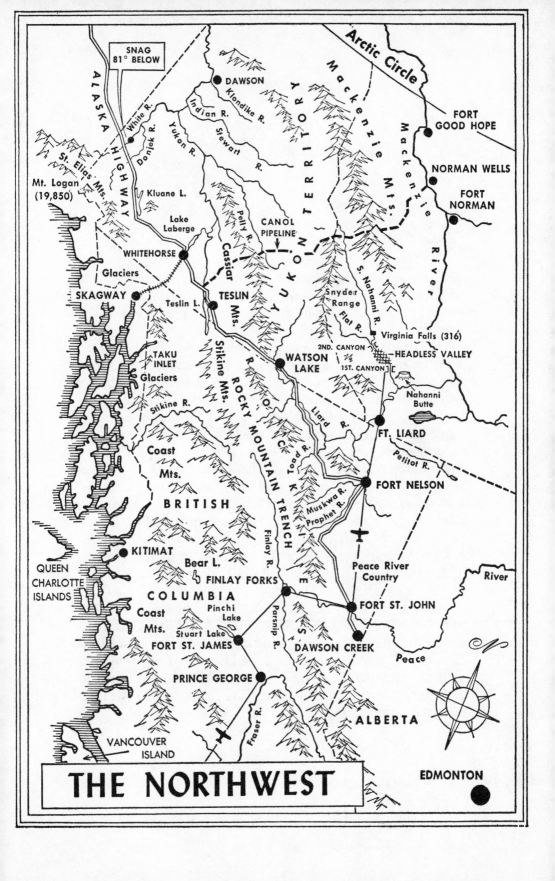

THE NORTHWEST

2 | Sixty-eight Below

Ed Hanratty, Baker's wiry little mechanic, had the Junkers warmed up before we woke the following morning. An hour later the four of us were winging across the white expanse of the lake and off into the emptiness of the northeast.

Half an hour later a curious spectacle unrolled below us. Here on the edge of a little lake rose a gnarled and ancient mountain, shaped somewhat like a cornucopia. As Baker banked the Junkers around the mountain, we could see an immense, yawning hole near the peak, almost like a volcanic crater. In the shadow of the mountain, cut out of the wilderness in a neat grid of streets and avenues, lay a little town large enough to hold about twenty-five hundred people. The houses were quite new, and freshly painted, and so were the stores and offices, the bowling alley, the movie theater and dance hall. Yet the stillness of the grave hung over this settlement. Nothing moved in the streets. No smoke curled up from the cottages and bunkhouses. There was no sign of a vehicle or a domestic animal, no tracks or footprints in the snow.

Here was one of the haunting sights of the Canadian north: the gnarled mountain, the little lake, the neat, dead town, and the wilderness rolling off to the horizon in every direction. When we landed by the lake shore, a single man walked down to greet us. He was the caretaker and the only resident of Pinchi Lake, B.C., one of the world's strangest ghost towns.

"You know," Russ Baker said, as we drank a cup of coffee in the caretaker's house, "this lake could have made me a rich man if I'd used my head back in the summer of 1938. There's a fortune in mercury ore hidden away in that mountain behind us."

In the summer of 1938 nobody realized that. In those days the little lake was just another piece of topography in the crazy-quilt pattern of northern B.C. In that hot lazy summer nobody could have guessed that by 1943 Pinchi Lake would be producing all the mercury for the Allies, that a boom town would spring up at the base of the twisted mountain, and that this would be the site of the biggest mercury mine on the continent. Nobody guessed— except a cook named Andy Ostrem and a bush pilot named Charlie Elliott and a prospector named Dan Miner. The knowledge brought death to two and a fortune to the third.

Ostrem had been around Fort St. James for years, a penniless hunchback who used to cook and do odd jobs for the government geological survey that was slowly charting the mineral wealth of the north. The previous summer, 1937, the survey had reached Pinchi Lake, and the geologists, sampling the ore, had found it fabulously rich. The government surveyors are notoriously tight-lipped. Their task is to chart the country, record the information on maps published a good many months later, and keep quiet about what they find.

But Ostrem, frying up bacon and beans, knew the secret and determined to stake the lake the following spring. It was a lean winter and by Christmas he was broke. He sold the story of the mountain full of mercury to Charlie Elliott, a bush pilot, for fifty dollars. When spring came, Elliott flew Dan Miner, an experienced prospector, off to Pinchi Lake to stake the area. Then tragedy struck.

The first to learn of it was Russ Baker, sitting on his

porch overlooking Stuart Lake on May 24, the Victoria
Day holiday, eating a salad lunch. Around the bend in a
canoe came a man who looked like an Indian. Baker, looking a second time, saw that it was really a white man, his
face stained with blood. He recognized him as Bill Martin, Charlie Elliott's mechanic.

Baker reached the beach at the same moment as Martin,
who was barely able to speak: "Charlie's all smashed to
hell . . . Nation Lakes. . . . Go get him." Then the in-
jured man fell forward on his face.

The Nation Lakes are fifty miles long. In May the land
is sheathed in a blue haze, beautiful, lonely, and empty.
Through this country for seventy miles, on foot and by
boat, with the blood caking his torn scalp and clothing,
Bill Martin had plunged, his face sticky red in the sunlight, the squaws running from him in panic as he staggered through the native encampments. Over it now Russ
Baker flew, searching for the telltale silver wing of Elliott's
crashed plane. He found it late in the afternoon sticking
out of one of the lakes near the shoreline.

Dan Miner, the prospector, lay dead in the plane's cabin.
Elliott lay dying on the shore. But before he expired he
whispered the secret of the mountain on Pinchi Lake.

"That's how I mean I could have been rich," Baker said,
sipping his coffee. "Of course I didn't pay any great attention to it. This country's full of rumors and legends about
gold and silver and mercury and copper. How was I to
know this one was real?"

But Andy Ostrem knew it was real. With Elliott dead,
he reasoned that the secret was his again. He confided it
to two penniless prospecting brothers, who had just sold
their car in order to eat. The three men let two more into
the secret in order to get a grubstake. The five partners
staked thirteen claims on the side of the gnarled mountain.

The claims paid off. The Consolidated Mining and

Smelting Company bought an eighty-five per cent interest in them for eighty-five thousand dollars. Andy Ostrem sold his share of the stock back to the company in return for a life pension of a hundred dollars a month and retired to Vancouver Island. The others collected thirty thousand dollars a year each when the mine went into production. The little town mushroomed up and by 1943 it was booming. But when the war ended, the mine and the town closed down. The ore is still there, thousands of tons of it, but, strange though it sounds, it is cheaper to bring mercury all the way from Spain than to mine it in northern B.C. Here in this empty shell of a town at the bottom of a million-dollar mountain is the perennial dilemma of the frontier country. Except for the sound of the caretaker's ax chopping firewood, Pinchi Lake was as silent as the day when Andy Ostrem first hammered his stakes into the mountainside.

We walked through the streets of the empty town and down to the plane sitting on the hard surface of the lake.

"I went through the ice in this damned lake once," Baker said as we climbed back into the cabin. "It was December and I took a chance that she was frozen solid. Well, she wasn't and we went right through thirty feet of water with the thermometer at twenty-eight below. By the time I got to shore, I tell you my teeth were chattering so hard they had to wedge a spoon between them to get the rum down."

We flew off again toward the great Rocky Mountain trench that cuts its way down the edge of British Columbia. This huge trough has been the natural pathway from north to south from the days of the fur traders to the days of the bush pilot. It is at least eleven hundred miles long, the most continuous gap on the face of the continent, stretching northwest from Idaho to the Yukon in an even diagonal. The Rockies form its eastern wall; the Cassiars and Ominecas guard it on the west. Five great rivers flow along its floor, some north and some south, for there are four drainage divides within the trench itself. Its width varies from two to ten miles, but its sides are almost box-like, so that, from the air, it lives up to its name—a great natural ditch in the shadow of the mountains. What caused this primeval highway? Its origin is still uncertain, but it was most likely produced by a folding of the earth's crust in those ancient times when the soft core of the continent was squeezed between the firm pincers of the Precambrian shield to the east and the Pacific shelf to the west.

The trench is not cut to a uniform level, but follows the natural ups and downs of the surrounding land. It is possible that it does not stop at the Liard but sweeps on along the upper Liard, the Pelly, and the Yukon into Alaska, following the diagonal grain of the continent. Anyone following the floor of the trench for a thousand miles or more will realize two things: that here is the most spectacular scenery in all of North America, and that here, too, is a route for a future railway or highway, dug by nature eons in the past.

Two of the trench's great rivers lay below us. Down from the north almost as straight as a plumb line came the Finlay. Down from the south to meet it swept the Parsnip. Both these rivers seem to be ruled on the map. When they come together they form the Peace, which plunges directly eastward through the mountain barrier into Alberta and thence north to Athabasca Lake and eventually to the Mackenzie. All this water forms part of the greatest river system on the continent next to the Mississippi-Missouri. In the end, all of it empties into the Arctic Ocean, some of it traveling twenty-six hundred miles to get there.

But we were seven hundred air miles south of the Arctic. Below us, at the juncture of the Finlay and the Parsnip, lay the settlement of Finlay Forks. On the map, in large letters, it looked like a metropolis. On the ground it consisted of a handful of log cabins, only two of them occupied when we arrived.

It was here in 1793 that a Highlander named Alexander Mackenzie arrived on his second famous continental trek. He was the greatest explorer of his day, a partner in the North West Company, like Fraser, who was to follow him. He looked not unlike his countryman Robert Burns, his features handsome, his mouth stubborn, his eyes poetic. He had just returned from the Arctic along the great river to which he gave his name, a feat of endurance and resolution that gave him no cheer at all, for it had not brought him to the prize he sought: the Northwest Passage. Now he was seeking a mysterious river beyond the mountains which the Hare and Dogrib Indians, far to the north, had told him about. With a single birchbark canoe, ten men, and a dog, he had portaged successfully past the awesome chasm of the Peace and stilled the mutinous murmurings of his paddlers with a regale of rum. Standing where no white man had stood before, on the floor of the mighty trench, the young explorer was faced with an agonizing dilemma: should he paddle north up the Finlay or south up the Parsnip? He chose to paddle south, and this route led him eventually to the Pacific, where he helped secure the western coastline for Britain. The Yukon, which he really sought, remained hidden for another half-century.

Except for the little cabins on the bank above the river, the land below was as aboriginal as it had been when Mackenzie first saw it. We swept down upon the broad river and came to rest beneath the bank. The weather had changed abruptly. It was four o'clock and the twilight was being hastened by a dark fog of fine snow particles blown almost horizontal by the rising wind. Out of this swirling haze a blurred figure in a parka emerged and identified himself as Paul Vatcher, telegraph operator, postmaster, weatherman, mining recorder and observer for the Department of Mines and Resources at Finlay Forks, B.C. (population: 5).

"It's a Peace River blow coming up, Russ," Paul Vatcher said. "Remember the last time, hey?"

"Sure do," said Baker, who was helping Hanratty lash down the Junkers. "The last time this happened, the drifts covered the plane. It took four men working with shovels all day to dig her out."

We began to unload some of our gear. The early darkness was already casting blue shadows over the white expanse of the river, and the dark profile of the hills, masked by the dusk and blowing snow, was rapidly merging into the blur of the sky.

We moved about clumsily. Art Jones, the photographer, and I were wearing heavy air-force parkas lined with blanket material, two pairs of socks, and two pairs of gloves. Yet in spite of this formidable covering I have never been so cold as I was that late January afternoon, scrambling through the deep snow of the Peace River and up the ice-sheathed banks with a duffel bag over my shoulder and a typewriter under my arm. The wind had risen swiftly now and we could hear it whining down the valley. The fine needle points of the snow bit into our faces. It was only a few hundred yards to the nearer of the two occupied cabins, but it seemed like a mile. At the top of the bank I paused and looked down on the river to see if I could see the plane. It was lost in the swirling snow.

We entered the first cabin and here Roy McDougall, a tall, lean trader who had spent most of his life in the north, and Florence, his daughter, served us innumerable cups of tea and great black slabs of moose meat.

"Peace River blow coming up," McDougall said. "It's unique, you know. The wind comes down the valley and the snow blows along with it. It's liable to cover the plane. A gull couldn't fly in this weather."

We bunked in the other cabin with Vatcher, the blond young telegrapher, whose wife was away on a trip Outside. We had expected to take off for Fort St. John the next morning, but when we trudged through the blowing snow we began to wonder. Hanratty, the tough little mechanic, was already working on the plane, but not with any great success. He seemed able to withstand the impossible cold without complaint. The thermometer stood at thirty-seven below, but he worked with his gloves off, while his hands went slowly blue. He didn't seem to notice the weather.

"All mechanics get that way," Baker remarked. "Their hands sort of go numb. They can't work with an engine wearing mitts, so they get mad and take them off. The only trouble is sooner or later all their fingers get like thumbs."

The thermometer was dropping, and the snow, as fine as white sand, had drifted well over the skis of the plane during the night and frozen to ice. We all set to work with shovels to loosen the skis. At this point Hanratty climbed out of the cockpit and announced that the battery was frozen. He'd have to take it up and shove it in Roy McDougall's oven before we could get the motor started. By the time we were ready to go, it was too cold and too dark to fly.

We were stranded for four days in Finlay Forks.

The following morning we tried again to escape. Down we went with shovels and axes and began the weary job of hacking the plane out of the ice that had formed during the night. While we worked, Hanratty draped a canvas tent over the naked engine and applied a blowtorch to it. It was four hours before the engine was warm enough to start. Then Hanratty took the battery out of Roy McDougall's oven and put it in the plane. Baker climbed into the cabin and gunned the motor. Jones and I ran out to the end of the wings and began to swing on them. As Baker revved the motor, the plane began to shake and Jones and I, each on a wingtip, tried to bounce it loose from its prison of ice. For a long time the Junkers refused to budge.

Finally it broke free. Baker looked at his watch and shook his head sadly. It was four thirty. Fort St. John was an hour's flight away on the eastern side of the mountains. It was too dark to start. We had been working all day in vain.

"Maybe we ought to open that bottle of overproof rum," Jones said that evening as we sat in front of McDougall's red-hot stove, eating more moose meat. The rum was in the plane with our other supplies, and Jones volunteered to go down to get it.

"No fear," Baker said. "A man never knows. We might need that rum when we reach the Nahanni."

"Okay," Jones said. "I guess you ought to know."

"I once had an awful fight with Skook Jamieson over a bottle of rum," Baker said. "It was up at Usilika Lake, and it all happened in forty feet of water and at zero temperature. That was some fight."

He settled back and began to reminisce about the time he had committed the deadly northern insult of refusing a drink, and of how Skook Jamieson, the horsepacker, had climbed into the cockpit with him and tried to force the rum down his throat. We all lived the fight again, blow by blow, as he told it: the first skirmish in the cockpit, the broken bottle on the floor, the two men dropping off on the floats, slugging as they went, the clinch and the fall into the freezing water, the battle seesawing back from the lake to the plane, until both men were too weak to fight any longer and could only haul themselves dripping onto the floats, open another bottle of rum, and collapse, exhausted but satisfied.

"We drank the whole bottle in half an hour, then rowed to shore, lay down on the beach, and slept sound until morning," Baker said. "My muscles were stiff for a week afterwards. Come on. Time for bed. We've got to get away early tomorrow."

But there was no hope of flying on the following day. By morning the thermometer was dropping steadily, and it continued to drop until it reached sixty-eight below. We did not know it then, but this was the coldest day in the recorded history of North America. At Snag, on the Alaska Highway, the thermometer dropped to eighty-three below. Men left vapor trails behind them as they walked. Gasoline turned to slush. A cup of water tossed into the air froze in mid-air and dropped to ground as hail. Icicles brought indoors where it was eighty above remained dry for a full five minutes before they started to melt. And Snag was on the same latitude as the Nahanni Valley.

The paradox was that, at the same time, the Arctic islands, a thousand miles to the north, were considerably warmer. Indeed, the coldest temperature ever recorded in the Arctic regions is sixty-three below zero, and on most Arctic islands the thermometer rarely drops below minus forty-five.

At Finlay Forks we did not attempt to venture out of doors unless it was unavoidable. I remember that Paul Vatcher had an outdoor toilet a few yards from his cabin. In order to reach it we were forced to dress as though we were going on a mile-long hike—double parkas, scarves, and double mitts. It was an experience I do not care to repeat. The wind had blown the privy door open and the snow was jammed against it so that it would not close, and there we crouched miserably in those brief but necessary bone-chilling moments from which there was no escape.

Once more, on the following morning, we packed our gear down to the plane. Once more we found ourselves shaking the plane free of the ice. Once more the oil in my typewriter froze solid so that I had to put it in the oven with the battery before I could use it. Once more Jones's film-packs grew so brittle with cold that they began breaking off in his hands.

But the temperature had started to rise. It was now around forty below, and it felt positively mild. By three p.m. the motor was warm. We waved good-by to Vatcher, who was standing on the ice ready to waggle the wings again to get us moving. He was relieved to see us go, I think. We had almost eaten him out of eggs, and that can be a serious thing in the north. The Vatchers bought all their food once a year, two tons of it, and had it shipped in by boat each summer. After that, if they wanted a beefsteak, they ordered it by one of the infrequent planes that happened by.

Jones and I piled into the little cabin in the rear of the covered cockpit. We were perched on top of our gear behind the two empty oil drums. We could see very little out of the frosted windows, but just after we cleared the trees we sensed something wrong. Baker banked the plane around, and a moment later we had bumped back onto the river.

The windshield was covered with black oil.

"It happens sometimes in cold weather," Baker said laconically. "If Ed can fix it, we'll still get away." Ed took off his mitts and fixed it.

A few moments later we were in the air again, winging down the wide Peace River toward the black hole in the mountains and fairly shaking with the cold. The gorge of the Peace lay below us, a clean break in the wall of the Rockies. While other rivers flow down the sides of the mountains, this remarkable stream cuts right through them to form the deepest pass of all in the continental barrier. How can this be? The answer is that the Peace is a very ancient river, older than the Rockies themselves. In that contorted period of crustal upheaval that geologists call the Laramide revolution, when continents were moved and oceans swept back and the earth's hide was wrinkled and warped, the Rockies were born. But the Peace was already there. And as the land split and folded and the great mountains erupted slowly over the ages, the Peace continued to cut its way down so that today it is less than two thousand feet above sea level while the surrounding peaks soar to seven thousand feet. Hence this gloomy gorge through which we now flew in the bitter cold of a January afternoon.

The Ice Age was still with us, here among these alpine pinnacles. The remnants of the ancient glaciers persist among these mountains as evidence of the time when half the continent was prostrate in their grip. The great cordilleran icecap, squeezed between the Rockies and the Coast Range, was once twelve hundred miles long and four hundred broad, formed in those ancient times when the summers inexplicably cooled and the little mountain glaciers began to expand down the slopes to the valley bottoms. When hundreds of these enlarging glaciers blended together into one massive sheet, an icecap was born. After thousands of years an enormous dome of ice built up, seven thousand feet thick, covering lakes, rivers, canyons, and plateau, until only the highest peaks poked their needle points above it like island cliffs. The ice tongues squeezed out from their mountain prisons through river passes to join with other icecaps to the east and enter the ocean to the west forming the lovely fiords that mark the northern Pacific coast of British Columbia and Alaska. Our own route was taking us across the mountain region where the cordilleran cap had its center, and on this chill afternoon it was not hard to believe that the remnants of it were still with us.

Dusk was already upon us when we reached the Peace River country on the other side of the mountains. Below us was the rich farmland that a few years before World War I had been unpopulated frontier. Now it supported some fifty thousand people, living off the black morainic soils that lie thickly on the broad benchland above the river. As a result of this turning-back of the wilderness, the phrase "Peace River" has become a symbol of optimism in the north. There are other valleys like it, and the hope is that in future years more Peace Rivers will be wrested from the hinterland.

For the first time now we saw the narrow strip of the Alaska Highway cutting through the forest in a white line to the northwest. We landed at the little settlement of Fort St. John, a town of nine hundred people, checked into the hotel, and had some supper. Then Art Jones and I walked through the deep snows to visit the Murray family, who run the *Alaska Highway News*.

It was the Murrays, really, who had started the recent wave of Headless Valley stories. Among them they were correspondents for a dozen papers all the way from the *Toronto Star* to the *Chicago Tribune*. Each of these papers had been carrying enthusiastic stories about the valley under a Fort St. John dateline and under the byline of one of the Murrays.

There are four Murrays: George and Margaret Murray and their two offspring, Georgina and Dan. The town, when we arrived, was still buzzing with stories of the monumental split that had occurred among them. There had been a provincial election a little over a year earlier. George Murray, an old campaigner, had run as usual as Liberal Party candidate in Lillooet, B.C. His wife, a galvanic, birdlike woman whom everybody calls "Ma," had unaccountably decided to run for the provincial legislature too, in the Peace River, not as a Liberal but under the banner of its bitter rival, the Social Credit Party. This made young Dan Murray so mad that he published a statement in the *Lillooet News* insisting his mother was related to the other Murrays only by blood. "What's Social Credit, Ma?" Georgina had asked. "I don't know, Georgie," Ma Murray replied jestingly. "But I'm running for it anyway." Both Murrays were beaten at election time, and now the entire family was back in journalism.

Mrs. Murray met us at the door, a chipper little woman with snapping blue eyes and a booming voice that is seldom silent. She began to talk as soon as we entered and she was still talking when we left. Her background is romantic enough. She started her career at the age of thirteen working in a saddle factory in Kansas, slipping sentimental notes in with the leather in the hope that a wealthy cowboy in Canada would marry her. Finally she left for Alberta, but got sidetracked in B.C. by George Murray, a newspaperman, to whom she was swiftly wed. The Murrays have both been in the newspaper business ever since. Georgina was born in the middle of a newspaper strike, and Danny arrived when his father was in trouble over a libel charge.

"You're not honest-to-goodness goin' to the Nahanni Valley this time of year?" Ma Murray boomed at us, as she poured out big slugs of rum. "Would you listen to that, Georgie! Why, I wouldn't take a chance like that. You don't know what you're going to find in there. It's an awful time of year to fly in there—nothing moving at all, and men going missing and all that."

She kept on talking and sipping rum. We left with her warnings ringing in our ears, and the following morning prepared to fly north again.

It was bitterly cold when we walked out to the plane. When it is really cold in the north, there is very little wind, simply a terrible stillness broken only by the sounds of the timbers in each house snapping with the frost, like a volley of pistol-shots.

Russ Baker came back from the control tower. "They won't let us go out," he said. "There's nothing flying today. They say it's too cold." He climbed into the cockpit and began to fiddle with the controls.

"I'm going anyway," he said suddenly.

I said I thought this would get him into a lot of trouble.

"I don't think so," he said. "You see, I offered to carry the mail—and that's going to get CPA's dander up. You watch now: I bet as soon as they hear we're away, they'll be right behind us. They won't stand being grounded if we're in the air."

And so we flew north again over the scrub timberland through which the long, white line of the Alaska Highway cuts like a chalk mark. Two hours later we landed at Fort Nelson, a lonely huddle of huts and airfields in the center of nowhere. Ten minutes after we landed, just as Baker predicted, the big CPA plane came in from Fort St. John.

3 | On the Rim of the Nahanni

We were stranded four more days in Fort Nelson.

Once again the cold came down like an iron clamp. On those brief moments when we ventured out of the Department of Transport bunkhouse where we were lodging, our eyelids froze together and our eyebrows and mustaches frosted up until we looked like whitened old men.

On the evening of our arrival a wiry little Indian trapper named Ed Gardner walked into the bunkhouse and engaged Russ Baker in conversation. His wife was a hundred miles away, in a lonely cabin on Deer River, expecting a baby at any moment. Gardner had been trying to get in on foot to bring her out, but the snow was so deep this year that he'd found it impossible. Would Baker take him in, and out again? Baker said he'd try as soon as the thermometer rose a bit.

On our second morning in Fort Nelson we decided to try it. We stripped the plane right down, throwing out everything movable, including the jack and the empty oil drums, and then took off into the northwest.

"Now you're going to find out what bush flying is really like," Baker shouted over his shoulder. "There'll be plenty of snow on that river and not much space to set down in. You watch."

We flew for an hour over the white tangle of bush and stream and then Gardner pointed down to a small speck on the edge of the crinkled pathway of the river. It was his cabin. As Baker circled to get lower, we could see an irregular line of small fir trees stuck in the snow to mark the best landing spot. There was about a quarter of a mile of ice to set the plane down in, not straight, but in a wide curve. After that the river bent sharply.

The instant the skis touched the top of the snow, the view from the cabin's windows was blotted out by a swirling fog of white. The plane bit deeper and deeper into the white blanket that covered the river until the snow touched the under edge of the wings. Then it came to a sluggish stop. Art Jones and the trapper and I jumped out into the snow up to our waists. Baker cut the motor a little and yelled at us.

"I'm going to keep her moving," he shouted. "Otherwise we'll be stuck here till spring."

He started to chug slowly down the river, then turned in a wide arc and moved back the other way again. The roar of the engine filled the tiny bowl in the hills, and the powdered snow shot skyward in great pillars almost obscuring the moving plane.

Jones and I tramped along the path cut by the plane's skis while Gardner floundered through the hip-deep snow toward his cabin on the bank.

A hundred yards away the plane plowed to a halt. The snow had stopped it. Jones and I struggled over. Ed Hanratty was already out of the cockpit, and the three of us clung to the wingtips rocking the plane as Baker gunned the motor. The Junkers started to move forward again, trailing us behind it.

A short time later Ed Gardner came through the snow pulling a sleigh with his wife in it. His mother, a bulky squaw, came along carrying a year-old baby. His eight-year-old son moved ahead swiftly on small snowshoes. Two huskies, leaping through the snow in mighty bounds, completed the entourage.

The Junkers was still thundering up and down the river.

Gardner made signals to the plane, and Baker brought it around to where the group of us were standing.

"Climb in as fast as you can," he shouted. "We're settling down into this snow."

We heaved the ponderous old woman and the baby into the plane and then the expectant mother. The rest of us followed. The little boy and the two dogs were staying behind, all alone in the wilderness.

Baker gunned the engine, but the Junkers wouldn't budge. We tumbled out into the snow again, rocked the wings, and got the plane moving forward while the propeller blast sent an artificial blizzard swirling around us. We climbed back into the cabin. Again the plane wouldn't move. We tried the same tactics three times more. No luck.

"All right, let's rustle some spruce boughs," Baker said.

We struggled back along the ski-trails, plucking up the small spruce-tree markers and piling them up in front of the skis. Then, by dint of waggling the wings and gunning the motor, Baker heaved the plane up on the boughs. Back again we clambered into the crowded cabin.

This time the Junkers lumbered into the air, just over the tops of the trees at the end of the crude runway. In the cabin at the rear Art Jones and I and the four Indians crowded as far forward as possible to lighten the tail. An hour later we were back safely at the Fort Nelson airport.

"For a moment there, I thought all of us were going to play stork in that cabin," Baker said. He looked down at his left foot, the one he uses for the floor controls.

"Frozen," he said. "That metal sure must have been cold."

The following morning the cold came down again, but we decided to chance a take-off. The snow, which had been falling most of the night, had ceased, leaving the sky a clear frosty blue. The sunlight spangled the snow, and

71

the glare would have been intolerable if we hadn't been wearing dark glasses.

"You could go blind in an hour up there without these," Baker said, adjusting his thirty-dollar lenses.

Hanratty, who wore neither glasses nor mitts, already had the plane warmed up. He hadn't needed to use the blowtorch this time. He borrowed the RCAF's hot-air blower instead.

The plane began to quiver for the take-off. Then there was a sharp explosion and the engine stopped. A cylinder head had blown out.

"We're lucky," Baker said as he climbed out of the cockpit and looked at the damage. "That baby must have been cracked for days. We might have blown it coming through the Peace Pass; then where'd we be, eh?"

Or in the Deer River country. Or later on in the Nahanni.

We were lucky, but we were delayed. Baker wired his office at Fort St. James to express the missing part by air. We sat it out playing cribbage in the Department of Transport quarters.

After the isolation of Finlay Forks, Fort Nelson seemed like a small metropolis. Trucks rumbled by up the Alaska Highway toward Whitehorse and Fairbanks. Scheduled aircraft came and went. The big hangars were clogged with Royal Navy Seafires and U.S. Mustangs. A division of the British Fleet Air Arm was on the spot attempting cold-weather maneuvers. The roar of the planes splintered the silence, and our Junkers looked like a has-been next to the war machines.

There were about thirty Royal Navy men on the job, most of them straight from England, and they were getting more cold weather than they'd bargained for. The pilots discovered that the motors of the Vampire jets were freezing at fifty-four below and that the cordite in the ammunition was freezing, too. One of the Seafires had burned out its bearings because the motor had to be kept running at two-thirds full throttle during the cold.

One evening Art Jones and I walked over to the old trapping town of Fort Nelson, which is set apart from the highway and Air Force base of the same name. Here, in contrast to the Quonset huts and the big new hangars, was the familiar huddle of log cabins that, until a few years ago, formed the distinctive architecture of the north.

The postmistress at the Musquaw post office stared at us as if we were mad when we told her we were flying into the Nahanni country.

"But this is the wrong time of the year," she said. "Even in the summer it's supposed to be dangerous country. There are all sorts of stories about it. We don't know what to believe."

It was quite clear that here in Fort Nelson they knew as little about Headless Valley as the people in Vancouver.

"I hope you know what you're doing," the postmistress said. "There was a man here last summer named Savoir or Savard or something. He was going into the Nahanni, too. He didn't know much. He vanished completely in there. Go on over see Art George, he'll tell you."

We wandered over to Art George's trading post.

"Sure, Savard came through here last spring," he told us. "He was a French Canadian, did a lot of trapping, some prospecting. He just wasn't equipped for travel up there. We told him. We warned him. He kept going anyway. Now he's dead in there somewhere."

Savard, it turned out later, wasn't dead at all. He had been in and out of the Nahanni and was very much alive on the Mackenzie.

When the new cylinder head arrived on the CPA plane, Hanratty and Baker worked like beavers getting the engine back in shape. While they were working, the Air

Force officer commanding the station dropped around to see us. He seemed to take it for granted that we would shortly be on the missing list and he asked me how many days we wanted him to wait before he started sending out search and rescue parties.

I told Baker, who said: "Oh, by golly, these guys will come and look for us before we even get there if we're not careful. Listen—nobody has ever had to look for me and nobody ever will. Tell him to wait at least eight days."

The wing commander took down a list of the supplies we had, the map positions of our route, and our radio wave length. This later turned out to be useless, for the radio was frozen stiff.

"We won't be able to start search and rescue proceedings for at least a couple of days," he said cheerfully. "Our aircraft is in Edmonton right now. But don't worry. We have a trained jump crew and we can get supplies and all that down to you when we find you. We've pulled quite a few out of this country."

The following morning we were ready. We taxied down to the main runway and then stopped short. An Air Force plow had already cleared the runway of the snow that had fallen during the night. The Junkers' skis stuck on the asphalt and wouldn't budge.

"First we had too much snow," Baker said. "Now we haven't got enough."

A plow came by and sheared off another six-foot strip of snow, and Baker shook his fist at it. We borrowed shovels and got enough snow back on the runway under the skis so that Baker could move the plane off into the deep snow at the side. We took off without using the runway at all.

Below us the Fort Nelson River wound its white way northwest through a ragged world of spruce trees stretching off to the Rockies. The thin line of the great highway slipped off over the edge of the horizon, and once again we were alone in the sky. There was no sign of man below us. A plane could drop down into this thick carpet and vanish as surely as a needle in a pile rug. More than one plane had done just that.

In Fort Nelson we had heard the strange story of a big U.S. Army transport that took off from the runway in February 1943 and was never seen again. According to the local people, it had fourteen passengers aboard and an army payroll estimated at two hundred thousand dollars. It had been held by weather for several days, and the thermometer stood at forty below when it roared out into the haze, heading for Fort Simpson on the Mackenzie. Although it had full radio facilities, no word was ever received from it. When the plane was last heard from, it was flying sixty miles north of Fort Nelson. The rest was silence. For weeks search planes combed the labyrinth of bush and stream between the two little towns. They found nothing. Somewhere, on one of the mountain peaks of the Mackenzie range, or on the slope of a lonely valley or in the matted forest below, the wreckage lay hidden. Already the story of the missing plane, with its neat packages of twenty-dollar bills, had become a northern fable. Somewhere, men liked to believe, the ground was green with banknotes dropped from the sky.

As we flew along the river line, the wisps of fog drifting below us began to thicken until finally the forest vanished and we were floating in the empty sky above a sea of billowing white. It didn't seem to bother Russ Baker. Occasionally he dove the plane into the fog in an attempt to see the ground below. Sometimes a small patch would open and Baker would peer down through it, looking for a familiar wriggle of the river. He was used to fog. Just as a passenger on a crowded streetcar can detect his own corner by peering at a small patch of pavement through a window, so Baker could tell where he was by peering at a patch of spruce forest through a window in the fog.

The fog lifted. Below us the world seemed exactly the same as it had the hour before—the winding river, the carpet of dull green. We mightn't have moved, but actually we had come more than a hundred miles.

A new river appeared out of the horizon. This could only be the great Liard, the Mackenzie's main tributary, which roars down out of the Yukon and—like the Peace—cuts through the mountains in a series of terrible rapids, to empty itself into the wide Mackenzie Valley not far from Great Slave Lake. We followed it north to the Petitot, where lay the trapping settlement of Fort Liard, peeking above the snow on the riverbank, a little huddle of huts, a church steeple, a Hudson's Bay post, and an RCMP barracks. There was a landing strip marked off on a frozen slough that joins the river, and on this slough there was a message for us. A series of ragged snowshoe trails laboriously spelled out in great ungainly letters the word SLUSH. Baker turned down onto the main river, and the Junkers landed in a series of bounces on its washboard surface just below the RCMP post on the bank.

A thin line of natives stood just above us, and two dog teams were already rushing down to meet us. Behind one rode the erect figure of Constable Jim Reid of the Royal Canadian Mounted Police in the handsome maroon parka and blue breeches of the force. Behind the other came a leathery little man, all gristle. This dark, bright-eyed creature was wearing a cassock under his thin parka. He could speak no English. He was an Oblate priest, one of a trio at Fort Liard, and although he handled the dogs like a professional and looked as if he were part of the land, he had been in the country for only six weeks. He had come straight from a seminary in Paris, to which he would never return.

We stayed the night in Fort Liard, a community that

has scarcely changed an iota in the past half century. Off on the northern horizon we could see the chisel-sharp limestone crags of the Nahanni, less than a hundred miles away. With luck we would land in the valley on the following day. That evening I went over all the information that I had been able to collect about it.

The whole business had begun here in this very settlement in 1900 when an Indian named Little Nahanni arrived with a sample of gold-bearing quartz. He claimed to have found it not far from the mouth of the Flat River, the main tributary of the South Nahanni. Until this time the Indians, with the silent co-operation of the Hudson's Bay Company and the Roman Catholic Church, had done their best to keep the white men out of their hunting grounds in the Nahanni country. Even in those days there were stories of fierce "Mountain Men" lurking in caves, ready to pounce upon the unwary traveler. Then four years after the first word of gold a second Indian found placer nuggets on a little stream called Bennett Creek running into the Flat River. There was a brief stampede into the country, but no further gold was found.

And there it might have ended save for the persistence of Willie McLeod, the halfbreed son of a Hudson's Bay Company post manager, a man born to the country, who could stalk a moose better than the Indians and who liked to live almost entirely off the land. In the spring of 1905 Willie and his brother Frank found the little creek and took some gold from it. They filled a box with quartz and placer samples, but lost it when their boat upset in the Flat River canyon. All they had left was a ten-ounce Eno's bottle plugged with coarse nuggets. They went back to Fort Liard, and here the two brothers teamed up with a Scottish engineer who to this day remains a mysterious figure in the story. His name has been given variously as Green, Wade, Wilkerson, and Weir. His origins and subsequent fate are unknown. What is known is that the three men headed back into the Nahanni Valley and were never seen alive again.

Three years later, after a prolonged search, a third McLeod brother, Charlie, found the skeletons of Frank and Willie on the right bank of the river some fifty miles upstream in a wide valley locked away from the rest of the country by steep mountains through which dizzy canyons had been cut. According to legend, the heads were missing. Some say the skeleton of their companion was found a mile away. Others say he vanished completely, only to be seen on the Pacific coast years later with sixteen thousand dollars in gold. On this point all accounts are vague. But ever since the skeletons were found, the valley has been known as Deadman's Valley. Popularly this was "Headless Valley," a term that soon came to encompass the whole watershed of the South Nahanni River.

Long before the McLeods' murder an earlier McLeod had been up the Nahanni River. In 1823 John McLeod of the Hudson's Bay Company reached the Nahanni from Fort Simpson. He visited it a second time the following year. Four years later the company planned to establish a trading post on the river, but for reasons now forgotten this was never done. In 1898 a party of Klondikers passed through the valley, leaving behind them log cabins built of vertical poles. It's doubtful if they ever reached the Klondike and more than possible that they died of starvation in the valley itself.

After the Klondikers came a former ex-Mounted Policeman and trader named Poole Field, over the mountains from the Yukon country, where he had done duty in the Klondike stampede. Field spent most of his life in the Nahanni, leaving a trail of cabins behind him.

Now a series of adventurous men trickled into the Nahanni, all seeking the lost McLeod mine. None of them found it but some made other discoveries, far stranger.

After World War I a young English traveler and explorer named Michael H. Mason studied the Nahanni Indians and reported they were "hostile to strangers" and that "many white pioneers have been done to death by them." Mason added that "the tribe was for many years under the complete domination of one woman, supposedly of European descent." Here was the White Queen story, in one sentence.

Mason's book, *The Arctic Forests,* intrigued an Oxford graduate named Raymond M. Patterson who had been invalided to Canada. He decided to explore the Nahanni and look for gold. He found the dizzy canyon on the tributary Flat River where the McLeods' boat had been wrecked—but nothing more. He went on up the Nahanni, however, past the mouth of the Flat, and discovered a giant waterfall, 316 feet high. It was later named Virginia Falls.

Harry Snyder, a millionaire oilman and big-game hunter, wanted to find the gold, too. He made several journeys into the Nahanni, bagging mountain sheep and grizzlies on the slopes bordering the river. He found no gold, either, but what he did discover, in 1936, was fantastic enough—a range of sawtooth mountains, twelve thousand feet in height and encompassing one of the largest snowfields in Canada, fifteen hundred square miles in size. They rose like a great triangular island, these mountains, above the ocean of mountains surrounding them. No white man had set eyes on them before, for they could not be seen from the deep floor of the Nahanni Valley.

All this time "Sourdough Jack" Stanier, of Fort Liard, had been doggedly searching year after year for the Mc-Leod mine. Between 1909 and 1934 he made nine trips into the Nahanni. His final journey had a *Treasure Island* flavor to it. He tracked down a priest who produced from the bottom of an old trunk a crude map drawn by Willie McLeod thirty years before, showing the site of the diggings on Bennett Creek. Stanier followed the map, and there, sure enough, were the rusty pans and shovels and rotting sluice-boxes. But there was no gold—nor has anybody found gold on the Nahanni or the Flat to this day.

Stanier and other prospectors have even been haunted by the belief that all the men who have met with foul play on the Nahanni have been looking for gold. There was Martin Jorgenson, who in 1917 sent out a message that he had struck it rich and whose headless skeleton was later found near his charred cabin. There was an outlaw named "Yukon" Fisher who used to buy shells with coarse nuggets at Poole Field's trading post and whose bones were found in 1927 on that same Bennett Creek where the McLeods had once hammered in their stakes. There was Phil Powers, whose charred remains were found among the ashes of his cabin on the Flat River in 1931. Stanier believes that Powers was murdered and his cabin burned around him to conceal the crime.

There have been other deaths in the Nahanni country, more easily explainable but often no less bizarre: two trappers wrecked in the swirling rapids of the dark canyon; another frozen to death as he crouched to try to light a fire. Finally there is the weird story of Poole Field's half-wit niece who tore off all her clothes and vanished up a hillside. The Indians said the devil had got her. All these tales, sometimes magnified and distorted, contributed to the aura of grotesquerie surrounding the land of canyons, waterfalls, and hot springs.

Jim Reid, the Mountie constable, took me over to the cabin of Willie McLeod, the halfbreed interpreter for the police, who was a nephew of the Willie who had vanished into the valley forty-two years before.

Yes, said Willie, he remembered his uncles and their
untimely end. He was a small boy when the deaths occurred, but he had heard the story many times from his
father and from the old men of the Slavey Indians who
had once occupied the valley.

But Willie's account only confused the mystery, for he
asserted that his uncles hadn't lost their heads at all. When
their skeletons were found, the skulls were intact, he said,
and the bodies were identified by the teeth. They had
been shot to death while they lay in their sleeping-bags on
opposite sides of a campfire. The truth will probably never
be known. At about the same time I was interviewing
Willie, another nephew in Calgary was telling a reporter
that the two men had been decapitated, and that his father
had buried them without their heads.

There are other variations of the McLeod story, each
one as plausible as the next. Whether the brothers were
murdered, whether they were shot and decapitated, or
whether they simply starved to death and their bones were
picked clean by wolves, there is now no way of knowing.
But they have long since become a northern fable.

"There are no more Indians in that valley," Willie was
saying. "They don't want to go into it. But they still talk
about men in there that kill people. You know, twenty-five
years ago they all believed the Nahanni country was
haunted. They're getting over that now, I think."

We sat in the dimness of Willie's cabin talking about
the dying race of Slavey Indians, whose main taboo is the
dead man. Because of this, Willie said, the Indians enter
the Nahanni only in groups.

"Not many left anyway," Willie said. "TB, flu, whooping cough, got most of them."

When the priests aren't about, medicine men still chant
over the sick, waving charms made of ducks' heads, and
beaver, and occasionally mink skins sprinkled with water.

Few Slaveys will shoot a wolf, because they think that it will kill the spirit of their grandmother. If one shoots a moose, he believes his gun will never shoot straight again. They are so afraid of the dead that they will occasionally burn the houses of the deceased. The drums of stretched moosehide still boom all along the Liard, and it is not hard to understand why the Nahanni country is a land of legend.

We walked down the trail through the woods to the cabin of Bill King, a ruddy and grizzled prospector, who has done some exploring in the Nahanni country. We found him sitting on his cot in his one-room cabin, a dark, spartan cave without a lamp of any kind.

"Sure, I was in them mountains in 1934," King said to us out of the gloom. "Big Charlie, the Indian, took me in. He said he knew all about a gold mine that would make us both rich. I guess he got scared. We'd done maybe one hundred seventy miles when he turned back. Frightened, I guess, though I don't know what of. I had to go back with him, of course. That's all I know about the Nahanni. Maybe there's gold there, but I sure didn't find it."

That evening a priest dropped around to tell Russ Baker that there was an Indian woman in the settlement with a broken collarbone. A plane had been sent for to take her to Fort Simpson on the Mackenzie River, but the cold had delayed it. If she waited any longer, they'd have to break the bone again to set it and she'd probably be crippled for life. Could Russ . . . ? Russ could.

The next morning we bundled Mrs. Joe Dutras and her cinnamon-colored baby into the Junkers, and headed for Fort Simpson, one hundred and fifty miles to the northeast. The Nahanni joins the Liard at a point almost exactly between the two settlements, so we would fly directly past its mouth. Jim Reid, who would normally have to make a dog-team patrol into the country, came along as a passenger. The airplane would save him two weeks of steady mushing.

"We'll drop this lady at Simpson, then double back and camp at the mouth of the Nahanni," Baker said. "Then we can fly into the valley next day—and out again if we're lucky."

Below us the Liard River corkscrewed its way through the flat plains and forests. Off to the southwest, dim on the horizon, we could see the foothills of the Rockies. Ahead of us lay the land of the Nahanni, the "people over there far away." We could see it plainly now, with its angry river writhing through the sharp peaks on its way to the Liard. They are strange pinnacles, these, the beginnings of the great Mackenzie Mountains. At first they were reckoned to be a northern continuation of the Rocky Mountain chain, but it is now fairly well established that the Rockies stop short at the Liard. What, then, caused this other range of mountains, so different in shape and in history, with the curious triangle of the newer, sharper Snyder Range rising above them? Nobody knows very much about these Mackenzie Mountains, though they cover more than seventy-five thousand square miles and are the largest single group of mountains in Canada. Their structure and history are virtually unknown, and it is so difficult to reach them that they have not yet been properly mapped.

There was the start of them on our left as we flew towards Fort Simpson—breath-taking limestone crags, like huge teeth jutting from the ground, some like giant bicuspids filed razor-sharp, others like monster molars with flattened tops, with the river cutting into them. I thought of Coleridge's river Alph that "ran through caverns measureless to man," and a little shiver of anticipation rippled through me. I could understand perhaps why this river and these mountains had frightened the Indians, for now they frightened me.

4 | Into the Valley

We reached Fort Simpson on the Mackenzie River two hours after leaving Fort Liard. The town lies on the river-bank, but the airfield and Department of Transport station are about fifteen miles away. The Indian woman and her child, neither of whom had uttered a sound during the trip, though they had each looked at us steadily and curiously, were taken into the DOT station to await transportation to the hospital. Then we were off again, back to the Nahanni.

The long shadows of the early northern twilight were already creeping across the blunt, forbidding bulk of Nahanni Butte when Baker dropped the Junkers on the ice at the mouth of the South Nahanni River. In the shadow of the five-thousand-foot Butte a single cabin crouched on the riverbank. It belonged to Jack laFlair, a trader who with his Indian wife had lived there for thirty years with-

out losing his head or his mind. He greeted us at the door
of his cabin, a moonfaced little man with a grizzle of black
hair at the chin, delighted but puzzled to find us on his
doorstep.

"You won't find nothing," he said as he squatted down
on the bunk in his two-room cabin. "All these crazy stories!
I been hearing 'em for years. Indians and trappers got
nothing better to talk about, I guess.

"I tell you how these things start up. Now, listen to this.
Up on the Liard a piece from here there's a spot where, if
you look back, you can see a rock shaped something like a
Maltese cross. It only looks like that from one side, and if
you're going down-river it only lasts for about a minute.
Then it's gone.

"All right. A couple of summers ago I'm in Simpson fix-
ing up my winter's supply and I happen to mention this
cross to some guys there, just like I told it to you.

"Last summer I go back for my grub and I get the whole
story told back to me, by Jeez, only this time they had
Indians and cave-dwellers molding crosses out of the rock.
That shows you how these stories start."

LaFlair's wife had baked some sausages and scrambled
some eggs, and we all crowded into the kitchen to eat.

"I been hearing these stories ever since I arrived here,"
the trader said. "That would be 1916–17, about the time
Jorgenson was killed. The Indians told me to stay out of
the country. They were afraid a gold stampede would
overrun their traplines.

"There was a professor up here a few years ago from
the States—Texas, I think. He went digging around in
those limestone caves up on the Butte, he and a bunch of
students. They dug down through a lot of leaf mold and I
think they found one old flint arrowhead. The Indians are
supposed to have moved this way on their trek from Siberia. I figure that's how the stories got started about the

cliff-dwellers and the prehistoric people. They were here all right—about a million years ago.

"I expect the fishing fella back this year. He was up here in 1938. Came all the way bringing a special boat of his own because he'd heard the trout fishing was good here. Imagine a guy coming all the way from California just to fish for trout. Well, he tried to get the boat through that first canyon and he couldn't do it. Boat drew too much water. He never did get any trout, but it didn't seem to worry him. He sat right down here in this cabin and started to design a new flat-bottomed boat that would get him through the canyons. He said he'd be back, but of course the war got in the way. I expect he'll be along one of these days."

We talked about the hot springs, which are supposed to keep the valley tropical and shroud it in a blanket of mist.

"That would be up near Gus Kraus's place, about forty miles upriver before you hit the first canyon," Jack laFlair said. "Gus there, he has a couple rigged up so he can go in swimming in the winter. They're hot all right. Sulphur springs. They come out of a little creek that runs into the river from the south.

"Gus and his wife—she's a squaw—they work a trapline between his cabin and the springs. They don't change the climate any. There's plenty of snow within a dozen feet or so. There's nothing tropical about the Nahanni. Hell, a fella named O'Brien was froze to death in there, about twenty miles from here at what they call the Splits. I remember it all. We found him crouched over his fire trying to light it. He'd froze right there, kneeling down. It looked like he was praying, but he wasn't. Just trying to get warm, poor fella.

"You'll find a lot of caves in this country. They're all along the edge of the canyons. You'll see 'em tomorrow. There was a trapper up here awhile ago who invented a bunch of stories about Mongol caves. He said there was copper kettles and things in them. Nothing to it. He did it to earn some spare-time cash taking in big-game parties."

LaFlair told us that the old diggings of the Klondikers could be seen on some of the creeks running into the valley. "They came up through the Nahanni and crossed over the divide to the Pelly country on their way to Dawson City," he said. "There's one of them buried down on Granger Creek, and the bank's been washing out near the grave. You can see his feet sticking out. This is all part of the Trail of '98."

He grinned ghoulishly and pushed back his chair, and we moved into the dim front room and began to lay out the sleeping-bags for the night.

LaFlair was still talking away. He had had nobody to talk to, save for his silent wife, for six months.

"Oh, they got lots of superstitions, these Indians around here. They won't eat a bear head, for instance. They'll throw it to the dogs every time. Just the same as we are, in a way. We won't eat horse meat. We won't walk under a ladder, and we figure it's seven years' bad luck to break a mirror, and when we spill salt, we throw it over the shoulder. What's your difference?"

Jack laFlair was something of a philosopher. On the bookshelf above his bunk I noted two copies of James's *Principles of Psychology*.

The following morning we got an early start. All of us were a little nervous because no one had ever landed a plane in the Nahanni in the winter and a good many people said it couldn't be done. LaFlair cautioned us about the ice in the river, which he told us was often rotten.

Once again Ed Hanratty was working on the engine with the blowtorch. Then we were into the sky and heading northwest along the Nahanni. On our right the sharp peaks marched off in a straight line into the haze. Below us the river split into a dozen channels meandering lazily across the floor of the wide valley. Ahead of us we could see the spot, some forty miles distant, where it seemed to bury itself in the mountains.

We reached this barrier within half an hour. Directly below us we could see the tiny square of Gus Kraus's cabin. Russ dipped down almost to ground level, but there was no sign of life. Close by the cabin was a little creek, its ice rotten and yellow, and not far away steam rose from the hot springs, which looked like greenish spots on the snow. This was the sole hint of tropical conditions.

It was obvious that the ice was too rotten to risk a landing, so we plunged directly into the gloomy canyon the river had cut through the limestone. On the far side of this mountain barrier lay the valley that the Indians had shunned for forty years, because long ago two white men had died seeking their gold.

The canyon was more than half a mile deep, and the rock walls rose a sheer fifteen hundred feet from the water's edge. Around us the chill blue mountains towered into the sky. This entire section seemed to be veined with labyrinthine canyons, each branching off the main canyon and biting deep into the surrounding limestone, sandstone, and slate. It was a fantastic sight—canyon upon canyon running off in every direction. Now, on each side of us, in this canyon country, so close that we could have tossed a rock into them, were the caves we had heard so much about. There were dozens of them—black irregular holes in the sheer cliffside, cut by the downward erosion of the water, stretching from the lip of the precipice to the river's edge. But they held no sign of life.

Over this dark and gloomy gorge, with its black caverns and its eerie winds, we flew for fifteen miles, the Junkers tossing about like a shuttlecock in the turbulent air. Then before we knew it, we had banked around a curve in the canyon and burst into Deadman's Valley.

If we had expected to find the mysterious mists of legend sheathing the ground from view, we were mistaken. The air was clear and the visibility unlimited. If we had expected to find the lush vegetation which, according to one chronicler of the valley, made the animals so fat they could hardly waddle, we were wrong again. The valley was as white and as silent as any other valley in the north. If any curse lay over it, then it was this silent curse of the tomb, shattered only by the reverberating drone of the Junkers.

It is like a gravy boat, this valley, an oval bowl ringed by mountains. Through it the river winds lazily, split into channels, to vanish again at the far end in more mountains. Baker swept along this ten-mile length of valley looking for a place to land on the river. The chances didn't look too good. The main channel was rent by an ugly scar of black water, which meant that the ice was rotten. Baker avoided this and came down a mile away where, from the air at least, the ice looked firm and flat.

We were a few feet above the surface when Baker suddenly gunned the dying motor and the plane rocketed skyward. He told us what happened later. He was about to touch the ice with his skis when he saw what appeared to be the shadow of the plane on the ice below. Then he remembered the sun wasn't shining. The movement could be only one thing: water running a few inches under thin ice. A few seconds more and we'd have been floundering in the freezing river.

We circled the valley again. Over on the north bank a little creek ran into the Nahanni. The water had overflowed and frozen on a sandbar. Baker decided to chance a landing here even though, from the air, the surface of ice and snow looked like a choppy ocean.

He took the measure of the surface carefully, making a couple of trial runs to look it over before coming down. Below us the snow had been whipped into frozen hillocks, some of them seven feet high. The plane shuddered at the first impact and bounced into the air again. Before we could collect our thoughts, it hit a second time and bounced again. The third time it heeled over on one side and the near wing scraped the snow. Ahead of us was a six-foot hillock and we were plunging straight for it. At this precise moment a little gust of wind caught the Junkers under its low wing and lifted it like a paper dart over the obstacle. We shot down the bumpy ice for a few hundred yards and came to a jerky halt.

"By God, we showed her who's boss!" Baker yelled triumphantly.

We climbed out and surveyed the saucer in the mountains which we had come so far to see. After the thrumming of the motor the silence seemed oppressive. Robert Service once called this northern calm "the silence that bludgeons you dumb," and this is a fair description. We had seen no signs of animals from the air and there wasn't the track of a beast on the ground, or the song of a bird in the sky. To all intents we were the only living things in this dead empty land.

But from the air we had seen two cabins on the south bank about a mile and a half from where we had landed. We decided to cross the river and find them. Hanratty tied down the plane's tail assembly so it wouldn't spin in the wind, picked up his little hatchet, and led off through the deep snow across the river. Because of the treacherous ice, he hacked at the surface with each step to make sure it would bear our weight. Twice he hit water with the first chop, and we had to change course.

On the far bank the snow was eight to fifteen feet deep, and as fine and dry as powder. We floundered through it, struggled up on the bank, and finally came upon the two crumbling cabins and three log caches set up on ten-foot stilts. The cabins were as empty as the valley. The damp hand of decay lay heavy upon them and it was impossible to enter their dank and gloomy confines without experiencing a shiver of depression. Who had lived here, and when? What had happened to them? A rubber boot, an ancient syrup can, a rusty tobacco tin, and a yellowed crumbling photo of a movie queen—these were the only clues available in the twilight of these man-made caves. We had a sign of our own which had been prepared by the newspaper's promotion department reading: THE VANCOUVER SUN—FIRST INTO HEADLESS VALLEY. We tacked it to a tree, and Jones took a picture of it. But here, beside these dead cabins in this dead valley, the sign seemed strangely out of place.

There was something about this place that puzzled us still. For one thing there were the great sculpted snowdrifts and hummocks. And then there were the fallen trees, thirty feet high some of them, six, eight, and ten inches in diameter, strewn about as if uprooted by a giant paw. What force had wrought this devastation?

The answer came to us as we stood on the bank in the ghostly silence looking across the lonely valley where our plane sat tethered beneath the sharp-peaked mountains. Slowly, as if from nowhere, a low moaning sound inserted itself into our consciousness. It increased until it became an eerie, chilling drone that rose in pitch and echoed across the valley. It was some moments before we realized that this banshee wailing was the wind, funneling down the natural wind-tunnels of the canyons and bursting out into the valley's bowl, like air pumped through an organ pipe. Frank Henderson's quoted remark came back to me: "The weird, continual wailing of the wind is something I won't soon forget." And Sourdough Jack's comment in a letter to me about the winds howling ceaselessly in the gloomy canyons, and the Indians' stories about the devil who howled in the mountains. This, then, was the spirit that haunted Headless Valley, the sound that chilled men's souls and helped build the folklore of the Nahanni.

Russ Baker was looking a little worried. "Come on," he said, "we ought to get moving fairly quickly. We'll never get out of here if that wind keeps on as it is."

We looked at each other, at the trees lying about on the forest floor, at the great drifts and hummocks of snow, at the little whirlpools of white, rising and pillaring in the air. And suddenly each of us wanted to leave Headless Valley. We floundered back in our own tracks, across the river, and along the valley floor to the spot where the Junkers was lashed down, a spot not very far from that ancient campfire where the McLeods' corpses had rotted four decades before. But there was no sign now of murdered men, only the white powder of the snow whirling about us. Baker stuck some small spruce trees into the rough surface of the overflow as a guide, and then we were off again into the gray skies.

We had a hundred miles or so of the Nahanni to explore from the air, and we flew steadily northwest, plunging almost immediately into the second canyon at the far end of Deadman's Valley. This gorge twists for twenty miles through the mountains, and it is a sheer thousand feet from its lip to the river below. Toward the end of the canyon we burst upon the peculiar limestone formation that travelers into the Nahanni have named Hell's Gate. Here was an immense pillar of rock rising in the very center of the canyon. Around this obstacle the river swirled, and then poured into a box canyon. Beyond this gate lay another silent valley.

Before it ends, the canyon descends to almost unbelievable depths and its walls soar to unbelievable heights.

Colonel Snyder measured the distance with an altimeter and found a sheer drop of 5,860 feet from rim to river surface. This makes it the deepest gorge on the continent, deeper even than the Grand Canyon of the Colorado and far dizzier, for it is a bare mile and a half across at the top.

To our left we could see the mouth of the Flat River, where so many men had died; it runs through country as flat as its name. A few miles farther upstream we came upon the spectacular Virginia Falls. They lay deep in the shadows of the fading afternoon and imprisoned in a mantle of ice, but even so, they were breath-taking to look at. They are twice as high as Niagara, and half a million horsepower is locked away in this one brief section of the South Nahanni River. Here was the supreme sight, the climax of the day—the sleeping falls, frozen hard against their guardian pinnacles of rock in the shadow of the mountains.

Above the falls the Nahanni wound north to the horizon in a long series of curves, so symmetrical that an artist might almost have painted them on the landscape. The mountains, too, drifted off into the unknown and vanished with the sinuous river on the rim of the horizon. There was nothing else to see. We turned about and headed southwest for Fort Liard.

The day had been uneventful except for our landing on the river, and yet it was perhaps the strangest I have ever spent. We had never expected to find anything in the Nahanni and yet we had heard and read so much about it that this valley, exactly like a hundred others hidden away in the north, could not fail to move us. All of us, I think, felt small shivers down our backs as we stood in the snows on that cold morning, expecting God knows what.

Now our flight from Headless Valley was capped by a final symbol. We were flying about a thousand feet above the hard surface of the Liard when Baker suddenly leaned back from the forward cabin and pointed off to the south-east. There on the horizon lay a magnificent range of rose-colored mountains. They were higher than any mountains I had ever seen, and as jagged and ruthless as the Nahanni's peaks. And each of these Everests was painted a Walt Disney color of rich red rose. Strangest of all, this range appeared on no map of the land.

I looked at the mountains again, and as I watched they began to ripple in the sunset, as if one were watching them through a sheet of water. The rippling increased until great wavy shadows seemed to be dashing across the mountain slopes at express-train speed. Then, suddenly, the mysterious mountain range was gone.

"Mirage!" Baker shouted, and turned back to the controls.

And with that we said good-by to the land of the wailing winds where, if you want to seek it, there is a mirage on the rim of every horizon, and a Shangri-La behind each mountain range.

5 | The Graveyard of Lost Planes

Russ Baker said he was going to take us home by way of Million Dollar Valley.

We were sitting in Fort Liard talking about the events

of the day and longing for a cup of rum. As soon as we landed, Art Jones had pulled out the papier-mâché box that contained the bottle of Lemon Hart, 150 proof. There was nothing left in it but broken glass. The rum had frozen solid in the biting cold and burst its bonds.

And so, rumless, we prepared to fly back by a different route, across the Yukon border to Watson Lake, and then south over the mountains of northern British Columbia in a land that is sometimes called "the graveyard of lost airplanes."

This was the country that was invaded during the war when the United States and Canada built the Northwest Staging Route to Alaska. A daisy chain of emergency landing strips was thrown across the northwest corner of the continent until it was said that you could fly from Edmonton to Fairbanks and never be more than one hundred miles from a landing spot. With each new rectangular scar chopped out of the forest mat, the skies grew darker with aircraft.

Here came planes the north had never known before: the swift darting Hurricanes, the delicate-looking Kittyhawks, the lumbering DC-3's, the speedy Mitchells and Black Widows, fast, powerful fighting craft that made the Junkers and Fairchilds look like buggies. The P-38's, they claimed, were so thick over Fort St. John one day that you couldn't see the skies at all.

Over the mountain graveyard of old planes the new planes roared. Down below like tombstones lay the wrecks of earlier days: a Fleet Freighter lying on a hill near Lower Post on the Liard, a Junkers broken in half at McConnell Creek, a Stinson in the trees north of Takla, a Fokker gone through the ice at Fort McLeod, a smashed Waco at McDame's Creek, another at Wolverine. To this roster of tragedy the war added new names.

Most of the young pilots who ferried aircraft to Alaska

during the war had never been in the north, and the staging posts were filled with men from Texas and Alabama. In those days of green pilots and strange terrains, some weird things were done in the name of navigation. One day at Dog Creek, far, far inland, a Hellcat pursuit fighter from an aircraft carrier out in the Pacific zoomed out of the sky and smashed up on the flightway, bone dry of gasoline. One day at Prince George, in central B.C., a U.S. Army transport set its wheels down on the runway. Out climbed the pilot, looking bewildered, and said, to nobody in particular: "My God—this doesn't look like Seattle." Seattle lies more than four hundred miles due south.

There is the tale of another transport that got trapped by weather at nine thousand feet coming south from Fairbanks to Whitehorse. The pilot flew west searching for a patch of sunlight and finally was able to set down on the shores of a sandy beach. He radioed Whitehorse that he'd landed on the shore of a large lake. Back came the message: "Taste the water." He did. It was salt. Only then did he realize, with a shiver, that he'd flown straight between the peaks of the St. Elias Range—the tallest mountains on the continent—and come out unscathed on the Pacific Ocean.

There is an almost legendary but true story of a twin-engined Beechcraft on a routine training flight from Comox on Vancouver Island south to Vancouver, only a few dozen miles away. The Beechcraft was flying blind on a beam, and it kept flying until it ran out of gas without ever reaching its destination. Its two occupants bailed out and found themselves in the wilds of central British Columbia over Germansen Landing, a good five hundred miles north of their destination.

There are other more tragic stories of the graveyard. At Whitehorse one night, so the story goes, the residents could hear a big plane circling overhead in the fog. Suddenly the man in the control tower realized with horror that the pilot thought the street lights along the road to the airport on the hill were the lights of the runway. The tower was afraid the big plane would crash into the town, so he was forced to order it away. Tower and pilot knew that this meant almost certain death for everyone in the aircraft, but there was nothing else to do. The big ship roared off into the fog and was not seen again. Months later, army pilots flying over Lake Laberge saw the silhouette of a big plane under the water.

It was into this land of lost planes that we were now venturing, over a terrain so stark and strange and empty that it looked almost prehistoric. This is the uninhabited land tucked away in the extreme southeast corner of the Yukon Territory, a land where the mountains, gnarled and contorted, seem to boil up out of the snows. There was nothing to be seen below us except these mountains, as twisted as an English oak—not even a lonely trader's cabin with its welcome curl of smoke.

About an hour out of Fort Liard, Russ brought the plane down low and skimmed into a narrow rugged valley wrinkled with rocks and empty stream bottoms. Here, beneath the naked mountains, we saw an incongruous sight: three big airplanes—Martin B-26's—apparently quite intact, lying belly-down in the snow in a direct line, about two miles apart, like great wounded eagles. This was Million Dollar Valley, so called because a million dollars' worth of aircraft were wrecked here.

The planes were en route to Alaska in the late fall of 1941 when the lead pilot lost his way. Fearful of running out of gas over the mountains, he brought his plane down in the first valley he saw. The others followed in behind him. Here the aircraft were trapped. So were the twenty-four members of the crew.

Baker told us the story of the valley after we landed at Watson Lake. It was he who had found the three planes during the search that followed and he who had landed his Junkers in the valley—between a mountain and a crevasse—to bring the men out. He told us that when he first went in for a landing, he almost got shot. To while away the time the airmen had taken the machine guns out of the bodies of the planes and were firing tracer bullets into the air and into the forest.

"Those boys never knew how close a call they had," he said. "They were all dressed light, and the weather that time of year could change in a minute. If it had, they would have all frozen." He took them out in shifts in the little Junkers, and some years later the U.S. government decorated him for the feat. When the Alaska Highway was built, the army bulldozed a road into Million Dollar Valley and salvaged some of the equipment. But the empty fuselages still lie on the ground looking from the air like brand-new planes on a runway. They add a bizarre touch to this already bizarre corner of the north.

At Watson Lake there were more stories of lost planes. The grisliest concerned a DC-3 that lumbered into the airport one winter's night only dimly visible through a swirling curtain of snowflakes. It made a stab at the runway, missed it, rose into the air again, recircled, and then vanished. For ten days ground parties searched for miles around without success. Then one party, coming back into the airport, lit a fire to brew some tea. As the snow started to melt, the members of the party noticed, to their horror, the outline of a body appearing under the surface. They kicked the embers away, brushed back the snow, and found one of the dead crew. The plane had crashed, it turned out, just two miles west of the airport, so close that nobody had bothered to look there.

We stayed overnight with the Air Force in Watson Lake.

The following morning we turned south across the choppy ocean of mountains that plugs the northern half of British Columbia from Rockies to seacoast.

For the next few hours we saw little but mountains. We were flying over the great rumpled land mass known as the B.C. Interior Plateau. It does not look like a plateau at all, for it is choked with many mountain ranges—the Stikines, the Cassiars, the Ominecas—peaks of five thousand feet caught between the two higher ramparts of the Rockies on the east and the Coasts on the west. This is unknown empty country. On the map the rivers and lakes are still marked by dotted lines. There are no settlements. Indeed, in all of northern British Columbia, an area far larger than California, there are only three thousand white men. Here are canyons of great beauty cut by rivers that wriggled downward as the mountains rose. Here are lakes of purest green—still, cold ponds imprisoned by dams of glacial debris left behind by the vanishing ice sheets. And everywhere there are mountains smothered in snows that never melt.

As dusk approached, we dropped between the peaks and landed on the hard white surface of a little lake not far from a huddle of cabins and tattered gray tents, and a square log trading post set a little apart from them.

"This is Bear Lake," Baker said. "I want you to meet Carl Hannawald."

We climbed the bank and entered the barrack-like trading post. Inside the log walls the military atmosphere persisted. The floor was scrubbed to a glossy whiteness, the counters were neat as a pin, there wasn't a spool of thread out of place. In this austere setting sat an enormous figure of a man in neatly pressed khaki trousers and a checkered bush shirt. He had a bullethead, and thick steel-rimmed spectacles that enlarged his watery blue eyes. This was Hannawald, the trader.

"Come in, gentlemen," he said. "Have supper! Good to see you, Russ."

And so we sat in the neat kitchen behind the neat storeroom, eating sausages neatly arranged on glistening plates and talked to Carl Hannawald, the Prussian army officer from World War I who had been living all alone except for the Indians on the shores of this lake since 1932.

He had come to Canada after the war, with his cousin. They had eighteen thousand dollars and with this sum they bought a ranch. It turned out to be a useless stretch of dessert. Hannawald drifted north, finally going to work in a trading post. When he learned enough about the business, he moved on, built his own private barracks at Bear Lake, and began to trade with the Indians.

Those who knew the history of the country said he wouldn't last a year. Others had tried to trade at Bear Lake; none had stayed very long. For the Bear Lake Indians are a curious tribe, with a history checkered by the white man's firewater and smeared with the white man's blood. Until Hannawald arrived, the country around this lake had been their domain and they had roamed the forest trails to the exclusion of almost everybody else. The Hudson's Bay post that had operated here before Hannawald's time had been burned to the ground and the clerk shot at from the bushes as he made his way up the lake by canoe. The company never rebuilt.

Hannawald talked at length about the Bear Lake Indians as the dusk gathered on the snows and the moon began to light up the white expanse of the ice sheet.

The tribe itself was a hybrid. In the veins of its bucks and squaws runs the blood of many bands—Babine, Coast, Sikanee, Carrier, Tahltan, and Hackwilgate. The reason for this mixed strain was also the reason for the lawlessness of the Bear Lakers. The tribe is made up of descendants of braves who, in the early years of the century, were outlawed by the other tribes for crimes of violence and banished to Bear Lake. Ever since, death and violence have been part and parcel of their existence.

Hannawald and Baker began to swap tales about the Bear Lakers; of the bloody battle between rival gangs, fought out in 1921 with axes, knives, and guns; of the wily little Indian who changed wives annually by getting each one pregnant, then jumping on her to cause a fatal miscarriage; of the policeman investigating a murder who was almost murdered himself by two natives who said, blandly, that they thought he was a moose; of the old man who, wanting to do Baker a favor, inquired brightly if there was anyone the pilot wanted killed.

Carl Hannawald leaned back reflectively. "It is no picnic here, you know," he said. "They hate us. They have scared quite a few out."

When I asked how he managed to stay, he looked at me sternly through the thick spectacles.

"With a club!" he said. "If they try to get tough with me, I get tough with them. Oh, I hear them talk. I hear them say to each other: 'One day I think we get that Meester Carl.' Well, they never get me yet.

"Come," said Hannawald. "I'll show you." He led the way into the storeroom, opened the heavy door, and pointed to the scars of bullets in the timbers. Then he told how, during a potlatch, the Indians would drink themselves into a fury, fight with clubs and knives, beat up the women, and then race to the trading post.

"They always shout the same thing," he said. "They shout: 'White man, you steal our country! We don't like you!' "

Hannawald would lie flat on the rough boards of the floor while the Indians fired at the door. The following day they would all be back amicably trading at the post.

These potlatches are the core of Bear Lake society.

Every time an Indian gives one for his friends, he moves higher in his totem, a sort of native fraternal order. The better the potlatch, the higher the Indian moves. As high totem gives him certain privileges—the right to trap on any line and to have other Indians work for him—each Indian strives to rise higher and higher. In 1929 the chief, Bear Lake Charlie, threw a memorable party that cost six thousand dollars and put him at the very top of the totem —a thirty-second-degree Mason, so to speak.

The basis of the potlatch is the "brew," a hellish mixture compounded of fruit, yeast, sugar, and anything else available, from pepper to tomatoes, mildly alcoholic, but more psychological than physical in its effects. Besides supplying the brew, it is the habit of the host at these parties to buy great quantities of merchandise and give it away; for the more gifts, the higher he ascends in his totem. There are many parallels to the Bear Lake society in our own world.

We bade Hannawald good-by and flew south to Fort St. James. Some years later I saw the trader's name in the newspapers. There had been another murder on the lake, and Hannawald had come to civilization to testify at the hearing. He announced that he would not return to the well-scrubbed trading post. Whether the Indians had been too much for him in the end, or whether he had at last grown rich by trading with them, I never learned.

The day after our visit to Bear Lake we were out of the mountain country and back at the bustling, modern little city of Prince George. My newspaper dispatches had preceded me, and Headless Valley had already achieved the immortality of a joke on the Jack Benny program and an editorial in the *New York Daily Mirror*. It was to prove, in the years that followed, an unkillable legend. Since that time few summers have passed without some new adventurer's beating a path to its canyons and waterfall to tell once again the story of the missing McLeods and the lost gold mine. In the fall of 1954 I came across an eight-column headline in the *Chicago Tribune* that had a familiar ring. "PROBE THIRTEEN DEATHS IN HEADLESS VALLEY," it read. The story went on to tell of "an apparently mythical place of eternal summer, vanishing men, prehistoric monsters and spirit winds."

Russ Baker had planned to come down to Vancouver with Art Jones and me for a brief holiday, but as usual there was no rest for him. He had hardly set down in Prince George airport before a B.C. provincial policeman came around to see him.

In a cabin on the Parsnip River a deranged trapper had to be picked up. A couple of years before, the wretched man had heard a radio news item about a man who had killed a fox and got a skin disease from the animal. The same week the trapper killed a mangy coyote, and the story preyed on his mind until he, too, believed he had a skin disease. He bought every known type of pill and ointment to rid himself of the imaginary ailment until finally his skin did become chafed and unhealthy. Sometimes he'd lie in the cold in his underwear to try to "freeze the bugs out." A few weeks ago he'd sent word that he'd run out of the pills that had now become as necessary to him as beans and bacon.

A day or so before Baker arrived in Prince George, a plane had flown up the Parsnip and the pilot had seen the trapper standing in the front door in his underwear. It was impossible to land on the river, but maybe Russ could get down on some near-by lake and mush in with the pills the trapper wanted. Could Russ . . . ?

Wearily, Baker said he could. He'd be ready right away.

The plane for Vancouver was due in an hour, and Art Jones and I had reserved seats on it. Baker was already deep in his plans for the new job. When we came to say

good-by, he was sitting in the tiny office of his Central
B.C. Airways, his parka hanging loosely from his shoul-
ders, his big beaver skin mitts beside him, poring over a
map of northern British Columbia, his stubby finger trac-
ing the line of the Parsnip River as it flows toward the
Peace down the great Rocky Mountain trench.

And that is the way we left him.

Postscript

When, in 1947, I first wrote about the rapids and gorges of the South Nahanni River for the *Vancouver Sun*, I predicted that some day a great tourist hotel would rise in the shadow of Virginia Falls and that the river itself would be harnessed for hydroelectric power. It seemed a plausible idea at the time. I was twenty-six years old and excited by the possibilities of the post-war boom.

By 1954 I found I had moderated my views. Travelling down the Mackenzie River by tugboat that summer, I felt a small tingle of apprehension when I learned that six major companies were searching for oil in the Nahanni country. Did I really want platoons of professional roustabouts, with bulldozers and drilling equipment, invading this harshly beautiful land? Did I really think a luxury hotel would enhance the natural beauty of Virginia Falls? Was a spur of the Alaska Highway, with its concomitant of gas stations and roadside eateries, really necessary? The possibility made me shudder.

Fortunately, the federal government came to the same conclusion some years later. In 1972, Parks Canada set aside one seventh of the South Nahanni watershed as a national park reserve – a wilderness corridor centred on the serpentine river. It was one of three great parks created in the north that year. In the southwest corner of the Yukon, sprawling across the peaks and glaciers of the St. Elias range and nudging the tip of the emerald lake that bears its name, is Kluane National Park Reserve. Far to the east, straddling the glacial interior of Baffin Island and covering one of the largest icecaps in the world, is the Auyuittuq Reserve. In 1984 and 1986 two more Arctic parks were set aside: the Northern Yukon National Park near the Alaska boundary on the Beaufort Sea and the Ellesmere Island National Reserve, an immense tract of glaciers, fiords, and mountain ranges at the very top of the world.

No roads lead to the Nahanni, and I hope never will. To reach it you must travel by small boat or by airplane. Every year about a thousand adventurers make that effort. No commercial activity is allowed within its boundaries and doubtless never will be, since the Park has also been named by UNESCO as a World Heritage Site.

Much of the Rocky Mountain Trench, which we crossed on that memorable flight to the Nahanni, is now under water. Finlay Forks, where

Postscript

I stayed with Paul Vatcher, the telegraph operator, now lies six miles out from shore, deep beneath the surface of Williston Lake, now the largest body of fresh water in British Columbia. Created by the Bennett Dam on the Peace River to produce hydro power, the lake stretches for one hundred and fifty miles, submerging much of the Finlay and Parsnip river systems. A second arm winds for another fifty miles from a new community (also called Finlay Forks) eastward down the trough of the Peace as far as Hudson Hope. A road links the forks with another new town, Mackenzie, a community of five thousand on the lake's southern tip.

The preservation of the Nahanni wilderness would have appealed to the romantic side of Russ Baker, but I doubt that he would have applauded the flooding of the great trench. He liked the country as it was – raw, sparsely inhabited, free. He flew his bush planes with all the panache of the paladins of old. But there was a practical side to his nature as well. If he took chances, he also figured the odds, which helps explain why he died in bed of a heart attack and not in the wreckage of a Junkers or a Beaver.

When I flew to the Nahanni with him, he had just formed his own company, Central British Columbia Airways. By 1953, having swallowed his competition and established his airline as the dominant carrier in B.C. and Alberta, he changed the name to Pacific Western Airlines. He had big ambitions. He wanted to create another national airline, as his friend and rival Grant McConachie had done with Canadian Pacific. He died in 1958 before he could achieve that goal. But thirty years later, the company he launched with a single-engine Junkers gobbled up its competitors to become Canadian Airlines, a major international carrier.

And the Junkers that took us to Headless Valley? You can see it today on display at the National Aviation Museum in Ottawa. It didn't have to be restored as so many other aircraft in that collection have been. It flew into the Rockcliffe Airport under its own power, and I have no doubt that, with a full tank of gas, it could fly right out again.

Part III

THE TRAIL OF '48

1 | The Gateway to the North

I was standing at the edge of the Edmonton airport on a warm morning in May 1948, waiting to fly to the Yukon with the Royal Canadian Air Force and feeling once again that I was on the very threshold of the frontier.

Edmonton is Canada's northernmost city and it rightly calls itself the Gateway to the North, for once you fly out of the airport and past the mixed farming country that fringes the town, there is little but scrub timber until you reach Fort McMurray on the Athabasca River two hundred and sixty miles away.

The north funnels through Edmonton. Men in bush jackets, Indians in fringed parkas, prospectors, trappers, bush pilots, and explorers walk its streets, many of them just a day out of Dawson, Fairbanks, Whitehorse, Aklavik, and Coppermine. Indeed, it is virtually impossible to reach any part of the western Arctic without going through this curious city that seems to be made up of eight or nine prairie villages all jammed together along the slender curve of the North Saskatchewan River.

Here into this airport, as I watched, poured the plunder of the north. Uranium ore from Great Bear Lake lay carelessly stacked in burlap bags in the corner of one of the big hangars. Sacks of whitefish, taken from Great Slave Lake, were being dumped on the tarmac, three quarters of a ton at a time. An American visitor was once flabbergasted to see a bush pilot unload half a ton of gold ingots at the airport without guard or armored car in sight. And they still talk of the day that J. F. C. Dalziell, the famous flying trapper, flew in with a record hundred and fifty thousand dollars' worth of stone-marten pelts.

Out from the airport flies the provender that keeps the north thriving: loads of steel cable, dynamite, nitroglycerin, boilers, bulldozers, Diesel engines, children's toys, crockery, the occasional horse, a piano for a mineowner's wife, a new wing for a stranded Stinson. A plane once took off from here carrying a ton of Pennsylvania hard coal for Yellowknife miners; they were willing to pay air freight on it because they needed it to temper their tools. And as I watched, they were loading an air-force North Star with provisions for men stationed in Whitehorse.

This is the hub of the northwest, and perhaps at no other airport in the world do sophistication and the frontier meet so squarely head-on. On a February morning the previous winter, an RCAF Dakota, its lights vying with the faint fingers of the aurora on the horizon, swept in from the Arctic. Airmen in parkas helped a child with enormous, astonished black eyes into a waiting ambulance. This was Kamiuk, a legless Eskimo boy from the settlement of Cresswell Bay, fifteen hundred miles away. In the same week a big Northwest Airlines transport roared in from Tokyo and a group of businessmen with briefcases and hard hats climbed out asking: "What day is it now?"

Because of the number of landings and take-offs the Edmonton airport has been reckoned one of the busiest in Canada. The town itself is one of the fastest-growing cities on the continent, and on that May morning it was bursting at its seams. At the very edge of the runways they were knocking together a new hotel out of a set of discarded army huts. Soon, by a curious northern alchemy, this vagrant assembly would be conjured into a class-A hostelry where you could sleep under electric blankets, wake to fresh coffee brought to your room, and eat the finest planked steaks and spareribs on the prairies.

Above me a fluttering helicopter drowned out the sound of the construction work. It was operated by one of the companies exploiting the subterranean ocean of oil upon which Edmonton sprawls. I went over to the airport lunch counter for a cup of coffee and got into conversation with a visiting oil executive from Texas.

"What a town!" the oilman said. "If this were Texas there'd be a bawdy house and three saloons in every block. And here—nothing!"

He was commenting on the unutterable dullness of the Canadian boom town in general and Edmonton in particular. I tried to explain that northern boom towns in Canada are seldom rowdy. In Dawson City at the height of the Klondike stampede in 1898 the Sabbath was observed so rigidly that the Mounted Police would, and did, put a man in jail for chopping his own kindling on Sunday. Edmonton, which has doubled its population since prewar days, just doesn't act like a boom town. A prospector or trapper in from the north can't buy a whisky sour or see a hootchy-kootchy dance at any time of the day or night. There aren't any bars or nightclubs. Two years can go by without a murder, and six weeks without a major crime. Jaywalkers get fined fifty cents.

Edmonton is the capital of Alberta, and the provincial Premier, Ernest Manning, somehow typifies the town. He is a blond, bespectacled Bible student whose thundering Daniel-style prophecies are broadcast each Sunday from a local tabernacle. The man who founded Edmonton in 1795, William Tomison, the "inland chief" of the Hudson's Bay Company, was of a similar breed. He was a strict Presbyterian, who lost trade because he refused to sell liquor to the Indians. To this day in Edmonton you can't buy a glass of anything harder than beer, and you still can't drink beer in public with your wife. A partition separates the ladies from the gentlemen in the Edmonton beverage rooms.

Yet Edmonton has been a boom town since the first log fort was thrown up on the riverbank and the torrent of furs began to pour down from the north. The north built Edmonton. The Klondike stampede in 1898 changed it from a village of eight hundred to a lusty town of four thousand. The air age that followed the First World War made it the Gateway to the North. The Yellowknife gold boom in 1935 boosted its population past that of its rival, Calgary, two hundred miles to the south. The Second War turned it into a madhouse: forty-three thousand Americans poured through it in a single year heading north and spending fortunes on the way. (Mike Jacobs still talks of the GI who marched into his newsstand and emerged with two hundred dollars' worth of fountain pens.) The boom has continued through the postwar years. First there was another Yellowknife boom: four thousand prospectors and a hundred mining corporations were funneled through Edmonton. Then there was an oil boom, one of the continent's greatest. This was followed by the Athabasca uranium boom. Edmonton has long since got used to booms, and through most of them its citizens have maintained the even tenor of their ways.

The central ganglion of these modern booms has been the airport—a seven-minute ride from the business section—the geographical as well as spiritual center of the town. The key to the airport is a slight, quick, brown-eyed Yorkshireman named Jim Bell, who has been the airport's manager since its beginning. I left my Texan acquaintance drinking his coffee and pondering on the paradox of a boom town that doesn't act like a boom town, and walked upstairs to talk to Bell.

He was swinging a big silver dollar on the end of his watch chain when I walked in. As surely as anything can, this coin symbolizes the global position of the Edmonton airport. Bell got the dollar from Wiley Post, who came through on his world-girdling flight in 1932. "This is the fastest dollar in the world," Post told him, and Bell kept it for luck. Later Bell lent the dollar to an Edmonton pilot. Before the coin got back on his watch chain it had been around the world again—by way of the Arctic and the Antarctic.

Bell tends to speak of the airport and the north with capitals in his voice. "This is the Key to the North," he kept saying. We were looking out on the tarmac, where nine Peterborough canoes destined for Great Bear Lake were being loaded into a Douglas transport marked "Eldorado Mining and Refining Limited." "You know, I keep thinking of the old Vikings, and the men of the old shipping days, when I watch this airport. Explorers and pioneers trying to extend their grasp beyond all the horizons. That's what's been going on at this air harbor all the days of its existence."

Bell likes to use the term "air harbor." The phrase was on his tongue back in 1919 before the word "airport" had been invented. Fresh out of the Royal Flying Corps, he went to the Edmonton city fathers with a suggestion: "Someday you're going to have a great air harbor here, and I want to be harbormaster."

He didn't get his wish until 1930, after a series of breath-taking excursions into the north by a new breed of *coureurs de bois* had focused the country's eyes on Edmonton. These new adventurers were loosely described as "bush pilots," a phrase originating among the aerial firefighters of the Ontario forest service, but they flew as well over mountain, tundra, river, and muskeg. In ancient Fokkers, Junkers, Vickers Vikings, de Havilland Moths, Avro

Avians, and a dozen other early flying craft, which seemed to be compounded of wire, string, cardboard, and sheet metal, they set off to conquer the north. Some of them lie now under mounds of charred and crumpled fuselage in various silent corners of the hinterland. Others survived to help write the history of the new frontier.

The two best-publicized figures in this wilderness aristocracy were a blond and owlish young air-corps veteran named "Wop" May and his commercial rival, a diminutive pilot of perennially boyish mien, "Punch" Dickins.

May had started his career as a captain in the Royal Flying Corps. It was he whom the German air ace von Richthofen was chasing at the time he was shot down by another Canadian, Roy Brown. May's exploits continued to make headlines and were climaxed in 1931 by his brilliant aerial pursuit of the Mad Trapper of Rat River across the snow-swept mountains of the Yukon divide on the very lip of the Arctic.

On a bleak January day in 1929 a remarkable feat of May's made Edmonton air-conscious. He and his partner climbed into a tiny open-cockpit biplane, hoisted thirty pounds of serum aboard, and, guided by trappers' smudges along the river, headed for a diphtheria-racked settlement in the Peace River country far to the northwest. This perilous journey in forty-below weather in a plane without skis caught the imagination of the continent. May and his partner froze their hands, faces, and lips. They spilled their last oil in the snow by accident, had to scoop it up into cans, heat it over a fire to steam out the water, and pour it back into the engine again. But they made it to their destination and back, and when they landed, ten thousand cheering people were on hand to greet them.

Meanwhile, Punch Dickins was also making history. He was employed by Western Canada Airways, the daddy of all northern flying lines. In 1928 in a Fokker seaplane he set off across the Barren Lands, whither no pilot had ever ventured, and traversed close to a thousand miles of naked tundra, most of it never before viewed by white man. Before his mission was accomplished he had described an enormous four-thousand-mile circle around the north and covered in just twelve days a journey that would have taken the old fur traders eighteen months.

Dickins performed a second feat of aerial exploration in 1929 when he made history's first fight up the Mackenzie to the Arctic, thus becoming the first pilot across the Circle. He returned in fifty-four-below weather with a payload of baled furs that brought his company four thousand dollars in freight profits. May's exploit with the diphtheria serum had appealed to Edmonton's heart; Dickins's appealed to the city's pocketbook. The mixture of sentiment and hard business sense worked magic. The city ripped down the old hangar that had rotted on the grassy airstrip for a decade, built a new one, named Jim Bell manager of a new class-A airport, and held the country's first air show.

Dickins and May continued to make news. It was May who took the first official airmail into the Arctic—a contract he managed to capture, in spite of Dickins's earlier feat. Enthusiastic stamp-collectors deluged him with four tons of letters—so many that he had to buy three new planes to handle all the mail. By this time a new era had dawned in the north—the era of the great mining discoveries opened up by aerial prospectors. One of these prospectors was a canny Toronto mining man named Gilbert LaBine. It was Punch Dickins who was flying him across the rocky cliffland that borders Great Bear Lake when LaBine spotted the telltale formation that led to North America's first radium and uranium mine.

Bell had a box seat as the drama of early flying unfolded and the greats of its golden age flew off on errands of mercy and discovery. One pilot flew across tundra and

Arctic to locate the position of the North Magnetic Pole. Another flew out of Edmonton across the Barrens to Amundsen Gulf on the frozen ocean and, with only an hour of daylight left and a compass needle whirling like a dervish, rescued eight sailors stranded in an ice-locked schooner. A third combed the lonely land between Great Bear Lake and Coppermine until he found his mark—an igloo made from the engine cowling of a wrecked plane— and flew its three starving occupants to civilization.

The record-breakers poured through the airport in a steady stream. Parker Cramer, the first man to fly from Siberia to New York, roared into Edmonton one night, misjudged his landing in the flickering light of oil flares, tore the belly out of his fabric Cessna, got it stitched together, and roared off again next morning. Ten U.S. bombers drifted through on the first military flight to Alaska, led by a young lieutenant colonel, Hap Arnold. Frank Hawks, the reigning speed champion of the day, whisked a mystery plane into town and dazzled the bush pilots by flying off to Fort McMurray, two hundred and sixty miles away, and back between breakfast and lunch.

"But it was Post and Gatty put this airport on the map," Bell said. "They landed here on their first trip in 1931 and that night we had a record rainfall. The *Winnie Mae* was bogged down in an ocean of mud. I remember Wiley Post climbing out of the plane and I remember exactly what he said: 'This is the end of it. We're finished.' "

But while the fliers slept in his office, Bell hustled up a farmer's stoneboat and had the plane towed out onto Portage Avenue, which borders the airport. This boulevard, since renamed Kingsway, had no houses on it then, thanks to the great land bubble that burst in 1913. It is two and a half miles long, and Post got the *Winnie Mae* off in five blocks.

"That was the era of big chances," Bell said. "You know,

the other day I was looking through my old logbook of pilots who checked through this airport. Fifty-five of those men have been killed in the air."

We talked about the early mining days, which the airplane fostered. After the radium strike the skies north of Edmonton came alive with planes. After the Yellowknife gold rush of 1935–6, pilots stuffed their passengers between machinery and bales of groceries so that they emerged from the low-ceilinged aircraft in a strange crouching position dubbed the "Fokker stoop."

The war made the airport big business. It was so busy at one time that there were twenty-seven planes in the air waiting for the signal to let down. Flights of six hundred aircraft came through at a time, and one day Bell counted one hundred and twenty DC-3's lined up along the edge of the tarmac, all waiting for the weather to clear and all loaded with aerial torpedoes.

"I clocked the landings over a two-and-a-half-hour period one day," Bell said, "and there was a plane landing every ten seconds."

Henry Wallace and Wendell Willkie stopped off at Edmonton. One day a plane from the Soviets asked priority to land. Bell couldn't give it, though Vyacheslav Molotov was aboard. Molotov stayed at the airport overnight, took over an entire building, and had holes bored in his bedroom floor so he could see what went on in the rooms beneath.

One day a girl from Prestwick, Scotland, arrived at the airport, stowed away in the front-wheel housing of a Liberator. She was hoping to get to Alaska to ferry planes to Russia. Another time a man in overalls walked into Bell's office to phone Tennessee. "They took me off my regular run and sent me up here ferrying a ship to Alaska," he explained. "I haven't been home yet. I better let my wife know I can't make dinner."

Bell was still reminiscing when it was time for me to catch my plane for the Yukon. I rose and said good-by to him.

"They're still coming through, you know," Jim Bell said as we walked out of his office. "There were two youngsters through here the other day, flying Piper Cubs around the world, and a couple of elderly ladies ferrying Aircoupes to Alaska. And I had a British housewife stranded here last spring. She was trying to go around the world, too."

I strolled over to the RCAF hangars in the bright morning sunlight. The Eldorado plane had loaded its canoes and was off. An oil company's helicopter hovered in the sky. The regular CPA flight to Yellowknife was leaving.

By late afternoon I myself was far away on the banks of the Yukon.

2 | The Cinderella City

I was standing once again on the main street of Whitehorse, the town where I was born. Behind me the familiar blue hills of the upper Yukon Valley rippled off in endless succession, like the waves of the ocean. Before me, the Yukon River—as blue as the hills, at this point—swept past on its two-thousand-mile journey to the Bering Sea.

The last time I had stood in this wide, dusty street, with its irregular line of old frame buildings, had been on a warm September day in 1939 when the hills were aflame with the autumn oranges and yellows of birch and aspen. In those days Whitehorse was a sleepy little village of four hundred people, with its history behind it and its future uncertain. Husky dogs snored in the dirt roadways and I remember that one had been kicked out of the way by a man who came over from the White Pass Hotel to accost my father and me. One carried on conversations in the middle of the street in Whitehorse, in those days. This man had come to tell us that Britain had declared war on Germany. Now the war had come and gone. It had wrecked many cities but it had transformed Whitehorse into the crossroads of the northwest.

The town that now greeted me, scattered along the river flats of volcanic ash, was a cluttered hodgepodge of war-time jerry-building—a wild mélange of tar-paper shacks, outhouses, bunkhouses, Quonset huts, corrugated-iron lean-tos, false-fronted frame structures, log cabins from an earlier day, a few trim little bungalows, and a few square blockhouses disguised by imitation brick—all mingled with piles of salvaged lumber and piping, rusted hulks of trucks and bulldozers, and scattered heaps of old oil drums. This was the mess left behind by the army of forty thousand soldiers and construction workers who had poured through Whitehorse to built the Alaska Highway, the Canol pipeline, and the airfields of the Northwest Staging Route. Whitehorse was still cleaning up after them.

I checked in at the Whitehorse Inn, the handsomest building in town, put up before the war, enlarged since, and operated by the town's greatest legend since Sam McGee. He was Thomas Cecil Richards, better known to everyone as "T. C.," a dapper figure, dressed from head to foot in pearl gray. He had once been a butcher in the Cariboo country of B.C. Now he was Whitehorse's leading citizen, controlling restaurants, taxi service, butcher shop, laundry, theater, and hotel. The story of his acquisition of the Whitehorse Inn is a variable tale and Richards himself has done little to clear it up. He has given several colorful versions of the affair. One of them goes like this:

"At four a.m. on September 1, 1936, I was playing black-jack against Ken Yoshida, a Japanese and owner of the hotel. I had already won a thousand dollars and then three thousand on the turn of two cards. Then I drew a king, a deuce, and a nine and got up from the table owner of the hotel. I went out fishing with a bottle of rum."

This is probably an oversimplification, but there is nobody in Whitehorse who does not believe that it is at least founded on fact. Richards has always answered the door when opportunity knocks. He made his first big money in 1921 by mechanizing a famous northern institution—the romantic but uncomfortable six-horse stage on sleigh runners that used to travel the winter road between Whitehorse and Dawson. The long journey, through a lonely world of frozen river and silvered forests, took five days, with overnight stops at log roadhouses. Richards figured the fare and the time could be cut almost in half by using tractors instead of horses, because the tractor trains could run all night. The scheme worked, and the passengers, who huddled on bales of freight for three solid days in fifty-below weather, were delivered, chilled to the bone but otherwise intact and on schedule.

"Well," Richards used to say when the passengers feebly protested the journey, "you wanted to get there fast, didn't you?"

Whitehorse, when I reached it that May afternoon in 1948, had come a long way since the days of the six-horse stage and the tractor train. It has always occupied a strategic position at the head of the Yukon River, and it is the only Canadian town north of the sixtieth parallel served by rail. Up through the sharp, spectacular mountain gorges of the famous White Pass runs a line of narrow-gauge steel from Skagway on the seacoast. It takes five locomotives to tug the little trains over the divide where half a century ago a thin file of gold-seekers plodded. Now Whitehorse had become a staging point for trucks and airplanes as well. The low benchland overlooking the town had been sheared off to make room for the biggest airport in the territories. The long, dusty ribbon of the Alaska Highway wove through the hills and around the town before stretching off into the mountains toward Fairbanks, Alaska. Whitehorse, the halfway point and nerve center of the highway, was no longer a sleepy village of four hundred or a roaring boom town of forty thousand. Its population had settled down to a stable three thousand, but Whitehorse itself was not yet a stable community. It was a town in transition, still reeling from a prosperous blow dealt it during the war, still clinging wistfully to a romantic past, and just starting to look forward to a rosy future.

The past had its monuments and its symbols. There was T. C. Richards's Inn, with its unlocked doors. After fifty years a key was still a curiosity in town. There was the Whitehorse Skyscraper, an extraordinary three-story log pagoda with stairways tacked onto the outside. There were the little old cabins of Sam McGee and Robert Service, twin shrines that had been the town's two main attractions before the war. Service had been a bank clerk in Whitehorse in 1905 when he borrowed the name of a depositor for his famous ballad "The Cremation of Sam McGee."

Down on the riverbank, slowly rotting to dust, were some of the most famous of the old Yukon river boats, straight from the days of the Klondike rush. They sat there on the ways, the paint long peeled from them, their timbers black with age, their paddlewheels crumbling to bits. There sat the old *Yukoner:* in the gold-rush days she puffed up the river with a cargo of chorus girls and champagne, and an orchestra playing on her deck. She had been owned by a onetime Montana sheriff who had struck it rich in the Klondike. The climax of her career came when she became the scene of the Yukon River's only mutiny. Now she was used to store lumber. Not far away was another rotting hulk, the famous *Bonanza King,* built and paid for by a millionaire miner from Eldorado Creek. In the blue-green waters of the river itself were newer steamers, the *Klondike, Casca,* and *Whitehorse,* with fat yellow smokestacks and white gingerbread fretwork trimming the cabins and bright red paddlewheels at the stern. They and others like them had been plying the long, cold river for half a century, but their days were numbered.

The past had its monument, too, in the weekly *Whitehorse Star,* in whose dusty files the first verses of Robert Service can still be found, and in its graying, erudite editor, Horace Moore, a soft-spoken, pipe-smoking old-countryman.

"Do you remember the last time we met?" he asked as we sat talking in the rear of his cluttered little office. "It was in 1937. You were going down-river to work on the creeks out of Dawson, and I was a waiter on the old *Casca.*"

I remembered quite well: the waiter who quoted Charles Lamb and wouldn't let me tip him because he said I couldn't afford it. When he had made enough money he ceased to be a waiter and became a publisher, thus fulfilling a long-held ambition. The war had intervened since

I had last seen him, and we soon got onto this universal topic of northern conversation.

Horace Moore had steered his little paper through those hysterical times without once giving the impression that Whitehorse was anything other than a respectable, well-behaved suburb. Outside his office in 1943 he could see men and women standing five deep in ten-block queues, lighting fires in the middle of the street to warm themselves while they waited ten hours to buy a bottle of whisky. Moore continued to print the church notices and write his quiet, scholarly editorials. Now, like the river boats', Horace Moore's days in Whitehorse were ending.

In the back room of the Army and Navy Club the Ace-Away game—a hangover from the war days played with three dice—still had its followers. The dice rattled out of the rubber cup, the men in Cowichan Indian sweaters leaned over the board, the dollar bills and ten-dollar bills mounted into a crumpled pile on the table, and the dealer sang out his familiar cajolery: "Jing-a-low for all that dough." Gambling is illegal under the criminal code of Canada, and Whitehorse in 1948 was the nearest thing to a Reno or Las Vegas the country has had since the Klondike era. The Royal Canadian Mounted Police, who keep the law in the Yukon, patrolled the streets, but the Ace-Away games rattled on behind closed doors. A man once made fifteen thousand dollars in a single night at Ace-Away, and a Chinese laundryman ran a small stake up to seventy-four thousand in a week. He left Whitehorse the following day and was never seen again.

But Ace-Away, too, was doomed. A year or so after I visited the town the police finally closed the games. They no more fitted the new Whitehorse than Horace Moore's venerable *Star* or the old stern-wheel steamer *Casca*. The same year Moore sold the *Star* for seven thousand dollars to a six-foot salesman who introduced aggressive methods, trebled the circulation, and printed gaudier news than church notices. Once he ran the story, names and all, of a prominent citizen's being charged with wife-beating. When the citizen arrived at the *Star* office brandishing a knife, the new owner threw him out.

As for the river steamers, they were retired from service about the time that T. C. Richards, plagued by a wave of burglaries, installed Yale locks in the Whitehorse Inn. The British-Yukon Navigation Company, which has controlled transportation through the territory since 1900, found the old stern-wheelers no longer paid their way. The airplanes skimming from the hill and the trucks lumbering up the highway had stolen the business. The *Casca* and the *Whitehorse* and the *Klondike* joined the *Yukoner* and the *Bonanza King* on the waterfront ways.

They have since been granted a reprieve, mainly because of an idea that has long been simmering in the mind of a onetime Yukon bush pilot named Grant McConachie, the president of Canadian Pacific Airlines. McConachie is a suave and smiling executive of husky build, fertile imagination, and romantic background. His early career, like that of most former bush pilots, was a garish mosaic of aerial adventure, mercy flights, crack-ups, and financial problems. In his youth he was called "the human airplane," a title he lived up to by hammering new engine parts out of scrap iron to save himself from being marooned on a frozen lake. He was a man of considerable resilience. When he cracked up one plane, sustaining broken ankles, kneecaps, wrists, and ribs, he recovered and married his nurse. When he owed hangar rent for another plane, he persuaded a mineowner to stake him and parlayed the result into an airline: Yukon Southern Air Transport. This was one of eleven hinterland companies bought up by the Canadian Pacific Railway and merged to form Canadian Pacific Airlines in 1942. McConachie joined the new firm and confidently predicted he would end up as president. Five years later the prediction came true.

Since then McConachie has turned the hodgepodge of bush lines into an air-travel system whose tentacles reach out to Hong Kong, Tokyo, Hawaii, Fiji, Australia, South America, Mexico, and—by way of the polar seas—Holland. His planes blanket the Canadian north, but McConachie still isn't satisfied. He wants to lure more people north by way of his airline, and in the winter of 1953–54 he decided to use the Yukon River steamboats as bait. He leased the old freighter *Klondike* and spent a hundred thousand dollars transforming her into a floating luxury hotel. He re-decked her, installed a cabaret and a cocktail bar (with murals of the dance-hall days), and organized a Klondike tour for wealthy travelers.

The tourists get their money's worth. CPA flies them to Whitehorse from Edmonton or Vancouver and pops them aboard the steamboat, which takes them four hundred and sixty miles down the winding Yukon to Dawson City and back. The tourists stake miniature claims, pan for gold, fish with willow rods, re-create the cremation of Sam McGee on Lake Laberge, and dance with old sourdoughs in the Nugget Dance Hall at Dawson. This is the first large-scale attempt to exploit the immense tourist potential of the Canadian north, a natural resource that may someday be as fruitful as all the muskrat pelts of the Mackenzie or all the nuggets of the Klondike.

Whitehorse, with its airport, its highway to Alaska, its railway from Skagway, and its new tourist trade, has become, beyond doubt, the most stable town in the north. It is now the capital of the Yukon, a prize finally wrested from the old city of Dawson. It has four bars, including one called the Rainbow Cocktail Lounge, paneled in blond wood and upholstered in mauve nylon, where the customers are fined ten cents a word for profanity. It has a Kiwanis Club, a branch of Alcoholics Anonymous, a Board of Trade, and a two-million-dollar Federal Building that is the costliest structure in the Yukon's history. All these things have come to pass in the decade since the war.

Yet this is only the beginning for Whitehorse. It sits in the heart of a vast mineral area that still awaits development. The Alaska Highway winds its way past deposits of copper and nickel in the mountains of the St. Elias Range, while up the muddy Pelly River, the Yukon's great tributary, lie lead, zinc, silver, and gold. Whitehorse is growing once more. Soon it will spill across the Yukon by way of a new steel bridge; three thousand lots will be available on the far side, and a three-million-dollar hospital will be built. For a new kind of stampede is about to begin on the shores of the Yukon River.

The reasons for all this sudden expansion could only be guessed at in the late spring of 1948 when I passed through my birthplace. Yet even then an extraordinary man named Thayer Lindsley was dreaming dreams and making plans to turn the entire valley of the southern Yukon into a new industrial empire. For years Lindsley has had his eye on the great river, which is one of the world's last easily available sources of hydro power. His plan is staggering: what he wants to do is to reverse the flow of the river so that it spills back over the Coast Mountains in which it rises, dropping a thousand feet through tunnels drilled in the granite to generate twice as much power as the St. Lawrence Seaway.

Lindsley is another northern legend, as mysterious as the country that has made him powerful. It is impossible to travel through the north without crossing the tracks or passing in the shadow of this remarkable man. When Gilbert LaBine was staking his silver and radium claims on Great Bear Lake, Lindsley's planes were flying overhead. When gold boomed Yellowknife, Lindsley's mine, the Giant, became the largest of all. When the lead, silver, and zinc of Keno Hill in the Yukon made stock-market history in 1950 and 1951, it turned out that Lindsley's company had the lion's share.

Yet, though he is the leading mining personality in Canada, Lindsley remains a recluse whom few men know, a mystery man with a genius for shunning the limelight, who has made millions but hasn't yet got around to buying a motorcar.

I met him once in Toronto when *Maclean's Magazine* was working on the first article about him ever published. He came into my office, a tall, sticklike creature in his seventieth year, with birdlike features and a frailty of body that belied his energies. He didn't want the article and he was trying to persuade us not to publish it, for publicity embarrasses him. Up to then no newspaper in the world had had a picture of him or a file on his career. Yet most mining men insist he has contributed more to Canadian mining than any other man in history.

It is hard to believe that the north's most imaginative industrial scheme lay locked in the brain of this mild-looking man with the neat white mustache and the sunken cheeks, who dresses so primly, who neither smokes nor drinks, who prefers apples and whole-wheat bread to exotic foods, who has never bothered with more than one servant, and who cares not a fig for money. Lindsley is willing to gamble hundreds of millions on reversing the continent's fifth largest river, yet often he forgets to carry enough funds on his person to buy a breakfast or hire a taxi.

He is a Harvard graduate from the same class as Franklin Delano Roosevelt (whose standing was a good deal lower than Lindsley's). He came to Canada in the mid-twenties, formed a holding company called Ventures Ltd., and laid the foundations of the international mining empire he now controls. Today, through Ventures, its twin Frobisher Ltd., and other holding companies, he holds in his palm some sixty subsidiary companies not only in Canada but also in Venezuela, Uganda, South Africa, Greece, Norway, Nicaragua, California, the Philippines, Costa Rica, Honduras, Nevada, and Massachusetts.

Lindsley proposes to make breath-taking changes in the upper Yukon River (formerly called the Lewes) around Whitehorse. By 1962 he expects to have spent two hundred and seventy million dollars on the first stage of a plan that may take half a century to complete. By then sixty thousand square miles of new country will be opened up, and smelters and refineries will be producing iron, steel, cobalt, nickel, and manganese at the rate of four hundred thousand tons a year.

This is merely the beginning. The storage capacity of the upper Yukon is enormous—the largest in the Western Hemisphere except that of the Great Lakes. Lindsley's surveys show that almost five million horsepower can be developed cheaply enough to make it pay. The St. Lawrence Seaway will produce only two and a half million.

Frobisher and Ventures, two of Lindsley's holding companies, plan eventually to spend seven hundred millions in developing the first 4.3 million horsepower. To do this Lindsley's men will back up the river with a series of dams and then spill it back over the Coast Mountains through a network of tunnels to the generating stations near Taku Inlet, a long, narrow arm of the Pacific that cuts through the slender Alaska panhandle near Juneau into British Columbia. Here a smelter town of twenty or thirty thousand will spring up.

The over-all plan for the great river stretches off into the mists of the future. It will probably take half a century or more and cost upward of a billion dollars. Fifty years from now three hundred miles of the river may be dammed—all the way north from Miles Canyon at Whitehorse to the century-old post of Fort Selkirk. It is a fair guess that by then as much as ten million horsepower will be in use.

Lindsley is banking on the world's hunger for cheap and easily available power, and the Yukon has both kinds. It will be cheap because of its abundance. It will be available because the tunnels and generating station need be only forty-five miles from the Pacific Ocean. Within a decade ore-carriers from all over the globe will steam up the Alaska-B.C. coastline to the new smelters. The ships will go to Taku Inlet, and barges will freight the ore up the shallow water to the new town just inside the Canadian border. Because ocean transport is still the cheapest kind, it will pay to ship unprocessed ore thousands of miles for refining and then float the finished product back to the markets.

Lindsley's own network of companies controls enough raw ore to keep the project busy in its first stages. He plans to bring nickel and cobalt from the South Pacific, manganese from South Africa, zinc and iron from Vancouver Island. By 1962 the nickel output alone will be nearly a third that of the giant International Nickel Company at Sudbury.

The series of man-made tunnels and dams will thread through some of the most picturesque country in the world. The dammed waters will rise almost to the edge of the White Pass railway, and the old gold-rush trail from Skagway. A dam will be built at the head of Miles Canyon and Whitehorse Rapids, where two hundred Klondikers lost their lives in the 1898 stampede. Backed-up water will bloat Tagish Lake, whose glacial emerald surface reflected the sails of twenty thousand homemade boats in 1898.

Much later a series of dams will back up Laberge, the lake north of Whitehorse made famous by Service and Sam McGee. Five Finger Rapids—the most spectacular navigation hazard on the river, where enormous pinnacles of rock loom out of the water—may vanish. Finally, Lindsley expects to trap the muddy waters of the Pelly, which pours down westward from the continental divide to join the Yukon at Selkirk, two hundred miles north of Whitehorse.

By this time all the great store of base metals known to lie in the Whitehorse area will be developed and no man can tell how large this Cinderella town may grow. Predictions are futile in the north: they are either too generous or too conservative. Certainly when I revisited my birthplace on that spring day in 1948 I had no more inkling of what was in Thayer Lindsley's mind than, a decade before, I could have guessed that the little town of four hundred would swell tenfold. But one thing is certain: of all the northern towns, Whitehorse has the shiniest future.

3 | **Ghosts on the Klondike**

I caught the weekly CPA plane out of Whitehorse for Dawson City, two hundred and seventy-five miles to the northwest. For two hours we flew across the rolling peneplain that geographers call "the Yukon interior plateau," a land of great rivers, green little sloughs, and broad, empty valleys clothed in spruce and birch and poplar. Here are the "mighty mouthed hollows" of Service's poems, snaking down through the blue hills, each with a tinsel trickle of water meandering across its broad floor. And beyond the rim of every valley lies another valley, identical with the last.

The Yukon plateau is a northern extension of the great interior plateau of British Columbia, and the Yukon River is its filament. It lies imprisoned between the two great cordilleran barriers that follow the curve of North America into the peninsula of Alaska—the Mackenzie Mountains, far to the northeast, and the St. Elias Mountains along the seacoast to the south. Although the summers here are blazing hot, the winters are as frigid as Greenland's, so that the word "Yukon" has become a synonym for fierce cold.

Yet, paradoxically enough, the glaciers that smothered all the rest of Canada during the Ice Age scarcely touched the heart of this country. While Iowa, Illinois, and Indiana lay prostrate under a mantle of ice, the Yukon River flowed north, much as it does today, through its broad forested valley. For it takes moisture to produce an ice cap—endless snows drifting from the sky—and the Yukon is semi-arid land. A mountain rampart, the tallest on the continent, bars the moisture-laden Pacific Ocean air from sweeping into the interior. It falls instead upon the southern slopes of Alaska, to feed some of the greatest and most spectacular glaciers in the world.

But there are no glaciers in the Yukon's heartland and, because of the dry climate, no lakes either, except for those alpine fingers of indescribable green that lie near the base of the mountains where the great river rises. The familiar flat checkerboard of water and forest that gives the rest of northern Canada its texture is absent here, but an ancient pattern of erosion, undisturbed by glacial invasion, is inscribed on the corrugated surface of the land. Here, for millions of years, the streams and rivers have been at work sculpturing the countryside down to a level as low as running water can ever reduce a land mass.

Thus the history of the land is graven in its valleys. Below us we could see the most familiar aspect of the Yukon country—the high benchland above the great river. The slopes seem to have been terraced by a giant hand, shaped into monumental staircases descending from the tops of the rounded hills to the water's edge. Each of these benches marks the bottom of an ancient stream course. Almost every Yukon valley is modeled in this manner so that the downward erosion of rivers and streams is clearly indicated.

The once-blue river, now soiled to dirty gray by the mud of the tributary Pelly, was directly beneath us, flowing endlessly north and west in a huge crescent that loops over the Arctic Circle and back through Alaska to the sea. It is the continent's fifth largest river. It rises within fifteen miles of salt water, but it takes a tortuous twenty-three-hundred-mile course to reach the ocean. It begins with a series of seepages and mountain springs on the northern rim of the Coast Mountains that wall off the Yukon Territory from the Pacific. The green glacial lakes feed it, and so do the dark little streams that ripple through the frozen mosses of northern British Columbia. Soon it swells in size to drain almost all of the Yukon and Alaska. The floor of permafrost that lies a foot beneath the soil forces almost all the surface water to run off into the Yukon and its tributaries so that, in flood, the volume of water in this huge river system rivals that of the Mississippi.

This is the old gold-rush route, the cold, wet road that links the White and Chilkoot passes with the Klondike.

Once, fifty years ago, its metallic surface was alive with boats, rafts, scows, and bateaux, as thirty thousand men poured down the river in the strange mass compulsion that gripped the continent and, indeed, most of the civilized world, in the dying days of the Victorian age. Today the river is empty and silent, unchanged except for the scars on the hills where the prospectors' fires have charred the landscape.

The river is a boatman's dream. Almost all of it, except for a few dozen miles at its source, is navigable. Salmon swim upstream for more than two thousand miles from the Bering Sea to Lake Bennett, high in the mountains. Between Whitehorse and the delta there are only three or four obstacles, and none of them is insurmountable. The beautiful, twisting section of the river colloquially known as the Thirtymile pours out of Lake Laberge, so blue and clear that you can see the wrecks of old steamboats lying on the bottom. It is considered by some pilots to be the most dangerous stretch of navigable water in the world, but ever since a daring skipper took its double-S turn at full steam to go to the aid of a stricken comrade, it has held few terrors for seasoned pilots. There are two sets of rapids, the more spectacular being Five Fingers, where the river has cut five channels through a rocky dike of conglomerate. Eight hundred miles downstream on the Alaska side lie the notorious Yukon flats, where the river spills out ten to twenty miles wide over a prehistoric lake bottom so shallow that boats cannot navigate it in low water. There in the golden age of the stern-wheelers the old ships used to jam up like customers in a movie queue. But for most of the summer season the Yukon can be easily negotiated. Without it, the Klondike might never have been discovered and the country would still be largely inaccessible.

The river and the land it drains present a strange paradox. In one sense the Yukon country is the oldest part of the north. In another sense it is the youngest.

The Klondike strike was the first important mining discovery made north of the sixtieth parallel. It predated by forty years the big gold strike at Yellowknife, eight hundred air miles to the southeast. Thus the Yukon was developed and civilized while its neighbor the Mackenzie country was still a primitive land existing only for the fur trade. For half a century Dawson City, with its banks, hotels, newspapers, high school, farms, electric light, telephones, and running water, has been the most civilized of the far northern towns.

Yet from an explorer's standpoint the Yukon is far younger than the Mackenzie. A century ago it was an unknown watercourse flowing through a dark land as silent as the grave, unexplored and unmapped. When Alexander Mackenzie traced his great river to its mouth, the Yukon was only a legend on the lips of the Dogrib Indians, who refused to take him across the mountains to seek it out. The fur traders and prospectors were slow to trickle into the Yukon plateau. Almost a century elapsed before the Yukon had its own Mackenzie. He was a U.S. cavalry lieutenant named Frederick Schwatka, who went down the entire river by raft and skin boat in 1883. There were other white men along the river by then, but Schwatka was the first to explore it thoroughly from the Chilkoot Pass to the Bering Sea. He named every feature he saw, and most of the names still hold with one notable exception. The little salmon stream known as the Deer River has long since become the Klondike.

And now the Klondike was below us, clogged with the white gravel tailing piles of the gold dredges, which for almost half a century have been tearing deep into the bowels of the river bed. A few moments later we landed a few miles out of Dawson City on Archie Fournier's cow pasture, which does duty as an airport.

I was home again after a nine-year absence. For though I was born in Whitehorse, I was brought up in Dawson, and I have always thought of it as my home town.

An old home town is many things to many people: faces, memories, old buildings and vacant lots, climate and history and low blue hills, dust and gravestones and old, old men—a shifting montage of sounds and impressions that sometimes stray through your dreams like the sound of an ancient school-bell or the bark of a dog long dead. It was to recapture some of these impressions that I had come back.

My home town is not an ordinary home town. There has been nothing conventional about it since the early days, in '97, when tents by the thousands began to bleach the swampy mile-and-a-half wedge of frozen ground where the Klondike meets the Yukon. The sourdough who staked it out named it for George Dawson, a hunchbacked government geologist. Since that time it has nurtured some of the most surprising people—all the way from General Evangeline Booth of the Salvation Army to a buxom brunette nicknamed the Oregon Mare because she could whinny across the dance floor of the Monte Carlo saloon like a colt in springtime.

Tex Rickard, the promoter, was a waiter in Dawson City, and so was Alexander Pantages, who became the greatest theater-owner of his time. Sid Grauman spent his boyhood here before he went to Hollywood to build the Chinese Theater. Jack Marchbanks, who later ran the track at Tia Juana, was a gambler in Dawson. Wilson Mizner, who operated Hollywood's Brown Derby restaurant and composed Broadway plays, began his career as a tenor soloist in the Dawson of the stampede days. Jack Kearns, who later managed Jack Dempsey, started his boxing career in Dawson, and there Frank Slavin, the heavyweight champion of Australia, ended his. A whole school of writers and poets—Joaquin Miller, Jack London, Rex Beach, James Oliver Curwood, and, finally, Robert W. Service—lived for years off the literary avails of the stampede city.

From the days of Diamond Tooth Gertie and Nellie the Pig (so called because she once bit off a bartender's ear), its citizens have shunned convention. When I returned to Dawson they were still talking about Eddie Rickard, the second-hand man who willed his estate to a fund for supplying every destitute sourdough with a bottle of whisky each Christmas.

The buildings, which seem to have sprung straight from a Gary Cooper Western, are no more conventional than the citizens, nor is the climate, which in the summer allows purple asters to grow to twice their normal size, then plunges to sixty below each winter. And there is nothing conventional about the river either: each spring it runs amok, roaring and grinding like a dozen express trains as it tosses elephant-sized cakes of ice high up on its banks.

It is, in some ways, a saddening experience to return as a stranger to a town that once belonged to you, because a stranger sees things differently from a native.

"You're going to see some changes," Ed Hickey said to me as he drove me, in Dawson's only taxicab, along the white gravel road that skirts the Klondike River. But there were few changes, really, in Dawson City. It was almost exactly the same town I had left. The real changes were in myself.

It shocked me to drive around the curve of the Klondike bluff after a decade and see once again the faded old buildings that had formed the backdrop to my childhood. Most of the buildings have been part of Dawson since the gold rush. Easily half of them are boarded up and empty, and there is hardly one that does not slant crazily along the plank sidewalks. Perhaps half are log; the rest are frame with corrugated-iron roofs. Their architecture is of that style familiar to students of the old West—the school of the false front, the bay window, the fluted pillar and covered entrance, the scrolled cornice and ornamental balcony. But now the architecture mocks the visitor because it is crumbling away.

Street after street is lined with empty buildings: old hotels and gambling houses, deserted dance halls, saloons and grocery stores with rotting porticoes and sightless windows. Nature is not kind to frame buildings set in permafrost. There was once a flat little park built in Dawson. It stayed flat for a year, then took on the roller-coaster contours characteristic of the terrain. Even the occupied structures slump drunkenly because the ground on which they are built—frozen permanently for some two hundred feet down—continually heaves and sinks.

The problem of permafrost plagues the north, and nowhere more than in this oldest of northern communities. Many of Dawson's buildings were erected a half century before modern engineers began to learn something about the various curious phenomena associated with permanently frozen ground. It is strange that it should take so long to begin to understand it, for one fifth of the land area of the world is underlain by permafrost, which may be only a few yards deep or may go down thirteen hundred feet as it does at Resolute Bay and on the Russian coast. (It was the Russians who made the first studies of permafrost, and it is to them that North American engineers owe much of their knowledge.)

Dawson with its washboard roads and its slanting buildings is a monument to man's futile attempts to struggle with the problem. The great fact of permafrost is that when it melts, the character of the ground changes completely. Often enough it shrinks in size and becomes as soft as gruel. When the protective insulating blanket of moss is torn aside by bulldozers building airstrips or roads, the ground, frozen for the past million years, begins to melt and chaos results. When a building is placed upon it, generating heat into the soil, a similar state of anarchy follows. It is impossible to fight permafrost with stronger materials or more rigid designs. In the past few years northern engineers have learned to construct roads by the "passive method," leaving the insulating moss alone so that the permafrost is undisturbed and remains as firm as bedrock. Similarly, masonry foundations have been found unsatisfactory in the north. The houses that remain erect are the ones that are built on stilts or pilings or raftlike platforms with ventilation or insulation between the floor and the frozen ground. In fact, northern construction firms have found it best to paint buildings white so that they will attract a minimum amount of heat to the frozen soil.

Dawson's tottering buildings surrounded me as I drove toward the river front. Tucked in between the ancient structures were the log cabins and neat white cottages of those townspeople still left in the community. About eight hundred people remained in a city that had once held twenty thousand. I found that some of the buildings I once knew had been torn down, and there were more vacant lots than I remembered as a boy, though God knows there were plenty even then.

The old Green Tree Hotel, where Babe Mitchell, the dance-hall girl, was shot, had long since vanished from Front Street, and so had the big frame warehouse where Jan Welzl, a Czech refugee, used to work vainly on his perpetual-motion machine. The Nugget Dance Hall, which used to be the Auditorium in the days when Alexander Pantages was a beer-slinger, had been boarded up.

The dim lettering of the old Red Feather Saloon still showed on the side of a rickety building opposite Billy Biggs's blacksmith shop. The padlocked saloon was just as I had remembered it, its interior, as seen through the grimy windows, jammed with second-hand machinery that all but crushed the splintered mahogany bar.

I checked into the Royal Alexandra Hotel on Front Street. On the wall there still hung three enormous oil paintings of nudes, each seven feet high and encased in gilded baroque frames. The walls and ceiling of the lobby were sheathed in the characteristic embossed metalwork that seems to earmark commercial interiors designed in Canada at the turn of the century. The same worn Edwardian chairs of black leather still sat there, and the same old men, it seemed, sat buried in them. Beyond the half-open door to the rear, the inevitable poker game was curtained in the inevitable blue fog of stale cigar smoke.

Sam Broughton was at the desk, as always, a big man with a generous Victorian mustache and black armlets and a faded green fedora tilted low over one eye.

"Hello there," Sam said, casually. "You came back, eh?"

Sam had come to Dawson fifty years before to stay five years. He never left again to go to the "Outside"—the term that northerners apply to the rest of the world. A year before, some of Sam's relatives had written in to ask if he was still alive. Sam hadn't yet got around to answering them.

The talk in the lobby of the Royal Alex was familiar talk, for it centered on the breakup of the river and the arrival of the first boat. Indeed, it seemed as if I had stepped out the door for only a moment or two.

The first boat had preceded me into town by a couple of days. The entire populace, as usual, had turned out to greet the stern-wheeler as she pulled into the dock on Front Street, and now the town was eating its first potatoes, fresh fruit, and lamb in weeks. Supplies had run out during the winter, and import by plane was too expensive. Dawson merchants order their food a year and a half in advance and, even so, it doesn't last the season. That winter bananas had sold for two dollars a dozen.

They were still talking, too, about the ice breakup—the other great spring event. There had been a snag in the big Ice Pool, the lottery into which Yukoners pay a dollar to guess the exact moment of the breakup. For the second year in succession the wire tied to the flag out on the frozen river had broken before it could stop the clock and mark the moment when the ice moved. The money had been held over for another year, and ten thousand dollars was now at stake.

I picked up my grip and climbed the sweeping and beautifully proportioned staircase to my room. The building had been settling again in the permafrost, and the floor of the long upstairs hall was warped and twisted as a result. There was no key, of course. A big brass-knobbed, white-quilted bed sat in the center of the room. A china pitcher and washbasin occupied a table beside it. An old-fashioned dresser, badly chipped, completed the furnishings. The windows overlooked the Dawson hills, capped by the tapering Midnight Dome, a mountain marked with the moosehide-shaped scar of a great slide that, according to legend, had fallen away in an enormous chunk and buried an Indian village in the days before the white man. The legend is romantic but geologically untenable. The rocky bluff from which the slide is cut is underlaid with mountain springs that force their way up through the permafrost, forming small glaciers each winter. By an inexorable process over the centuries they have laid bare the face of the vertical cliff so that each year a little more of it crumbles away and the "slide" always seems fresh and new. There are springs everywhere in this part of the country, and each winter they form domes of ice, which often block roads and pathways and occasionally come up through the cellars and fill the cabins themselves.

I walked downstairs again and out into the sunshine of Front Street. The Royal Alex used to be the Dominion gambling house, the scene of the Klondike's only holdup; the Arcade Café, next door ("House of Good Eats," Harry Gleaves, Prop.), had been the Flora Dora dance hall. I walked in and drank a chocolate milkshake at the original mahogany bar. The golden letters *Flora Dora* were still inscribed over a doorway that now leads into the kitchen.

For most of my formative years I had lived in these surroundings without once realizing that it was the most famous ghost town in the world. The streets in which I played as a boy had never seemed romantic or out of the ordinary, nor do they seem so to the few who live there today. The weathered, abandoned buildings I used to pass on the way to school had never seemed shoddy or decrepit in the old days. Yet they looked that way now.

If the town had changed at all, it had shrunken within itself. Another fire had swept Front Street, though it had once again spared the Royal Alex, to make it the oldest building remaining on the block. But Apple Jimmie's place, two doors down, was gone, and so was Jimmie, the little pock-marked Greek greengrocer who had got his name selling apples at a dollar apiece in the gold-rush days. The Front Street fire had razed the Yukonia Hotel, which silent Sam Bonnifield, the gambler, had lost and won again in a single night. And the Orpheum Theater, where eleven-year-old Margie Newman, the child singer, once stood heel-deep in nuggets thrown to her from the boxes, was also burned to the ground.

I walked across the street to the firehall. A big polished steam pumper still sat there. Legend said it had been stolen from the Victoria, B.C., Fire Department in 1900.

It had long been a tourist attraction, but Bull Ballantyne, the fire chief, had brought it out of retirement the previous year for the Front Street fire.

I sat down on a bench beside Bull, a tremendous granite-slab of a man who packed a record load of two hundred and fifty pounds up the forty-five-degree ice slopes of the Chilkoot in '98. We talked nostalgically of the old days.

"I came to Dawson intending to make a quick stake and get out—same as your dad," Bull said. "Well, I'm still here."

Bull Ballantyne ran the Dawson firehall with the help of his son, Jimmy, a veteran of World War II. Jimmy was also president of the Yukon Order of Pioneers, a brotherhood of prospectors formed in Circle City, Alaska, in 1894. My father had been a member and in his time you'd had to be a sourdough of '98 to get into the lodge. Now you could qualify if you'd arrived by 1910. On Discovery Day (August 17), which commemorates the finding of gold on Bonanza Creek, the Pioneers don their purple and gold sashes and parade through town. The parade has been dwindling with the years. Every winter the Y.O.O.P. pays for the funerals of more men who worked all their lives on the gold creeks and died penniless.

Jimmy Ballantyne was as big as his father and looked just like him. He told me he expected to spend his life in Dawson, as his father had. He had spent five years overseas, some of the time in Italy, and then, like so many of Dawson's native sons, he had come back to his birthplace. In the *Dawson News* building I looked at a photo of the 1925 hockey team. Of the nine young players shown, six were still in town. So were some of the boys I had gone to school with: most of them were working on the gold dredges out along the Klondike.

I left the firehall and walked north on Front Street along the riverbank, past piles of rusting machinery, old boats rotting on the sand, and cabins overgrown with weeds. The willows were already encroaching on the town, the boards of the sidewalk were green with moss, and the smell of decay hung heavy on the summer air. Snuggled against the hillside was St. Mary's Hospital. It had stood here for fifty years, and here the Sisters of St. Anne took care of the feeble old men who had nowhere else to go. I knew most of the old men. There was Fred Case, who used to drive the stage from Whitehorse. He was ninety-four years old now, one of thirty-two indigent sourdoughs cared for in the hospital. Eight had died of old age the month before I arrived. Others had lost their minds. Some lived only part of the time in the hospital and spent the summers in their own cabins. A few even worked part of the year on their claims.

The following day I wandered down toward the center of town, where the Federal and Territorial Administration building, a big, gray structure, stood in the shade of the cottonwoods beside a little park. Although the sidewalks are wooden, the streets of Dawson were once literally paved with gold. In depression days, unemployed men made good wages panning the dust that had filtered from the pockets of the men from the creeks. The richest pay-dirt was to be panned right in this section of Fifth Avenue, which had once been the "Paradise Alley" of the red-light district. Harry Gleaves, at the Arcade Café, told me he had once panned a thousand dollars in dust from under the floor of the old Orpheum Theater, and two carpenters who were repairing the Bank of Commerce panned fifteen hundred dollars right on the premises.

Dawson's days as capital of the Yukon were numbered, for though a group of young businessmen were protesting violently to Ottawa, the territorial seat would soon move to Whitehorse. Meanwhile the controller, J. E. Gibben, a spruce, well-groomed civil servant, acted as the Premier of the Yukon and the Mayor of all her towns. Although Dawson is still an incorporated city, she has elected no mayor or council for almost half a century. A delegation once arrived from the Prairies bearing letters of greeting from prairie mayors to mayors of Dawson, Keno, Mayo, and Whitehorse; the incumbent controller gravely accepted them all. The Yukon has always been a sort of benevolent dictatorship run by the federal government at Ottawa. The five-man elected territorial council can pass only on measures that cost no money. The morning I saw him, the controller was answering a plea for a new fire hydrant, getting a ferry to take a missionary's horse to the Indian village of Moosehide, and settling a dispute between two miners over water rights. Such were the immemorial problems of the post.

But there was something new in Dawson City—a strange restlessness that had the town in its grip. Dawson has never minded being cut off from the Outside, but now it was discovering its isolation from the rest of the north. The Alaska Highway had passed it by, several hundred miles to the south. So had the Northwest Staging Route from Edmonton to Fairbanks. Worse still, Whitehorse was growing as Dawson declined. This, perhaps, was the bitterest pill of all, for there has been no love lost between the little hamlet at the head of the river and the proud city on the Klondike. Even the politics of the two communities have differed. Dawson as long as I knew it was a Conservative town; Whitehorse was Liberal.

Since I revisited Dawson in 1948 the rot has set in deeper. The river traffic has vanished, save for the single tourist boat. The Royal Alexandra Hotel has been condemned. St. Mary's Hospital has burned down. The *Dawson News* has ceased publication. The government has moved, and the administration building is now a hospital. The population has dropped to fewer than five hundred.

Moss and willow are growing over the untrodden sidewalks on the edge of town. The elements have erased some of the names on the white wooden slabs in the Pioneers' Cemetery under the hill, so that only the bright Golden Rule of the Order remains. Each year a few more buildings vanish, a few more sourdoughs die, a few more people leave. Even Jimmy Ballantyne has gone.

Is this, then, the fate of the mightiest boom town of all —to cling tenaciously to life and then to expire slowly and grudgingly, like the old-timers who sun themselves on Front Street in the summer?

Those who are left in Dawson still refuse to believe it. Everyone is waiting for another boom. The optimism of the north—it almost amounts to Micawberism—is never brighter than it is here among the ghosts of an earlier, braver day. During my week in Dawson several bulldozers were imported for use in mining, and the *Dawson News* ran a story about them that started with the cheerful sentence: "Front Street is starting to look like the main street of a small Outside city these days."

But only one reason remains for Dawson's existence, and that is the reason for its birth. As long as there is gold along the Klondike, there will be someone living in Dawson. When the gold is gone, Dawson will go too. The geologists of the Yukon Consolidated Gold Corporation say about twenty-five years' production is left along the various creeks where the dredges work. When the dredges stop working, Dawson's heart will cease to beat.

4 | The Smell of Gold

After half a century the faint smell of gold still lingers in the Klondike. The housewives stir their tea with nugget-handled spoons, and the sourdoughs sport nugget chains across their vests. You can buy an ounce of gold dust from the teller at the Bank of Commerce if the spirit moves you, or slide a plan into the old tailings along the creeks and see the dull, greenish glint in the bottom when the gravel has washed away.

No one will ever know exactly how much gold has been torn from the Klondike Valley, but the sum is certainly greater than three hundred million dollars. There is perhaps fifty million dollars' worth left, hidden in the bedrock fissures of such storied creeks as Gold Run, Last Chance, Eldorado, Bonanza, Hunker, Quartz, Dominion, and Sulphur. Today the lion's share of this Crœsus hoard is controlled by one big company, rich in history, poor in profits: the Yukon Consolidated Gold Corporation.

On my second-last day in Dawson I drove out along the network of roads that lace a thousand square miles of rolling gravel foothills—the watersheds of the Indian and Klondike rivers, which outsiders lump together as "the Klondike" and insiders label simply "the creeks." I wanted to see once again the intricate and expensive system that has been devised for extracting every last ounce of gold from the frozen muck and bedrock in which it has reposed for eons.

The Klondike gold country is bisected by a high divide

that lies about thirty miles from Dawson City. The creeks that flow down one side of the divide empty into the Klondike, which joins the Yukon at Dawson. The creeks flowing down the other side join the Indian River, which also flows into the Yukon about fifty miles upstream. I was heading for the divide in a little green pickup truck, supplied by the company, along a hard, winding road paved with white gravel washed out of the hillsides by hydraulic nozzles.

The Klondike hadn't changed greatly since those prewar summers when I had worked for the Yukon Consolidated as a laborer. It was still choked with high dunes of gravel—the tailing piles that are the dung of the great gold dredges. The flat benchland had long since been denuded of timber, and the blemishes left by hydraulic nozzles tearing into the hillsides were as raw as ever. Halfway up each slope was a white wavering line marking an abandoned flume or ditch that had once carried water to individual prospectors.

The valleys were perhaps a little cleaner than I had known them. In my time each valley floor had been a sort of garbage dump from the stampede days, littered with old shovels and picks and rusting wheelbarrows, timbers scattered like jackstraws, the skeletons of log cabins lined with newspapers of Victorian vintage, ancient boilers and winches, rotting sluice-boxes, worn-out engines and keystone drills, bedsprings, furniture, old stoves, and thousands of tin cans. There was a fortune in brass parts in 1937 when I worked on Dominion Creek, if they could have been shipped out cheaply. When war came and brass was scarce, it could at last be salvaged. Much of the rest of the debris has been swept away before the company's huge water jets, which rip the floor from the valleys of the Klondike so the dredges that follow may grope nearer for the gold.

We passed between two mountains of gravel, rounded a bluff, and slid through the village of Bear Creek, a huddle of little flower-decked cottages and iron-roofed machine shops. Here, to the company's gold-room, the wealth of the Klondike eventually finds its way, and here, red-hot and molten, the gold is poured into bricks to be airmailed to the Ottawa mint.

We turned up Hunker Creek, past Last Chance and Gold Bottom, and began the long zigzag climb in second gear that would take us over the wooded divide between the Klondike and the Indian. At Joe Fournier's roadhouse, on top of King Solomon's Dome, we paused and looked at the gold country, scarred and pitted by men and machines, stretching off in every direction. On the horizon the white-capped Ogilvie Mountains marched into the haze. The thin far-off whine of the dredges and the muted roar of the great nozzles floated up the slopes through the still summer air. From the Dome itself the gold-bearing creeks radiated in all directions like the spokes of a wheel.

Here, in 1896, stood a gaunt and dispirited Nova Scotian named Robert Henderson, the first prospector to enter the Klondike watershed. Henderson is listed as "co-discoverer" of Dawson and his descendants still live in Dawson. The other discoverer was George Washington Carmack, a squaw man from California, whom Henderson found fishing for salmon at the Klondike's mouth later in the same season. It was Carmack and not Henderson who touched off the great stampede. On Henderson's tip he trudged up through the swamps of Bonanza Creek, and here he found gold in quantity. Without bothering to relay the news to Henderson, Carmack rushed off down the Yukon River to record his find and spread the story. Here was the north at its most capricious: the lean, diligent Nova Scotian, who had spent all his life searching for gold, got nothing from the Klondike except a belated pension from the Canadian government; the heavy-jowled salmon-fisherman, indolent, boastful, and erratic, garnered a king's ransom within a year.

Anyone who stands on the Dome and looks out across the Klondike hills can quickly discern the structure of the gold country. The hills are generally flat-topped and, save for the occasional peak, of identical height. They are not really hills at all, but the remnants of an ancient plateau, grooved and pitted by eons of erosion. The valleys are great trenches cut into the peneplain, and the mountain peaks mark its former level.

In the five and a half million years since this tableland was hoisted up by unknown turmoils deep within the global womb, the creeks of the Klondike have ground down and borne away sixteen hundred billion tons of rock. In the story of this incredible abrasive process lies the secret of the Klondike's gold.

Long ago, when the young Yukon began to dig out its original channel, the rains that fell upon the land carved out small V-shaped valleys to drain the water to the central river. The Dome was then a small knoll rising above a smooth plateau, and it was from this central hub that the little streams began to radiate. As the great river dug deeper, the creeks kept pace with it, biting farther into the rock and grinding the sides into gravel. Some of the rock from which this gravel slid was gold-bearing. Now the creeks acted as sluice-boxes, the lighter gravel washing away to the river, the heavier gold particles sinking into crevices in the bedrock from which they could not be dislodged. As the tributaries reached the level of the mother river they moved more sluggishly, the valleys broadening out in U-shapes until the water meandered in lazy curves back and forth across the valley floor. Then a second period of erosion started; the Yukon River once more began to work its way down and the tributary streams followed suit, digging new V-shaped troughs in the floors of the old valleys. There were three such periods of erosion in the Klondike region, and wherever a V-shaped valley was formed, a line of gold caught in the bedrock marks the ancient course of the stream. These golden pathways, which are called "pay streaks," bear no relation to the present-day creeks. Some pay streaks are found high in the benchland above the valleys; others meander across the valley floor deep beneath the moss and muskeg and black muck that cloaks the old stream bottoms to depths as great as one hundred feet. Embedded in this frozen muck are the bones and skulls and even the flesh of animals that have long since vanished from the earth—the hairy mammoth, the great tusked mastodon, and varieties of bison, deer, and horse long extinct. The curved ivory mastodon tusks are a familiar feature of Dawson stores and cabins. On our way down from the Dome we passed a little cabin where two of them decorated the porch.

We were now dipping into the thirty-mile valley of Dominion Creek. This was familiar ground, for it was here that I worked as a member of a thawing crew in the seasons of 1937, 1938, and 1939. Now, a decade later, the thawing process—unique to the Yukon and Alaska—was still going on. The valley floor was black with mud and crisscrossed by a network of pipes. Water lay everywhere, oozing from the mud, squirting from breaks in the pipes, gushing from craters in the ground. The figures of men moved awkwardly through this morass, and suddenly I could picture myself floundering in high boots in the ice-cold water, ten years earlier, trying to fix a sagging pipeline. Farther downstream we could see the white flash of nozzles, and the antlike figures of the men operating them, ripping down the banks with tremendous jets of water under pressure.

The valley was literally being torn to pieces before my

eyes, a hundred men undoing, in the space of three or four years, the work of an epoch. Here was erosion gone mad, the valley bottom being peeled away to lay bare the gravels and the gold.

When we stopped at Middle Dominion camp, a man in whipcord breeches, light shirt, and high boots emerged from the bushes.

"Hello," he said. "Have you come back to the points?"

It was my old boss. He was born in Dawson City, and his whole life has been bound up with gold.

"You see, it's just the same as ever," he said, waving his hand at the scarred and ravaged valley.

They had been attacking each segment of the valley in four yearly stages. First they had stripped the surface of every bush and tree. Then bulldozers had moved in to smash the old prospectors' cabins and tear up the rotting sluice-boxes. The nozzle men followed to blast off the frozen moss and topsoil with pressures great enough to tear a man to shreds. Thus a ten-foot layer of valley floor was stripped off and sent down the stream to join the Yukon and eventually find its way to the silty delta on the Bering Sea. Finally, the thawing crew would arrive to melt the permafrost so that the dredge could operate. We could see spread out along a segment of the broad valley each stage in operation below us.

The clumsy process by which the land is thawed and the gold removed is the result of a fifty-year evolution in northern mining methods. The permanently frozen soil has always been the great obstacle to mining placer gold in the Klondike. The ground is as hard as granite within eighteen inches of the surface. Because the gold lies on the bedrock in the form of nuggets and fine dust, men have had to devise ways of thawing the intervening earth to reach it.

The first prospectors in the Yukon relied on the heat of

the summer sun, which can melt about two feet of soil a day. Each day they removed the thawed earth and exposed the next layer to the sun's rays. By this laborious method they were finally able to sink shafts to bedrock.

Wood fires soon replaced the sun's heat. All winter long, men would burn their way downward, thawing the ground at night with fires, until the valleys glowed like infernos, and then clawing away the ashes and soil in the morning and building new fires the following night. Once down to bedrock, the miners burned lateral tunnels until, wheezing and choking in these smoking dungeons, they encountered the ancient stream bed that contained the pay streak.

When the big companies moved in they decided to parboil the earth with live steam. Long lengths of pipe with chisel bits on the end—called "points"—were hammered into the ground, and steam was pumped through them. My father worked with steam points in his day and used to describe the seas of hot bubbling mud, the jets of steam rising from the ground all over the valley, the men standing on stepladders swinging their sledges, the pressure building up as the ground baked around the base of the point. (Occasionally it exploded and a point driver was scalded and sometimes killed.)

Soon the hills were stripped of fuel to feed the fires that built up the steam. A Nome inventor, reasoning that even cold water was warmer than ice, devised a method of pumping it into the ground, and this is the system now used in the Klondike. It is ten times cheaper than steam thawing, and without this economy all gold mining would have ceased in the Yukon long ago.

Below us we could see the point drivers at work, forcing the steel pipes into the ground with slide hammers. Point driving is one of the nastiest jobs in the world. The driver has a line of points he must hammer to bedrock. Standing deep in the icy black muck, he drives each point a few feet at a time with prodigious blows from his thirty-pound slide hammer. After each shower of blows he twists the pipe a little to force it deeper into the permafrost. Cold water continually courses through the pipe, spurting up all around him and drenching him with a freezing spray. He works seven days a week, including holidays, eight hours a day (it was ten hours in my time), and when he wakes in the morning he has to force his fists open, for they have stiffened from their perpetual grasp on the cold narrow pipe.

They used to tell a story about one of the company bosses who came out to Dominion Creek from Dawson one day on an inspection tour. He stood watching the thawing operation for a time, then turned to the foreman on the job and pointed to a man standing stock-still in the valley. "Fire him," the boss said, "he hasn't moved for half an hour." The foreman went across to the worker and found he couldn't move: he was up to his hips in mud.

The tale is plausible enough. By the time the points have pumped water into the vitals of the earth for three weeks, the whole valley has become a giant wet sponge. Water begins to boil up from nowhere. Great pools, some of them twenty feet deep, form all over the valley. Soon the whole land turns into an ocean of mud.

The pipelines begin to sink. The supports that keep them aboveground start to heave and buckle. The pipe bends at the joints, and the bolts begin to spring. The baling wire that holds the smaller pipes together snaps. Small geysers spring up all over the valley as the mud grows thicker and the water grows deeper. The members of the pipeline crew wade and scramble and ferry themselves on rafts through the mud and water, propping up a pipe here, driving a wooden pile there, ramming the sprung pipes together, repairing leaks and breaches in a desperate effort to keep the pressure up and the water pouring into the saturated earth. When things reach their worst, it usually begins to rain. Yukon rains can be more uncomfortable than any others I know, for the water comes down from the sky in a fine needle-point spray only a few degrees above freezing, and the wind drives it up the valley in an icy cloud. And yet, I remember, on those summer days when it wasn't raining, the temperature was almost tropical. I recall cutting survey lines along Dominion Creek one stifling July. We were stripped to the waist swinging machetes—jungle knives—for the growth was jungle-like. The sweat poured off us, soaking our garments. Clouds of flies and mosquitoes almost obscured the sky. The sun blackened our bodies and blistered our faces. But often enough in the early mornings we would have to break ice on the water to shave.

I left the camp and drove off along the dusty road that skirts the black sponge of Dominion. At a curve in the road an ancient hotel, long since left to rot, stood as a monument to the days of the six-horse stage. A few cabins lay crumbling beside it. Not far away an old Italian lived, still working his claim as he had for half a century. I'd known him when I worked on Dominion, a grizzled and lonely man, pathetically glad to see any passer-by. In those days he was taking thirty-five hundred dollars a year from his claim. Each summer he went in to Dawson and blew his whole roll on a wild three-day spree, buying new suits at breakneck speed and burning them up when they didn't suit his fancy, lighting his cigars with five-dollar bills, flinging his loose change on the sidewalk, and throwing the rest of his small fortune into the blackjack pot at the Central Hotel. This ritual observed, he would return to Dominion Creek and his little cabin, not one whit abashed, and begin once again to work the ground in preparation for the next year's escapade.

Not far away another cabin stood empty. I remembered

it, too. In the summer of 1938 a prospector had gone crazy in it from living alone too long and had tried to shoot down the postal truck. Out from Dawson came a truck-load of Mounted Police; there was a brief gun battle among the aspens and a new grave in the Pioneers' Cemetery in Dawson.

We left Dominion Creek, swung through Granville on the Indian River, and headed up Sulphur Creek toward the Dome again. In the distance we could hear the steady shrieking whine of another gold dredge—a haunting sound as familiar to the Klondiker as the howl of a husky under the winter moon.

A big dredge is an awe-inspiring sight, a squat, square monster three stories high. From its maw a long tongue of ax-sharp buckets licks down into the gold-bearing bedrock. From its rear a stacker spews out the useless gravel onto the tailing piles behind. There the dredge sits, floating in a pond it digs itself from the stream bed, surrounded by its own offal, its cables and winches screaming and whining like the souls of the damned.

When we reached it the big boat was swinging slowly from side to side on a thirty-ton anchor or "spud," its long bucket line gouging deeper and deeper. Finally it dug to depth and, as we watched, the bucket line came up, the spud was yanked from the muck, and the dredge lurched forward on its cables about six feet, like a man hopping on one leg. Once again it began to swing slowly, gnawing away at the creek bed, each bucket—a ton and a half of manganese steel—scooping up sixteen cubic feet of bedrock gravel in one bit. Some dredges have as many as eighty of these buckets.

The dredge is a combination digger and sluice-box. The bucket chain disgorges its loot inside, the coarse gravel is screened and washed away, and the heavier gold caught in the riffles and coco matting of the sluice system. The dredge, indeed, is duplicating the action of the natural riffles in the bedrock which originally captured the gold when the raw land was being worn away by the young streams.

As we dropped down from the Dome toward Dawson, I found myself pondering once again the curious and dramatic chain of circumstance that had created the Yukon Consolidated and so, ultimately, led to the violation of the green Klondike valleys by its men and its mechanical monsters.

The tale goes back to two extraordinary adventurers, both of whom juggled millions during their lives and both of whom died penniless. One was an Oxford don and classics student, a shaggy little man with a ragged blond mustache, a descendant of Sir Isaac Newton named Arthur Newton Christian Treadgold. The other was a strapping, heavy-jawed prizefighter named Joseph Whiteside Boyle.

Klondike Joe Boyle began as a bouncer in the Monte Carlo saloon in Dawson, but soon went on to better things. In 1902 he wangled from the Canadian government a vast lease of land—a seven-mile, twenty-five-thousand-acre chunk of the Klondike Valley. How he did it is still a mystery, but the resultant uproar so embarrassed the government that it granted no more leases. Boyle raised money in England and proceeded to build the biggest dredges in the world. No one thought they would work. Boyle was laughed at. But the fact is that they worked very well. Indeed, two of them were still operating when I drove along the Klondike road past the mouth of Bonanza. Between them they had dug up twelve million dollars since 1902. Another had been dismantled after thirty-two seasons—a longer life than any other dredge in history. It had found six and a half million dollars' worth of gold.

Before Boyle left the Klondike, he controlled half of Dawson. But the sequel to his Yukon sojourn far overshadowed what had gone before. The story has been told many times—of how he raised a battery of machine-gunners to go to the war, made himself a colonel, molded lapel badges of solid Yukon gold, went to Russia with an Allied commission, got caught up in the Revolution, and proceeded to lead a Graustarkian existence, drifting into Romania, befriending the beleaguered Queen, running the country almost singlehanded, plucking Balkan nobility from the grasp of the Bolsheviks, and earning a chestful of medals and decorations. And all this while his company in the Yukon slowly went broke, so that when Boyle died, in 1923, in England, he was virtually penniless.

Meanwhile, Treadgold, the Greek scholar, had been doing his own promoting. He had mushed in over the trail of '98 and worked, like the rest, with pick and shovel until he suddenly thought of dredging the creeks with huge floating machines. He walked into the New York office of Daniel Guggenheim, the mining king, told his story, and emerged with a check for sixty-five thousand dollars. With the Guggenheim money Treadgold built nine dredges, all smaller than Boyle's, and got the company under way; then he quarreled with his new associates and finally sold out to them for a million dollars.

He took the money and began to buy up every claim he could get his hands on. The Guggenheims, having skimmed the cream from the country, fled to the tin mines of Malaya, taking some of their dredges with them. Treadgold bought up their assets. His ambition was simple: he wanted to rule the Klondike. When Boyle's company went into receivership, Treadgold bought that, too, and merged the lot into the Yukon Consolidated.

He became a living legend. A diminutive man, he had a Napoleonic ego. Once when he was two days late on a trip west, he sent a wire from Winnipeg to the Canadian Pacific Steamship Company in Vancouver that read: "Hold the boat; *I* am coming." His memory was prodigious. After a twelve-year absence from the Klondike (1912 to 1924) he was still able to walk into the messhall at Bear Creek, shake hands with fifty men, call each by his first name, and recall the details of their first meeting.

But he spent the stockholders' money like water. He hated the dredges that had made him powerful, and he devoted the latter part of his life to a futile attempt to replace them with some new device, until the valleys were sown with monuments to his follies.

I remember walking down the Dominion Creek valley one evening in 1938 and stumbling across an enormous land-going digger, a gaunt skeleton of rusting steel two stories high, sitting on a neat line of railway tracks laid across the valley floor. It had moved no more than six feet, and only half its buckets had dug into the ground. Treadgold had imported two of these machines at a cost of half a million dollars each, but they hadn't worked. He left the one where it stalled and never bothered to uncrate the other.

Farther down the creek stood another memorial to the little man's costly imagination. He had devised a huge cableway slung across the valley between two giant towers. It had a scraper bucket that was supposed to scoop up the dirt as it flew along the cable, thus stripping off the topsoil. It, too, didn't work. He bought assorted types of suction pumps intended to suck up rock and gravel. They wouldn't work either.

In the early 1930's the stockholders began to get restless and an investigation confirmed what had long been suspected: Treadgold had been shuffling the stock with the aid of rubber-stamp directors in an effort to get sole control of the company. A long legal battle ensued and Treadgold was defeated. He left the courtroom a pauper, went back to England, and died there. He was the last of a long roster of Klondike kings who had millions in their grasp and ended life penniless. There has been a legion of them: Alec MacDonald, the Big Moose from Antigonish, who was worth nine millions in 1900 and nothing at all when he died chopping his own wood a decade later; Charley Anderson, "the lucky Swede," who bought a claim when he was drunk, took a million from it, and ended his days as a sawmill laborer; Dick Lowe, who staked a sixty-foot sliver of ground on an impulse, took six hundred thousand from it, and ended life pawning his watch; Tom Lippy, the physical-culture instructor who got a million-dollar claim on a trade, became a tycoon, and died bankrupt in Seattle. The list runs into hundreds.

As we neared Dawson, we passed a few more scattered cabins, most of them empty but a few still occupied by that dwindling tribe of optimists, the lone-wolf prospectors. There were still a handful of them left, but none made much money. One had taken thirteen hundred dollars from his claim that year. Another had managed to scratch out four hundred. The men who scaled the Chilkoot are tired now, and so is the ground they work.

But the company can still wring gold from the tired ground. Even though the Klondike has been mined and re-mined, Yukon Consolidated takes between two and three millions a year from the creek beds. On Bonanza, I watched one of Boyle's old dredges digging into ground already worked over by individual miners and then dredged by the Guggenheims. The ground was still paying its way and will probably continue to do so for a generation.

Indeed, a prospector who owns a seemingly worthless claim may find himself moderately well off if the dredge goes through his property. If the company cannot buy a man's claim outright, it pays a royalty, usually around eight per cent, of everything the dredge takes from it. Gus Nelson, a wizened, aging sourdough who shot the Whitehorse Rapids in '98 with a raftload of burros, mules, and horses, got thirty thousand dollars as his share of the gold found by the dredge on his Bonanza Creek claim. Another prospector, on relief, and unable to scrape an ounce from his exhausted property, got fifteen thousand in dredge royalties. A third got nine thousand; it helped pay his bills in the mental hospital which claimed him as it had claimed so many cabin-lonely miners.

And yet, in spite of the big holdings of the company and the scantiness of the gold found by the old sourdoughs, younger men were still seeking their fortunes in the old way when I visited my home town. In the little moss-chinked cabins along the river the magic term "mother lode" was still whispered. For men still ask the old question in the Klondike: where did all the gold dust come from? Surely there must be a vein of hard-rock ore somewhere, waiting to be mined!

The company's geologists don't agree. They say the gold veins have long since been ground to dust by the long erosion of the past. But like so many other northern questions, this one is still not conclusively answered. Many a sourdough has climbed to the top of King Solomon's Dome, surveyed the rich, storied little creeks running out from its base, and reasoned that the mother lode must lie somewhere under the shaggy head of the old mountain.

Before I left Dawson, I went to see Grant Henderson, a burly and powerful prospector and the son of Robert Henderson, the co-discoverer of the Klondike. Like his father before him, Grant Henderson had spent his life vainly seeking gold. For the past decade he had been picking away at the white quartz near the base of the Dome on whose summit his father had stood, fifty-two years before. In his ore samples there was a faint glitter to match the glitter in his eyes when he spoke of the mother lode. But shortly after I left town Grant Henderson died, without finding the will-o'-the-wisp he sought. The chances are that nobody will ever find it, and in another generation the monsters that chew up the creek beds will lie rotting in the sunlight along with the shovels and sluice-boxes of the early prospectors who first dug for buried treasure in the Yukon.

5 | **The Trail of '48**

I left memory behind and flew south again to Whitehorse. The army had just thrown the Alaska Highway open to unrestricted tourist travel and I wanted to see something of this long, lonely ribbon of gravel that, by the accident of the war, coils through some of the wildest and loveliest country in the world.

From the air we could see the threadline of the great road stitched upon the dark mantle of the spruce forest. It took fourteen thousand men to build it in 1942 and 1943, and each of its 1,523 unsurfaced miles cost almost one hundred thousand dollars. It begins far to the southeast, in the flat little farming community of Dawson Creek in the Peace River country of British Columbia, not far from the Alberta border. It ends at Fairbanks, a lusty, modern city deep in the low, blue hills of central Alaska. The route between Dawson Creek and Fairbanks is barred by unending obstacles: five mountain ranges, one hundred and twenty-nine rivers, eight thousand alpine torrents. The highway-builders managed to breast them all.

Whitehorse, nine hundred miles northwest of Mile Zero, is the big road's nerve center. Here was the headquarters of the Royal Canadian Engineers, who control and maintain the highway. The brigadier in charge was driving up to the Alaska border, three hundred miles to the northwest, and he offered to take me along. The following day we drove out onto the dusty road, in a khaki-colored staff car with the brigadier's flag flying, so that every soldier along the way saluted us smartly as we passed.

The brigadier was responsible for the main thoroughfare as well as the seven emergency landing fields along the way and for the two hundred miles of access road leading into them. He had more than seven hundred maintenance men strung out along the right of way, a vehicle and a half for every man, forty thousand spare parts to keep them going, and a five-million-dollar annual budget, which he hinted wasn't nearly adequate. Any road at all is a problem in the north. Fifteen hundred miles of class-A gravel highway is an enormous and expensive headache.

We slid out of Whitehorse on a beautiful section of road, thirty-six feet wide, the gravel deep, the curves gentle and well banked. But we had driven only a few dozen miles when its character underwent a remarkable change. The road narrowed and began to writhe and squirm in a zigzag series of hairpin turns, loops, and cutbacks. These contorted stretches reappear all along the length of the highway and they puzzle everybody who travels it. The explanation lies in its brief but erratic history. It was about half completed in 1943 when the Japanese threat in the Aleutians began to ease off and the United States Congress cut the highway appropriation. A pioneer bulldozer trail had already been completed over the easiest course, skirting mountains and muskeg. Strung out along this route from the Peace River to Alaska were seventy-seven contracting firms engaged in straightening, widening, grading, and banking the zigzag course. When the money ceased, the uncompleted sections were hurriedly graded and the highway left just about as it is today.

Now, five years later, on this bright spring day, the settlers were rolling north in their covered trucks and trailers, and the scenes along the highway were strangely reminiscent of the paintings of wagon trains moving west in the pioneer days. "One of everybody has traveled the Alaska Highway," a tourist-camp operator had remarked in Whitehorse. The vehicles of the new pioneers seemed to bear him out: two-ton trucks with houses built on top of them, jeeps with hinged Plexiglas tops, old delivery wagons, motorcycles, converted school buses, big custom sedans, thirty-five-foot four-roomed trailers, model-T Fords, and even bicycles. Every license seemed to be represented on the road, from the canary and robin's-egg blue of Alaska to the black and yellow of Hawaii. It looked as though everyone was bent on seeing the north now that the highway was open at last. The following month thirty-five hundred cars, buses, and trucks drove north along the highway.

A few miles out of Whitehorse we stopped and talked to a harried-looking man from New Jersey. He had his wife and five children packed into a model-A Ford and all his worldly goods jammed into a canvas-topped trailer. He was heading for Fairbanks, looking for work. He wasn't sure what there was, but he'd heard there was plenty. There were many like that, some with jobs to go to, others with nothing but hope. They were the vanguard of the great rush up the highway that took place in the summer of 1948—just fifty years after that earlier rush into the Yukon and Alaska. The settlers came first, in May and June; the tourists followed in July, August, and September.

Hitherto anyone traveling the highway had needed permission from the Mounted Police in Edmonton and there had been some weird requests. The astonished Mounties had had to deal with such people as the black-bearded Baptist preacher from Texas who proposed to navigate the entire road in a motor scooter in the company of a black spaniel bitch and her litter of seven puppies. The police had turned him back, but now the bars were down and the rush was on.

A truck with a Nevada license overtook us. It was crammed with apples going through Canada in bond. The driver hoped to sell them in Fairbanks before they all rotted, and he had an extra engine stored in the back in case he suffered a mechanical breakdown. A brand-new Buick, driven by two pretty girls, raced by in a swirl of dust. An older car followed. The owner was a retired railroad man, eighty years old. He and his wife were inveterate travelers. They expected to make the return trip in the comfortable period of two weeks. It has been done in less. Three Harvard students once drove all the way from New York City to Alaska in just nine and a half days.

The blue snow-flecked Coast Mountains lay ahead of us. We passed one of the highway maintenance camps— five men and their families living in a ghost town of old, black Quonset huts left over from the war days. There are eighteen of these camps strewn along the highway at intervals of about seventy miles, all with names rich in the flavor of the north: Blueberry, Sikanni Chief, Swift River, and Stony Creek.

We rolled west along the Takhini Valley in the shadow of the tall mountains, past the crumbling community of Champagne, where some of the Klondikers had burst through the mountains from the seacoast fifty years before. An ancient wagon, used by the Mounted Police in the days before the highway, rotted on its wheels by the roadside, flanked by a group of fat, impassive squaws with kerchiefs on their heads, scrubbing their washing in a tiny creek.

Sixteen travelers were eating lunch at Maw Perrins's when we stopped on Canyon Creek at noon. Two were geology graduates from the University of Arizona, driving the highway in a red delivery truck and prospecting as they went, hoping to find enough gold to finance their doctorates. A young Idaho farmer was heading for Alaska's rich Matanuska Valley. A correspondent for the *Trailer Times* was driving north—not unexpectedly, in an immense trailer. There were two young Texans, ex-GI's, still wearing their uniforms. Most of them would end up selling their trailers for food, or bartering their spare parts for gas. The north is not yet a land of unlimited plenty.

We sat down beside a surveyor from Arlington, Virginia, on his way to do summer fieldwork in Anchorage. He was traveling with his wife and two children in a violently green jeep with a trailer. The children were having the time of their lives, for they had just seen their first wolf pelt. The family wore the uniform of the highway: blue denims and loud checkered shirts. Nothing else is practical because of the heavy dusts that cake cars and permanent waves alike.

Mrs. Harvey Perrins, a buxom, black-haired woman

known as the best cook on the highway, began to pile on the food: homemade tomato soup, salad, fried chicken, new potatoes, two vegetables, grape jelly, hot biscuits, peaches, cake, and coffee, all for two dollars and a quarter.

"I'm doin' my level best to get a beer license," Maw Perrins announced. The standard highway price for beer was seventy-five cents.

Then we were off again, rolling north to Haines Junction at Mile 1016. From here you can drive straight south through the mountains to the Pacific Ocean near Skagway on the Haines cutoff road, a tributary of the great highway. This was a onetime cattle trail broken by Jack Dalton, a gun-toting sourdough, in the days before the Klondike rush. The problems of keeping a highway operating all year round in the north are dramatically illustrated by this beautiful but maddening side-road knifing through the mountain snows. All roads in the winter tend to form frost dams that hold back the water until it flows over the thoroughfare, freezes, and effectively blocks traffic. On the Haines road the previous year an untended glacier, formed in this fashion, had swelled until it was a mile long and seven feet thick.

We stopped at one of the highway's twenty-nine gas stations and added our signatures to hundreds of others in the visitors' book. The preceding signatures came from Cheyenne, Las Vegas, Iron Mountain, Cape Cod, and Miami. Then on we went, past the McIntosh trading post run by an Oxford graduate, and past the Dominion experimental farm where, in the shadow of the St. Elias Range, they are growing everything from wheat to watermelons. The highway was admirably marked, a yellow warning sign on every curve and hill, a red flag at every bump and frost boil. Occasionally we passed one of the big pieces of yellow road machinery—the trucks, graders, plows, cats, blades, scrapers, shovels, and cranes that are needed to keep the road open. Nine hundred and fifty of them were at work that summer. It took eleven thousand of them to build the highway in the first place.

Now the road twisted down through the Shakwak Valley to Kluane Lake, a long serpent of turquoise, as haunting as its name. (You pronounce it Kloo-*wan*-ee, and it sounds like a cry in the night.) For sixty miles the road clung to the west side of the lake, while down from the sky in shadowy slabs of purple the great St. Elias Mountains tumbled sheer into the green water. These are among the tallest mountains on the continent, far more imposing than the Rockies, and they form a prodigious block one hundred and fifty miles broad in the southwest corner of the Yukon. The northern wall of this block is practically vertical, and the scenery itself is reckoned the most spectacular in all of North America—a frozen wilderness of mountain peaks, swept by endless snows, and of valleys choked by long alpine glaciers. The peaks are still young and unworn by the abrasion of the ages. They average fourteen thousand feet in height, and one, Logan, is almost twenty thousand feet tall. It is this granite barrier that guards the interior from the wet sea-winds and keeps the rainfall down.

We slid past Destruction Bay, whose deceptively innocent waters had risen in all their fury to smash to kindling the rafts of the early sourdoughs. Then we came upon Burwash Landing, nestling under the mountains, and a big hunting lodge built of peeled spruce logs which belongs to Gene Jacquot, a sixty-seven-year-old French pastry cook. This dark little man came into the country in 1904 and was now doing a thriving business taking big-game hunters into the mountains after grizzly bear, moose, and mountain sheep, and fishermen out into the lake for trout. One caught that week had been so big it fed twenty men two meals.

We drank a bottle of beer here, served by a bent old man of seventy-two, with a flowing white beard. He answered only to the name of "Old Bert," and he might have been Methuselah himself.

"I'm the oldest bartender in the Yukon, I am," Old Bert told us proudly. "I walked into this country from Edmonton in 1903 on my own two feet before there was even a trail through the bush." Now he was serving beer to tourists from Texas and Virginia parked in sleek station wagons beside the log houses.

We drove on north, past the white mileposts and the neat little green-and-white buildings put up by the Canadian government for the convenience of tourists. The highway's brief, flamboyant history was written in the relics along the wayside: the scores of old tires suspended from the limbs of trees, a worn sign reading: "Beer, Wine and Women: Blackie's Dive," a cairn built in memory of an infantry officer killed during construction work, a honeymoon cabin with the words "Our First Home" carved into the log wall, and endless clusters of windowless tar-paper shacks and black Quonset huts, their roofs crushed by the winters' snows.

We drove through country that ten years before had hardly known the echo of a human voice—a country of wide valleys strewn with enormous boulders, through which thin trickles of water picked their way. They are treacherous and deceptive, these little streams. When a glacier melts or rain falls they swell to torrents that fill the troughs of the valleys and rip up roads and bridges as easily as they move boulders.

We rolled out on the wide, matted floor of the biggest valley of all, where the unpredictable, many-channeled

Donjek River pursues its braided course. Seven bridges spanned this river. Each year the water had defied the engineers by sneaking around a span and forming a new channel so that another bridge must be built. Now the engineers were coming to grips with the problem by building a single steel span, more than a quarter of a mile long, to replace the seven trestles. Their camp bordered the road, a modern village moved there by truck, complete with billiard rooms, Ping-pong tables, movie theater, library, canteen, and bowling alley.

On we drove, past streams that would make a fisherman's mouth water—Pickhandle Lake, where, the brigadier claimed, you could pull the whitefish out with your hands, and Swede Johnson Creek, where the grayling ran thick, and an unnamed pond where the pike were so plentiful that some tourists got them with spears.

The road swept down the green banks of the White River, a watercourse almost parallel to the Alaska line, which seems to be running with soiled milk, for we were in volcanic country and the whole land was deep in the white ash that smothered the southwest Yukon when a mountain blew up in the days before the white man.

Then on north past Onion Lake, where some travelers stop to make a wild onion salad, and past the road into the Snag airport, the coldest spot on the continent, and then diagonally to the Alaska border, where the powder-white mountains with the curious names stretch off in a long, even line toward the Aleutian Islands—Niggerhead Mountain and Beaver, Chair and Hump, Starvation and Cottonwood, Wienerwurst and Sanpete Hill.

We drove a few miles over the border into Alaska, far enough to come upon our first Pepsi-Cola sign and to realize that in all its twelve hundred miles to the border the highway boasts not a single twenty-four-sheet billboard. We stopped at the Border Trading Post, run by Bob

Jordan, a navy veteran with a blond mustache who had spent four years in the South Pacific and experienced enough heat to last for the rest of his life. His only neighbor was another navy veteran, still sporting his wartime beard, who ran a second post not far away.

We sat and talked about the highway and drank a little beer. Jordan told us about Yerrick Creek at Mile 1340, a northern oddity that, instead of flowing along a valley bottom, insists on running along the ridge of a hill, seventy feet above the surrounding countryside.

"The engineers are afraid it'll slip someday and spill over into the valley," Jordan said. "If that happens, it'll wash out the road and leave a bridge on top of the hill, all by itself. That'll look pretty silly, won't it?"

The next day we retraced our route to Whitehorse. I wanted to see the southern end of the highway—the nine-hundred-mile section between Whitehouse and the Peace River. The highway's chief maintenance officer was starting off for Dawson Creek the following day and offered to take me along. He was a big, black-mustached man with a gleam in his eye, who liked to sing raucous and moderately bawdy songs as he wheeled over the roller-coaster hills of the Yukon.

"My God, you're not driving with the maintenance officer?" a young subaltern said to me in the mess at Whitehorse. "That's suicide, man! He drives like an absolute fiend. Back out of it. Take the plane. Walk if need be. But don't get inside a staff car with him driving."

I went anyway. The maintenance officer had a driver allotted to him, but preferred to drive himself. The driver crawled into the back seat, and the maintenance officer and I got into the front. He threw in the clutch, put his foot down hard on the accelerator, and kept it there. The car spurted forward and was soon hitting an even sixty miles an hour, which on a gravel road is very fast indeed.

The maintenance officer began to sing.

"All hail Cathusalem, the harlot of Jerusalem,
All hail Cathusalem, the daughter of the rabbi . . ."

A hairpin turn loomed ahead. The officer kept on singing and, without slackening pace, took it neatly.

"I get in about eight thousand miles every month, you know," he remarked, interrupting his singing at an interesting point. "I have to keep checking the road all the time."

The bluebells and lupins made a bright fringe along the highway as we skirted the shores of Marsh Lake, a sheet of blue glass spattered with islands and ringed with shadowy lavender mountains. Snuggled into the shoreline was another peeled-log tourist lodge, run by a former Mountie who was doing twenty thousand dollars' worth of business every hunting season. To these shores each fall came wealthy Californians to shoot the grizzly, goat, moose, and caribou that roam the forests and crags within thirty miles of the lodge. A thirty-six-foot cabin cruiser was moored at the dock to take paying guests on two-week cruises in and out of the slender lake system that winds for three hundred miles through the Cassiar Mountains. Some tourists have been known to take seventy-five pounds of Arctic trout from Marsh Lake in forty-five minutes.

"Nothing rough here," the lodge's owner told us as we drank coffee with him. "Why, we set a real table with a cloth, silverware, and china right out there in the bush. It's just like home."

We were off again in a swirl of dust, and the officer began to sing:

"Now this young man was a brave young man,
So up the stairs he sped,

And very surprised was he to find
The chandler's wife in bed. . . ."

"Bridge!" cried the maintenance officer, and brought the car to a screeching stop. He got out, inspected the bridge carefully, and then off we shot once more.

"And in the bed was a sailor boy
Of quite considerable size . . ."

"You know," said the officer, interrupting the song again, "if you laid all the bridges on this highway end to end they'd stretch seven miles, and if you laid all the culverts end to end they'd stretch fifty miles. Every year we have to replace fifty culverts and a thousand feet of bridging. We're bridging all the time. I guess you saw that mess up at Donjek, didn't you?"

We were entering a new kind of country as he spoke, a country where the valleys seemed to have been scooped out of the land by a giant paw. We rounded another curve and burst upon Teslin Lake, which cuts across the British Columbia border. Everything about the Teslin country was blue that day. The water was a deep abiding blue, the mountains a hazy cornflower blue; even the mists that sifted up through the valleys seemed tinged with blue. The world was a blue monochrome, slightly out of focus in the summer heat.

A few miles farther on we came upon another spotless log lodge run by a Yukon sourdough. A private-plane-load of wealthy fishermen had just come in from Saskatchewan. The maintenance officer kept right on singing:

"Last night, the other night, when I came home at three,
I saw a hat upon the rack where my hat ought to
be. . . ."

We were rolling through the lake country along the border between the Yukon and British Columbia: past the

Morley River in a burned-over land where the gaunt shells of trees stood like specters in a haunted forest . . . into the broad moose pastures of the Smart and the Swift rivers . . . through the anvil-shaped hills and the tiny, lily-strewn lakes of Rancheria Valley, where the grayling lie thick beneath the surface.

Guileless rivers, these, in June and July: dark, limpid streams meandering through the black mosses and the blue lupins like the quiet brooks of England, babbling as they go. Yet in spring there streams go berserk. This was the country of the flash flood, and I remembered the remark of a staff officer back at Whitehorse: "You'd never believe that the same innocent water you drink out of a glass could do what these flash floods do."

A flash flood is a terrifying thing. It comes when you least expect it, bursting with a sound like exploding dynamite from the bushes where no stream ran before. It gives no warning. In a matter of seconds it can force a new channel two hundred yards long and twelve feet deep—one had done this on the Smart River the year before. Of all the problems facing the men who keep the highway open, the flash flood is the greatest. One spring the Little Rancheria River rose twelve feet in ten minutes flat, bursting its bonds, tearing out the bridge as if it were matchwood, sweeping away the pilings of a new trestle, and effectively closing the highway.

The engineers have to work fast and hard to keep the highway open.

"We once banged through a hundred-and-sixty-foot pile-driven span with a seventy-ton load in just three and a half days," the major told me as we rattled along.

The ribbon of gravel unrolled in front of us. Occasionally we saw a man or two working along the road, living the lonely life that members of the highway maintenance crews accept—men like Einar Nelson, a grizzled, barrel-chested, bull-strong Scandinavian boss of the crew at Little Rancheria, who had the reputation of working stripped to the waist in forty-below weather and had been known to run through the snow in his stocking feet when the mess bell sounded.

The officer stopped the car to talk to one of the work crews, and we both got out. Instantly we were faced with one of the most formidable problems of the north: the mosquito. The workmen were draped in heavy netting, drawn tightly around their necks so that no areas of naked flesh were exposed, but we were entirely vulnerable. The insects were so thick that we sucked them in involuntarily as we breathed. It was impossible to stand the torture of their presence for more than a few moments, for they encircled us in thick clouds, driving us almost frantic. We retreated to the car, closed the windows tightly, and drove on. There is little doubt that the mosquito has helped retard northern development. Even Vilhjalmur Stefansson, that incurable optimist of "the friendly Arctic," balks at them. Stefansson once reported mosquitoes so thick that he found it impossible to sight a rifle. In 1907 Ernest Thompson Seton, the naturalist and writer, found that out on the tundra more than a hundred of the insects landed on his hand in the space of five seconds. The Defense Research Board, which is vitally concerned with black flies and mosquitoes in the north (there are twenty species of mosquito alone), has clocked a hundred bites a minute on one man's exposed leg. The day may come when a pill is invented to give men protection against insect bites, but until that happens the mosquito and the black fly will remain to torture anyone who travels through the north in June and July.

We were still winding back and forth across the Yukon border, following the long, smoke-blue valley of the Liard, with the highway a jagged, khaki scar notching the hills

ahead of us. At Mile 588 we hit Contact Creek, where the
bulldozers from the north joined the bulldozers from the
south in November 1942. We rattled over the bridge that
spans the Coal River (so named because the water is
black with lignite) and then entered more burned-over
country, a blackened landscape, weirdly punctuated with
naked white birches, nervous aspens, and gaunt deformed
spruce.

There was fire ahead. The air was pungent with acrid
smoke and we could see it pillaring ahead of us on the
hillsides.

"By golly, I think she's jumping the road," the officer
said, and stepped on the gas pedal, already close to the
floor.

We hit a steady sixty and through the dust we could see
flames and hear the crackling of burning timber.

Then we were in the middle of it. The piles of felled
timber that line the road were burning fiercely, and the
whole land was obscured by a mantle of red-brown wood
smoke. We plunged into this murky world. Flaming missiles, like tiny meteors, soared overhead. The heat bore
down on us from both sides. Spruce trees, their pitch boiling within the bark, exploded on either side of us with a
"whoo-oosh!" that sent a ripple of flame shooting up the
entire length of the trunk. The scenery vanished and we
were alone in an envelope of smoke and flame.

Then, coughing and choking, we were out of it as
swiftly as we had entered. A few miles down the road the
officer spotted a crew of men and brought the car to a halt.

"You'd better close the road," he said.

"Already have, sir," said one of the men. "Yours was the
last car through. We're keeping them all back until this is
over."

We stopped for the night at an old army hut rigged by
the British-Yukon Navigation Company as a hotel. The

company was operating one of the two bus lines on the highway that year, and these makeshift hotels, all converted from army H-huts, were strung out the full length of the road. Each one had twenty or thirty beds. They were comfortable, cheap (two dollars a night), but primitive.

We were on our way again early next morning. The officer bought a stack of comic books, turned the staff car over to the driver, climbed into the back seat, and read his way through the lot of them during the morning. While he read we rolled past creeks with names like Washout and Log Jam, names that hint at some of the problems facing highway engineers in the north. When the road first crossed Washout Creek, only a tiny culvert was needed to span it. Now the culvert had become a steel trestle, one hundred feet long.

To our left lay the Grand Canyon of the Liard. But we were leaving the Liard country now and moving up the valley of the Trout and into a harsh mountain land.

Ahead of us lay the great barrier of the Rocky Mountains, their flanks wrinkled and grooved by centuries of erosion. All around us the land was scarred by wide pathways left by long-dead glaciers. The broad valley we now ascended was strewn with great pyramid piles of naked rock. Ahead of us the road bit through the treeless peaks of granite, sandstone, and lava. For the next hundred and sixty miles we drove among these giant obelisks. We could see the strata in them, wriggling red- and purple-veined lines that seemed to have been painted there. In some the strata ran horizontally, in others vertically or diagonally: it was as if the mountains had been tossed like boulders into the valley and some had rolled on their sides.

The whole country had a prehistoric look to it. Except for the thin highway snaking between the granite spires, the land was unmarred by human corrosion. The mountains seemed as raw and new as they were when the claws of the cordilleran icecap gouged them into their present shapes.

There was nothing distant about the scenery here; it was right on top of us, and it was a numbing sight. The whole land seemed to have been chewed up by the ice-fields. Glacial fans—some of them five miles wide—had been scooped out of the granite like natural amphitheaters. White waterfalls tumbled from the precipices above. We skirted the most beautiful lake of all, Muncho, just fifteen miles long and pure mint-green, cuddled in a curve of the highway in the shadow of the ice-cream mountains. The officer put down his comic books and took the wheel again as we climbed slowly, right through the clouds, toward the summit of the big road.

The officer was singing a song about a girl named Nellie "who had hair on her belly like the branches of a tree" when we passed Mile 419, the junction of the Toad and Racing rivers. There were hot springs here and I recalled that this innocent-looking spot was the once famous tropical valley that had inflamed Sunday-supplement readers in the twenties, before the myths moved north to the Nahanni.

Now the highway was gouging its way through the naked rock of McDonald Valley, higher and higher into the mountains, until at last we reached Summit Lake, forty-two hundred feet above sea level, the highest point on the road. We stayed here overnight, and the following day began to slip down the eastern side of the continental divide toward the Peace River country.

Down we went, over the camel-humped foothills and around Mud Hill, a strange mountain undermined by subterranean streams. This is the worst section of the Alaska Highway, where entire chunks of the thoroughfare threaten to slide off down the mountain slope. We crawled around the edge of Steamboat Mountain, a high mesa with a natural figurehead named by an old Indian who thought the top looked like the prow of a ship. Below us, two thousand feet of rock cliff dropped sheer to the floor of the Muskwa Valley, five miles wide.

On we went, the officer singing and driving, the driver sitting in the back reading the officer's comic books. We crossed the unpredictable Muskwa, which once rose twenty-six feet in a single July day and jammed a million board feet of lumber against a steel trestle. Miraculously the trestle held fast. We skirted the airfield at Fort Nelson, where I had been delayed the previous year en route to the Nahanni, and then we plunged south through twenty-five miles of wet muskeg, where the road never stops heaving and sinking.

"If we ever get the money, we'll build a detour here," the officer said, as the car bumped along. "But we probably won't get the money."

Now we were rounding Trutch Hill on the very lip of the Prophet Valley. The officer stopped the car and we both got out and looked back the way we had come. A vast and empty land stretched off a thousand feet below us—the parallel twin valleys of the Prophet and the Muskwa, long, shaggy carpets of stunted evergreens patterned with little ponds, fading off into the haze. Here was all the grandeur and all the emptiness of the north. On these occasions it is impossible not to recall Service, who sings of "the great, big, broad land 'way up yonder . . . the forests where silence has lease . . . the beauty that thrills me with wonder . . . the stillness that fills me with peace."

We rattled off again, the dust clouds rising behind us and obscuring the view. Dust is a great hazard of the highway each summer. It is so bad that convoys have to drive at "dust distance," each vehicle five hundred yards

behind the next. The dust plays havoc with civilian auto-
mobiles, and the wise travelers had dustproofed their cars
and brought along extra oil filters.

The scenery settled down now to rolling foothills. The
road widened again into a broad class-A highway boring
straight into the Peace River country. We cut through the
deep gorge of the Sikanni Chief River, then followed the
route of the Blueberry southeast. Finally we reached Joe's
Place, a little tar-papered eating-house at Mile 40 on the
lip of the broad Peace. Above us, the hundred-foot-high
garland of the Peace River suspension bridge was slung
across the river. This is the largest bridge of its kind in
northern Canada, and it cost four million dollars to build
in the early days of the highway. There was trouble here
already: the original construction crew had dropped the
piers twenty feet below the river bed but hadn't succeeded in anchoring it to bedrock. Long strips of metal
left behind on the bottom had caused eddies, which had
undermined the piers, and the bridge had tilted over two
inches. All winter, divers had been working under five feet
of ice trying to remedy the trouble. It was, of course,
warmer under water in a diving suit than it was above.

The bridge led us almost directly into Fort St. John,
past the bright checkerboard of chocolate and green farms
with their neat houses of peeled logs. From here it was a
brief run to Dawson Creek, the anchor point on the highway. We stopped the car in front of the hotel and here,
standing beside a big dust-caked station wagon, I met a
retired colonel of the U.S. Marines. He had left Clearwa-
ter, Florida, in February and he had already been all the
way up the highway to Fairbanks and back again. He was
tired and dusty, but he had that look of grim satisfaction
that is the hallmark of the professional tourist. He had
wanted to make the trip while the country was still part
of the frontier, and he had succeeded. He had been the

first tourist to navigate the highway. But, as we had seen, there were many in his wake. More cars were traversing the bumpy road up from Edmonton that weaves into Dawson Creek, and even as I bade good-by to the singing officer, some of them were moving off on the long trek north.

I walked over to the CPA office to pick up a plane for the Outside. The officer waved again, and when I last saw him he was going into the drugstore to buy some more comic books, humming a ballad to himself about the peculiar mathematical deformities of a young man from Bengal. The sign on the street corner pointed back the way he had come, and it said simply: TO ALASKA.

Postscript

Of the four geographical regions described in this book, the northwest has seen the greatest change. Edmonton, Whitehorse, even Dawson have been transformed in the forty years since I first wrote about them – and not always for the better.

Edmonton is unrecognizable. It has grown fivefold since I described it here. Alas, in doing so, it has lost its soul. Most of the heritage buildings that once gave it the texture of history have been knocked down to be replaced by a forest of steel and glass that has turned the core area into a miniature Houston. At night, the downtown streets are empty; it is hard to find so much as a cup of coffee outside the major hotels. The business district has been sucked dry by the suburban shopping centres, including the much-touted West Edmonton Mall, with its ersatz beach and fake ocean waves.

Rather than celebrate its own rich history – the fur trade, the bush pilot era – Edmonton has opted for somebody else's. Klondike Days has never achieved the kind of success that its rival, the Calgary Stampede, has enjoyed. But Calgary's festival is indigenous; Edmonton's isn't. I once suggested that Dawson City inaugurate an "Edmonton Days," complete with a replica of Rowand's Folly, the great log castle that goes back to the community's beginnings. My plan was simple: after a successful season in which the Klondikers dressed up as fur traders, Dawson would rent a large billboard on Jasper Avenue with the simple query: WANNA TRADE? Nothing came of it.

Meanwhile Edmonton continues to grow. The little downtown airport I described as the Gateway to the North caters only to private planes and the Calgary airbus. The big jets land at a newer airport miles from the city limits.

Whitehorse, a few hours away by plane, has also boomed, but not, I'm happy to say, in the way I predicted. Thayer Lindsley's plans came to nothing, and the river continues to flow past the town as it always has. As the anchor point on the Alaska Highway, with a population exceeding fifteen thousand, Whitehorse has become the biggest community in the north – sprawling now for miles along both banks of the Yukon. Only a few structures remain to remind the visitor of the gold-rush days – a scattering of log cabins, the old railway station, Grant McConachie's steamboat *Klondike*, which ran for a single season and has since become a

Parks Canada museum, and a few restored buildings on the main street. Except for the backdrop of blue hills, the drive from the airport into town might easily be mistaken for any other commercial strip – a typical Franchise Alley of chicken palaces, automobile lots, hamburger drive-ins, and motels.

The magnificent sternwheelers that once sat on the river bank as authentic reminders of a bygone era are no more. The *Casca* and the *Whitehorse* burned to the ground one night because nobody took the trouble to secure them. The flames brought tears to the eyes of hundreds who saw their heritage destroyed and who realized, belatedly, that they had lost something more precious than gold.

The narrow-gauge railway that ran through the White Pass between Whitehorse and Skagway is gone, too, replaced by a modern highway blasted at huge expense through the rock of the Coastal Mountains. It didn't occur to those who pushed so hard for a road that its construction would render the railway obsolete. Fortunately, a section of that spectacular line – perhaps the most breathtaking in all of North America – has been restored. Tourists from the cruise ships that dock in Skagway can now travel by rail to the summit, but not yet as far as Whitehorse.

The Alaska Highway remains the key to the community's prosperity. Some 150,000 travellers, most of them tourists, pour through Whitehorse every year by bus, private car, camper, or trailer. Since I first travelled that long, dusty road, the tight curves have been straightened, the roadbed has been widened and improved, and most of it has been paved or hard-surfaced with bituminous tar and gravel. The highway has also spawned a network of feeder lines, so that Dawson City is now easily reached by automobile. In fact, you can drive all the way to Inuvik on the new Dempster Highway that runs north out of the Klondike.

I remember driving into Dawson with my family in the summer of 1962 on one of these feeders – the breathtaking Top of the World Highway that branches off from the main road just over the Alaska border. Here the vistas stretch off for miles on both sides of the high ridge to which the highway clings for sixty miles. In the hot haze of summer, the hills roll on seemingly forever to the blur of the horizon.

We were going to Dawson that year to take part in the Gold Rush Festival, a brainchild of Tom Patterson. Having launched a somewhat similar event at Stratford, Ontario, he now turned his eyes northward, spurred on, so he claimed, by reading my book *Klondike*. This prompted the federal government to restore Arizona Charley's famous Palace Grand Theatre (which, in my boyhood, I knew as the Nugget Dance Hall), and also the little *Keno*, the only sternwheeler left from the steamboat era (the *Klondike* was not built until long after the original steamboats ceased operation). That flurry of heritage reconstruction helped touch off the remarkable renaissance of Dawson City.

In spite of this, much of the old Dawson that I knew as a boy and revisited for this book is no more. All of Front Street, including the Royal Alexandra Hotel, the Arcade Café, the Floradora Dance Hall, and the Dominion Gambling House, has burned down. The great dredges that once churned up the gold creeks were discontinued in 1966. The tailing piles that rose starkly along the Klondike are already furred with new growth. Soon they will vanish behind a screen of willows and alders.

Yet despite fire and decay – and the loss of its seat as territorial capital – Dawson has experienced a revival. The ounce of gold that sold for thirty-five dollars in 1948 is now worth four hundred. Old claims once thought to be worked out are again yielding profits. Bonanza Creek is being ripped apart again, in some places for the fourth time, not by dredges but by bulldozers. Old Number Four dredge, Joe Boyle's most famous monster, has become a tourist attraction. It sits in a bed of silt, stabilized by Parks Canada for the benefit of visitors who drive out to the site of George Carmack's original find to peer at the old diggings (some of the original stakes are still in place) and to goggle at the new.

But the gold will not last forever and Dawson realizes that truth. It has chosen a different path to prosperity. Thanks to an infusion of federal money from Parks Canada it has been able to preserve what is left of its history. More than twenty original buildings have been restored or are in the process of restoration; another dozen have been stabilized and marked as historic sites. Robert Service's cabin, in which he wrote *Ballads of a Cheechako*, has been rehabilitated as a shrine. The Administration Building, where my father worked, has become a museum. Government House, the United Church manse, the old RCMP barracks, Madame Tremblay's famous dress shop all look today as if they had been built last week. If anything they look too much like a movie set. When the CBC produced my mother's *I Married the Klondike* as a TV drama, the old buildings looked suspiciously fresh while the sets, built in Ontario and suitably aged, looked more authentic than the original. Many viewers confused them.

Back in 1948 there was no talk of heritage preservation, in Dawson or elsewhere. Now, with the realization that history is not a depleting resource, Dawson is in better shape than it was in my boyhood. Close to fifteen hundred people now live and work in Dawson and vicinity. The town has got rid of the refuse that was once piled among the weeds of the vacant lots. The mayor and council have established an architectural design for new houses, patterned after the turn-of-the-century style. Log construction is returning, and so are the flower gardens for which the community used to be famous.

Last year forty thousand tourists visited Dawson City, suggesting that in the north, what's above the ground can be just as valuable as – and often more enduring than – what's found beneath the surface.

Part IV

LANDS FORSAKEN AND SEAS FORLORN

1 | The Tracks of the Ice Sheet

Just before five o'clock on a hot June afternoon in 1954, a telephone call from Montreal came into my Toronto office at *Maclean's Magazine*. The voice on the other end belonged to a veteran Arctic and Antarctic pilot named Red Lymburner.

"I heard you wanted to go to Baffin Island," Lymburner was saying. "Well, there's a plane leaving Ottawa at two in the morning. If you can manage it in time, you can go along for the ride. We'll be back in a few days. Try and meet me at the Ottawa airport around one thirty."

I raced home, threw a few things into a suitcase, rolled up my sleeping-bag, and pulled on some heavy clothing. Thus unsuitably clad for the ninety-degree heat of southern Ontario, I drove past my long bed of iris, now in full flower, made Malton airport in twenty minutes, and caught an evening plane to the capital. In less than two days I would be standing on the frozen surface of the Arctic.

Lymburner, a stocky man with an unruly mass of red hair who had once flown with Lincoln Ellsworth and Sir Hubert Wilkins in the Antarctic, picked me up in a car at Ottawa and drove me across the tarmac to a waiting DC-3. I could see the red letters SPARTAN AIR SERVICES stenciled on the fuselage, but this was the only clue I had to this sudden and mysterious expedition into the high north.

"What's it all about?" I asked Red.

"Just a minute," he said; "here's Pat Patterson, our pilot. He's going all the way. I'm dropping off at Churchill. He'll give you the gen when he's got time."

Pat Patterson was tall and laconic and shaggily mustached.

"Details later," he said. "We're on our way. Climb into the back there and find yourself a seat."

I clambered into the plane. In the gloom I could just make out a jumble of freight roped tightly to the floor. The aircraft seemed to be full of people and I could hear women's voices. I found a space, sat down, and buckled the seat belt. A moment later we roared off into the night. Our destination was Pond Inlet at the very tip of Baffin Island. It lay due north, two thousand miles, almost a continent's width away. To reach it we would have to describe a great three-thousand-mile semicircle, skirting the western shores of Hudson Bay to Churchill, and then flying northeast across the top of the bay to our goal.

Next to me, a stocky man with a Scandinavian accent introduced himself above the roar of the engine as Axel Rosin, a Danish American. His wife, Katharine, a pretty, dark woman in a parka, sat next to him. It turned out that Rosin was, of all things, vice-president and treasurer of the Book-of-the-Month Club.

This urbane detail gave me a sudden sense of unreality. The whole affair did not carry the proper savor of an Arctic safari. What would a book-club executive be doing heading north off the edge of the map? And taking his wife? They belonged on an American Airlines flagship heading for Chicago, not on a Spartan Aircraft DC-3 winging over the black-spruce forest of northern Ontario.

Rosin began to tell me the story, and it steadied my perspective.

It went back to a summer's day several years before when he and his wife, both ardent alpinists and bird-

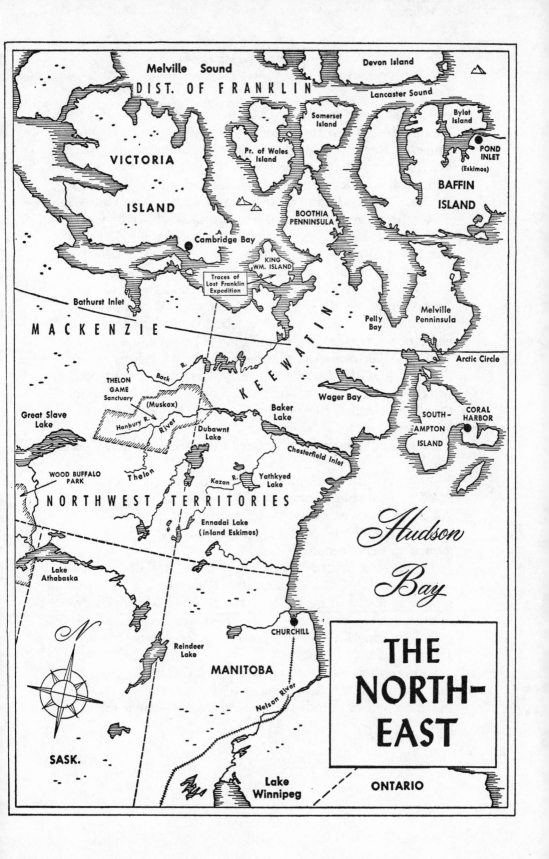

Melville Sound

DEVON Island

DIST. OF FRANKLIN

Lancaster Sound

Bylot Island

VICTORIA

Somerset Island

Pr. of Wales Island

POND INLET
(Eskimos)

BAFFIN

ISLAND

BOOTHIA PENNINSULA

Cambridge Bay

KING WM. ISLAND

Traces of Lost Franklin Expedition

Bathurst Inlet

M A C K E N Z I E

Pelly Bay

Melville Penninsula

Arctic Circle

Back R.

THELON GAME Sanctuary

(Muskox)

Hanbury R.

River

Wager Bay

Baker Lake

SOUTH-AMPTON ISLAND

CORAL HARBOR

Great Slave Lake

Dubawnt Lake

Chesterfield Inlet

WOOD BUFFALO PARK

Thelon

Kazan R.

Yathkyed Lake

N O R T H W E S T   T E R R I T O R I E S

Ennadai Lake (inland Eskimos)

Lake Athabaska

Hudson

Bay

Reindeer Lake

CHURCHILL

MANITOBA

THE NORTH-EAST

SASK.

Nelson River

Lake Winnipeg

ONTARIO

watchers, were climbing Mount Washington in New Hampshire. When they reached the summit, they found someone there before them, a forthright individual with an enormous mane of wavy hair, naked to the waist. Around his neck hung two cameras and a pair of binoculars, and he was taking a photograph with a third camera.

"Getting some scenics?" Mrs. Rosin asked brightly.

"I don't take scenics," came the scornful reply. "Yesterday I saw a winter wren singing here. I am now taking a photograph of the bush I found her in."

His name was Rosario Mazzeo and he proved to be a bass clarinetist with the Boston Symphony Orchestra. He, too, climbed mountains and watched birds. The three became close friends. Each time the orchestra came to New York and performed in Carnegie Hall, the Rosins would drink beer with Mazzeo and talk of adventure and bird-watching in far places. Most of the time they talked about the Arctic, which they had never seen but had dreamed of visiting.

"We should go to the Arctic!" Mazzeo would say excitedly.

"But you just can't pick up and go like that, Rosario," Axel Rosin would answer. "To do a thing like that you've got to have an expedition—scientists, that sort of thing."

"All right, then!" Mazzeo said to him one day. "I'll *organize* an expedition."

The Rosins laughed and forgot about it. Then, some time later, they got a message from Mazzeo: "I have five scientists ready to go to the Arctic." He had indeed got them together, secured a grant from the Arctic Institute of North America and the New York Zoological Society, and formed an expedition.

So here they were, crowded into a DC-3 flying over the dark northern forests on their way to an Arctic island that few men had explored: the two Rosins, five scientists, and one scientist's wife. Only one man was missing: Rosario Mazzeo himself. At the last moment, to his bitter disappointment, his musical duties had kept him from going on the cherished adventure. Thus there was a seat left in the plane, and, thanks to Red Lymburner and Spartan Air Services, I was aboard.

We slept, awkwardly twisted in our seats or sprawled over the boxes of supplies that crammed most of the body of the plane. We awoke in the blanched thin light of a northern morning to find ourselves coasting into the landing strip at Kapuskasing, the northern Ontario bush town more familiarly known as the Kap. The air was heady with a familiar fragrance, the pungent odor of the balm-of-Gilead tree, the common perfume of the north. From the Yukon to Quebec, this tall, quivering poplar with the sticky buds dominates the forest country and scents the crisp air with its incense. It is the *liard* of the *voyageurs,* and the Liard River in the Yukon is named for it.

We were soon away, heading for Churchill, a historic seaport on the western shore of Hudson Bay, and the gateway to the eastern Canadian Arctic. As the broad scroll of forestland slowly unrolled below us, Dr. William Drury, a thin, bespectacled Harvard professor who was leader of the expedition in Mazzeo's absence, told me what he and his colleagues planned to do.

They had decided to spend a summer of investigation on Bylot Island, a spectacular but almost unknown blob in the frozen ocean just off Pond Inlet, on the northern coast of Baffin. Not many scientists have visited Bylot, and that is why they had chosen it. They had been startled, therefore, to find, hanging on the walls of the National Gallery in Ottawa, a dramatic painting of Bylot's jagged blue mountains and green icefields. The painting was by Lawren Harris, an heir to the Massey-Harris farm-machine fortune (the same dynasty that produced the first Cana-

dian-born Governor-General, Vincent Massey) and one of
the nation's finest artists. Harris and his colleagues formed
the influential school known as the Group of Seven in the
mid-twenties and resolved, severally, to paint the Canadian hinterland. As a result many obscure corners of the
north are now on canvas.

Now the scientists were following the artists to Bylot
Island to try to fit another piece or two into the jigsaw
puzzle of the north. One would study the population dy-
namics of the northern fauna—the lemming, the Arctic
hare, the snowy owl. One would study bird life. Another
would try to discover the effect of permafrost on vegetation. A fourth would investigate the ecology of the Eskimo.
A fifth would climb the mountains. Dr. Drury's wife,
Mary, a cheerful twenty-four-year-old, would do the cooking for the expedition in between her studies of nesting
behavior. They would all remain in the Arctic for six
weeks, until another plane came up from Quebec to take
them home again. I would be returning with the DC-3
after it dropped them on the coast of Baffin.

A strange crew to be flying into the glacial wilderness,
these studious young professors in their shapeless khaki
parkas. Here was Dr. Benjamin Ferris, physician and
alpinist, seated on an upended packing case, reading
Mathematics for the Million and working algebra problems in his notebook. Here was Edward Ames, Harvard
undergrad and botanist, deep in Voltaire's *Candide*. Here
was the man from the book club, reading Prescott's *Con-
quest of Mexico*, with the pack ice of Hudson Bay just
over the horizon. Sprawled face-down on the floor, sound
asleep, lay the two women, looking for all the world like
rag dolls with their tousled black hair, heavy coats, blue
denims, and boots.

Below us the poplars had given way to a ragged monochrome of gray-green lichen, broken by patches of stunted

spruce and thousands upon thousands of round little ponds. From horizon to horizon this was the unchanging view. Here was the gray twilight land that skirts the southwestern shore of Henry Hudson's huge inland sea. It runs back from the shoreline for a hundred and fifty miles, flat and uninspiring, never rising to a height of more than six hundred feet above sea level and very rarely exceeding two hundred feet. There is no drainage here, only a vast tract of bewildering swampland.

It is known as the most monotonous country on the continent. Scarcely a human, Indian or white, lives or travels here. No telltale pillar of smoke curls up from the land. No trails or traplines cross it. No hut or cabin breaks the tedium. Even animals are scarce. For this is ancient seabottom, a wet, flat, forbidding country of silt and moss, lichen and muskeg.

Only from the air does this dismal terrain take on a certain interest, for now, as we watched, a startling formation showed through the ragged cotton-wool clouds below. The whole country seemed to have been forced into a single pattern, as though a giant magnet had been passed over the land and all the features had rearranged themselves, as iron filings will, in obedience to a natural law. The lakes were no longer in freeform shapes, but straight as rulers, looking more like canals. The bays and the islands followed the same geometry. Long ridges, straight as Roman walls, appeared between the even lines of water. The whole land presented a neat, grooved appearance, like a carefully plowed field after a rainstorm, the furrows running methodically from north to south. These strange ridges, called *drumlins,* are found intermittently from Hudson Bay to the Barren Lands. They are the tracks of the great Keewatin ice sheet, which moved south grooving the soft land in this fashion.

Of the three great ice sheets that blanketed the north

during that geological epoch of upheaval, erosion, and fearful cold known as the Pleistocene, the Keewatin was by far the largest. Its core lay somewhere to the northwest of Hudson Bay. Here, a million years ago, as the snows began to fall ceaselessly on the once-temperate northern lands, the great icecap was born. The snow fell so thickly that the pale summer sun could not melt all of it, and some was left over to be added to the next winter's fall. Soon a permanent field began to grow, and as it increased in depth the snow crystals were packed together by the pressure of the ever-expanding mass until they turned to ice. As the pressures became more terrible, this staggering lobe of ice, now a mile or more thick, began to creep outward in all directions. It has been likened to a mass of pitch poured from a barrel, slowly spreading outward by the force of its own weight, flowing in a plastic motion over mountains, hills, valleys, and rivers. The icecap radiated north beyond the Arctic Circle, crawled west to the Rockies, south to the Missouri and Mississippi (as far as the site of St. Louis), and east into the depression of Hudson Bay, which vanished and was replaced by an icy tableland. Not once, but at least four times over a million years did this great icecap form and advance and retreat again. In the same period its sister icecap, the cordilleran, on the far side of the Rockies, was sending its long, alpine tongues forking up into the Yukon and down to Montana; while on the opposite side of the continent the Labrador cap was forcing its way north to Baffin Island, east into the Atlantic, south to New England and the Ohio country, and west to join the Keewatin in the trough of Hudson Bay.

On at least two occasions the three great caps came together so that half the continent, perhaps four million square miles, was submerged under a single enormous dome of ice twelve thousand feet thick. Inexorably the great frozen wall ground on, choking the valleys, smothering the mountains, diverting the rivers, and changing the face of the land. Today, save for some final remnants in the Rockies and on Baffin Island, the ice has vanished, but its claw marks remain. It was these ancient scars that we saw below us.

Now another queer sight presented itself: shapeless, tawny patches stretched out between the lakes, with black uneven lines painted upon them. They looked rather like enormous tiger skins. The black lines were actually peat ridges, and there is yet no complete explanation for them. Most scientists believe they are caused by the yellow bogs alternately freezing and thawing and humping the peat into wavering ridges across the sphagnum mosses.

All the while, below us, the slender ribbon of the Canadian National's "muskeg railway" stretched off toward Churchill on Hudson Bay. This is the railway that took fifty years to build, for it was contemplated as far back as 1880, contracted for in 1911, but not actually completed until 1928. For half a century it was a Canadian byword, as controversial in its own day as the St. Lawrence Seaway. Now the railway is a reality, and wheat from the prairies is trundled across the muskeg to Churchill. The town is as close to Liverpool as is Montreal or New York, and no farther from the Canadian grain belt than are the ports at the head of the Great Lakes.

As we flew onward, paralleling the curve of the bay, the land below became more and more moth-eaten. The forests began to thin, coming and going in wide splashes of dark green on the tawny pattern of the bog. Occasionally a wriggling little stream, showing white flashes of rapids, hesitated through the flat country, but the large rivers meandered majestically, their sides as even and unbroken as any canal's. They cut their way neatly into the soft silt and seem to be painted on the landscape.

The little lakes began to curve in slim crescents following the contours of the great bay. The land sloped off gently toward the water in a series of terraces marking each successive beach line in the gradual shrinking of the inland sea.

For Hudson Bay *is* shrinking. In preglacial times it was a great river flowing over a wide plain. Some scientists believe the Missouri once flowed into it before the ice barrier blocked it off and diverted it south to its present course. When the invading ice wall ground its way down from the north, it compressed the land beneath it, forcing it some twelve hundred feet lower. Then, as the ice retreated again, the land, freed of its weight, began to expand like a sponge. Thus far it has risen between two hundred and fifty and eight hundred feet, and the rise is measurable in the memory of man. Certain Eskimo dwellings originally built near the shoreline, and certain fish traps originally constructed between high and low tide, are now thirty to eighty feet above sea level. Eons hence, Hudson Bay will once again be a river surrounded by a monotonous realm of lakes and muskeg. But the chances are that the land will be far more habitable than it is now, for the great cold bay does nothing to moderate the present climate.

On the shorelines below us we could see evidence of the bay's shrinkage. In the distance we could see the bay itself and the faint glint of its pack ice. This was the same spectacle that, in 1662, greeted those two ragged rascals of the woods, Médart Chouart, Sieur des Groseilliers, and his brother-in-law, Pierre Esprit Radisson, the first white men to penetrate the forests and stumble upon the fabled inland sea that lay one thousand miles from the Atlantic. Here was the route to the heart of the continental fur empire. Within eight years Radisson and Groseilliers (known to generations of Canadian schoolboys as "Radishes and

Gooseberries") had sparked the formation of the great company that took its name from the inland sea and for two centuries owned and ruled the north.

Suddenly we saw that the lakes below us were frozen and white and it was winter again. The army base of Churchill, Canada's most northerly grain port, lay over the horizon at the northeast corner of Manitoba. We were heading toward it and by late afternoon we were above it, a stark and dreary cluster of gray and white buildings that blended into the monochrome of the landscape. Except for a few stunted trees, the whole effect was gray. The waters of the bay were gun-metal; the gravel of the beach was dun; the lichens and the grasses were yellow-gray, and the rock on which the town is built was blue-gray. Even the sky was gray on this gray June afternoon. The tundra lay a few brief miles away and the striated Precambrian stone of the great Canadian shield, so familiar to northerners, came up to meet us as we skimmed into the airport. The bitter wind, blowing off the ice pack, told me that once again I was in the heart of the north.

The ancient rock was everywhere, jutting from the thin soil in rippling contours. The telephone poles, unable to penetrate it, were fixed to it by guy wires. The road between the airport and the town, over which we now rattled in a station wagon, was hacked out of it. The steam pipes heating the army quarters were laid in tunnels expensively blasted into it. As much as the beaver and the maple leaf, this Precambrian rock deserves to rank as the Canadian emblem. It is stark, but, as some of our painters have discovered, it is not unlovely. And it is fruitful. From this vast armored horseshoe, stretching from the uranium deposits of Great Bear Lake on the west, to the iron troves of Labrador on the east, the north draws its mineral sustenance. The edge of the shield is sprinkled with some of Canada's richest and most famous mining developments and the prospectors' favorite slogan is that the shield has only been scratched.

The shield sprawls across two fifths of the nation. It is the mighty anchor to which the continent is fixed. Its gneisses and its granites, its schists and its basalts, are among the oldest rocks in the world; some go back two billion years, as far as geological history can take us. They are so old that our knowledge of them is still uncertain, but because they contain no fossils, the suspicion is that some of them were here before life itself. They are the roots of long-forgotten mountain ranges sandpapered to dust by eons of erosion, or twisted and deformed and compressed out of all recognition by the terrible pressures and upheavals to which they have been subjected for the last two thousand million years.

This Precambrian stratum forms what geologists call "the basement complex," for, being the oldest of all, it lies at the base of every mountain range, far beneath the blanket of younger rocks that clothes the rest of the continent. But here, in the Canadian north, the Precambrian lies naked to the elements, an incredible rocky wilderness stretching from the sheer Atlantic shoreline, across Ungava, under the waters of Hudson Bay, and over eight hundred miles of tundra to the shores of the huge northern lakes—Great Bear and Great Slave.

There are other Precambrian shields in the world (in Africa, for example), but the Canadian shield is the largest and the most easily studied. To these deformed rocks we owe much of our knowledge of earlier epochs. The shield is an area of stability that has stood relatively firm while fierce continental upheavals changed the shape of the land, but even this great natural buttress has risen and fallen occasionally over the ages, allowing the seas to sweep in over it and retreat again.

The road through the rock took us from the airport to

the gray little town on the edge of the bay. It lies near the mouth of the Churchill River, which pours in from the frozen tundra to help form a natural harbor, in use for more than three centuries. On this very beach, three hundred and thirty-five years ago, Jens Munck, the seafaring son of a Danish nobleman, sat resolutely writing in his journal and committing his soul into the hands of God. Around him the ravens wheeled and shrieked and picked at the frozen corpses of his shipmates who had died, one by one, of scurvy, starvation, exposure, frostbite, and gangrene until only Munck and two cadaverous comrades were left to steer a tiny cockleshell of a boat home across the sea in a miraculous return from the dead.

Not far away, chiseled into the rock of Sloop's Cove, is the name of the greatest of all northern explorers, Samuel Hearne. Though he smarted under the iron hand of his future father-in-law, Moses Norton, who was the half-breed Governor of the fort and "a selfish debauchee," Hearne set out across the unknown tundra to search for a copper mine on the Arctic's rim and, in doing so, completed a journey that has never been equaled.

Near here, at Eskimo Point, after two centuries, stands an awesome and ancient fort, Prince of Wales, one of the continent's most intriguing military ruins. It was almost half a century in the building, and its walls, forty feet thick, are made from great blocks of quartzite cut by old-country stonemasons. This most formidable of all fortifications was in use only a decade. A French admiral captured it from the British without firing a shot. Hearne had become its commander, and the Frenchman took him prisoner. He treated the explorer like a literary celebrity and agreed to his ransom on the condition that he immediately publish his journal of exploration to the Arctic.

Today Churchill, a town of seven hundred, has become the great funnel that leads to the eastern Arctic. Indeed, in this the cold and treeless eastern land of rock and water, it is the only settlement that harbors more than a handful of white men. The nearest northern village, Yellowknife, lies seven hundred miles across the Barrens to the northwest. To the north, in the districts of Keewatin and Franklin, lies nothing but a few scattered trading posts.

Everything goes through Churchill. The grain boats steam out of here stuffed with wheat—eleven million bushels a season—for Britain, Switzerland, Italy, Greece, Holland, Germany, Panama, and Ireland. The aircraft of a unique corporation, Arctic Wings, soar off from here for the bleak glacial islands that represent the ultimate land on the continent. (The firm was once owned by the Oblate priests of Mary Immaculate, who wanted to set up a supply line to their missions. Once the line was established and flourishing, they sold it.) Prospectors, too, pour through Churchill. Since the publication, in 1953, of a thorough geological report on the Keewatin region of the Northwest Territories, they have been fanning out over the tundra from the town. Each summer the hunters arrive to slaughter some seven hundred of the white whales that can be seen basking on the surface of the bay at the mouth of the river and whose carcasses can be transformed into hand lotion, soap, perfumes, cooking oil, mink food, medicines, and tonics.

We were all exhausted when we reached Churchill. We had been traveling since two the previous morning, with little sleep and only a sandwich for brunch. Now it was eight in the evening. We ate a steak apiece in the hotel restaurant, while the inevitable juke box played the inevitable cowboy music that drenches the north. Then we drank a cold beer in the chrome-and-arborite tavern and tumbled into bed. We had one thousand miles of flying ahead of us the following day before we would finally reach the wrinkled hide of Baffin Island.

2 | The Island of Big Flat Stones

We were now to fly off into an entirely different kind of north from the one in which I had been reared. The western north of my boyhood—the land of big rivers, thick forests, gold mines and boom towns—is the banana belt of the frontier. The eastern north is entirely dissimilar. The vast wastes of Keewatin and Franklin stretch off to the east and the northeast, still partly unmapped and largely unpopulated, quite useless for agriculture or forestry and scarcely scratched by the prospector's pick. This was the first part of the north to be reached by white men, but the last to be conquered by them. Indeed, save for a handful of trading settlements, it has not changed appreciably since the bleak summer in 1611 when Henry Hudson's starving and diseased crew cast him adrift without food or water in a tossing shallop on the leaden surface of the bay that now bears his name.

These are lands that still know starvation and tragedy. On Boothia Peninsula not long ago a forty-five-year-old Eskimo woman, racked by the final stages of tuberculosis, pleaded with her son to kill her. He complied with the ancient tradition. The mother quietly placed her head within a loop of sealskin line suspended from a tent pole, while the youth pressed down upon her until she died. On Foxe Basin, in the winter of 1948, a man and two boys died of cold and starvation after devouring their dogs, their clothes, and their sleeping-skins. The wife and daughter survived by eating the cadavers and using the fat to light their seal-oil lamps.

Before invading this raw and empty land Pat Patterson, our pilot, walked up to the operations office above the airstrip to get a line on the weather. The big weather map on the wall showed the isobars curling like snakes around the great ice-capped bulk of Baffin Island, which lay northeast across the bay. Green patches near Greenland marked areas of falling snow. A second map showed formations of broken cloud.

"Well, how do things look?" Patterson asked the weatherman on duty.

"Not bad. There's snow at Arctic Bay, though."

"It's been snowing there all week," Patterson said. "I guess there's ice in those clouds, too, eh?"

"Hard to say. Maybe not. Could be only rain," the weatherman said, a little vaguely.

"Will Coral be open if we have to turn back?"

"Sure. I think so. This map's only valid till noon, you know."

"Do you mean things are going to get better or deteriorate?"

"Coral will be all right. Around Pond, well, they might deteriorate. Looks a bit like you might get snow. There's no bloody station in there, that's the trouble. There's no saying you couldn't bring these isobars in and draw another row. There could be a trough in there, and in the trough there should be overcast skies and snow."

"Well, how's Resolute as an alternate?" Patterson asked.

"Snow showers there, but the visibility is now ten miles," the weatherman said. He pulled a strip off the Teletype beside him. "Wait a minute. It's okay. Resolute is broken now and Arctic Bay is scattered."

"Let's go!" Patterson said.

"Let's go before it gets worse," said Mac MacIntosh, his co-pilot, a stocky young Spitfire veteran.

"Well, we can always get into Resolute anyway," Patterson said hopefully.

"Yeah, you can get in there okay. It looks like the trough is north of Arctic Bay and south of Pond," the weatherman said. "Of course, by the time you get there . . ."

"Yeah, I know," Patterson said. "Anything can happen. Well, let's go."

"Wait," said the weatherman, pulling another paper off the Teletype. "Resolute is calling for ten miles visibility varying with six miles visibility with snow. I wouldn't be surprised if you ran into that stuff all the way."

"We could sure use a few more weather stations in the north," Patterson said.

"You can say that again," said Mac MacIntosh.

We walked out to the landing strip, past the orderly rows of army and air-force buildings. Out from this great base, for sixty miles across the tundra, stretches the huge outdoor defense research laboratory in which equipment, men, and tactics are tested each winter against the event of the coldest kind of hot war. Here each year the most northerly military exercises in the nation take place, under spartan conditions. As a contrast, the steam-heated permanent quarters are a simulated spa, equipped with movie theater, newsstand, library, billiard room, clothing stores, jewelry and drug stores, cocktail bar, and officers' club, all tied together into a single labyrinthine unit by connecting passageways that make it unnecessary to poke one's nose outside, of a winter, except when engaged on maneuvers.

A chill wind was whipping across the airstrip as we climbed into the plane. It came from the pack ice, a white, slowly shifting mass several hundred yards out from shore in the dark waters of the bay. A few minutes later the ice was below us, stretching from horizon to horizon, broken and veined, with the sun gleaming on the black water that showed through the slushy channels. It was slowly breaking up as spring inched north.

We flew across this mottled world for four hours. It is a comment on our ignorance of the Canadian north that until 1948 no one knew for certain whether Hudson Bay froze all the way across. The general belief was that it never froze completely and that there was open water in the center. Finally an RCAF plane charted the bay in the winter and found it solid. But for three hundred and thirty-seven years—from the time the gray-bearded Hudson first entered it and thereby sealed his own doom—the bay had retained this secret.

Another secret it will always retain, and that is the fate of the first explorer to enter it. What became of Hudson, the stubborn mariner who, sailing across the great sheet of water, believed he had at last reached the Pacific? What was the fate of this iron-willed man who would neither brook opposition nor heed advice until his panicky crew, fearing he was leading them to disaster, cast him adrift? The odds are that he perished in the icy bay, but some historians and explorers have been nagged by the theory that he and his small son and the seven men cast off with him might have made their way to James Bay in the south, where some scanty fragments of legend suggest that a group of white seamen built cabins and lived for years among the Indians. The truth will never be known. As one Arctic chronicler has written: "Of all the dark mysteries of the merciless ocean, no mystery lies wrapped in deeper shadow than that which hangs over the fate of Hudson."

At noon the piebald sheet below us was broken by the desolate expanse of Southampton Island, a naked lowland almost as big as Ireland, rising from the ice in an enormous triangle. Not since I landed on the Aleutians had I seen anything more uninviting. In the bitter northern spring the island looked exactly like a lake disturbed by ripples. The ripples were formed by low ridges of Precambrian rock. The dead snow of winter was still caught in the troughs between them.

On this cheerless desert the oldest Eskimo civilization to overlap that of the white man came to its end. Here, completely independent of the white man, lived the Sagdlirmiuts with their bow-and-arrow culture, existing entirely on whale, walrus, seal, caribou, birds, and fish without a shred of vegetable ration, and living in houses built of stones, whose ruins can still be found. It was a white man's disease, typhoid fever, that wiped them out in 1903.

We landed at Coral Harbor—an airstrip and a huddle of buildings. Twelve men lived here: three RCAF enlisted men and nine Department of Transport employees. It is an all-male community, and I was reminded of the standing joke on the Aleutian Islands: "There's a woman behind every tree; only there aren't any trees."

An air-force staff sergeant greeted us as we landed. "Did you bring the beer, Pat?" he asked anxiously.

"Two cases," said Patterson.

"Thank God," said the airman. "I lose my bet. I bet the cook two dollars you wouldn't bring it. Hot diggity, I lost!"

"I told you I'd bring it," said Patterson. "I wouldn't of dared land without it."

"Some change since you was here last, eh, Pat?" said the airman. "Snow and everything was here last time. 'Course there's still *some* snow."

"When is summer?" I asked him.

"Hell, man, this *is* summer," said the airman. "C'mon up to the inn."

Once again I was reminded that in the north, latitude is

no guarantor of climate. Southampton Island actually lies south of the Arctic Circle. Over in the Mackenzie Valley, towns like Aklavik, far north of the Circle, would now be basking in the seventy-degree June heat. Cabbages would be fattening in the mission gardens, and poppies would be budding. Along the Arctic Circle the average July temperature varies from forty-two degrees on southern Baffin Island to sixty degrees around Arctic Red River on the Mackenzie. The cause of this curious contrast is the giant thermostat of Hudson Bay, three hundred thousand square miles of it, in constant intercourse with the Arctic and the North Atlantic. In spring and summer the cold seas keep the thermometer down in the eastern Arctic; in the fall they retard the drop in air temperature.

We had arrived at a long, low building that bore the chipper sign: SOUTHAMPTON INN: VISITORS WELCOME. This was the Coral Harbor messhall. Piled like bricks on the long veranda were several tons of ice blocks, the camp's fresh water supply. Some of the scientists produced cameras and began to take photographs, and some began looking through binoculars for birds. But there were no birds.

"More bird-watchers, eh, Pat?" the sergeant said. "What you do with that last lot you had?"

"Those weren't bird-watchers," Patterson said. "Those were geologists. They look at rocks, not birds. They're still up there on Baffin."

"I got three more coming in next week," the sergeant said. "I just got the message. The country's full of bird-watchers this year. There were some here last year, too. Used to rush out of the tents with nets, and the 'skimo kids would all look at them and shout: 'Clazy! Clazy!' Before they was through they had the 'skimos working for them, too."

We went inside for coffee and sandwiches. A few men sat around in worn easy chairs reading worn magazines,

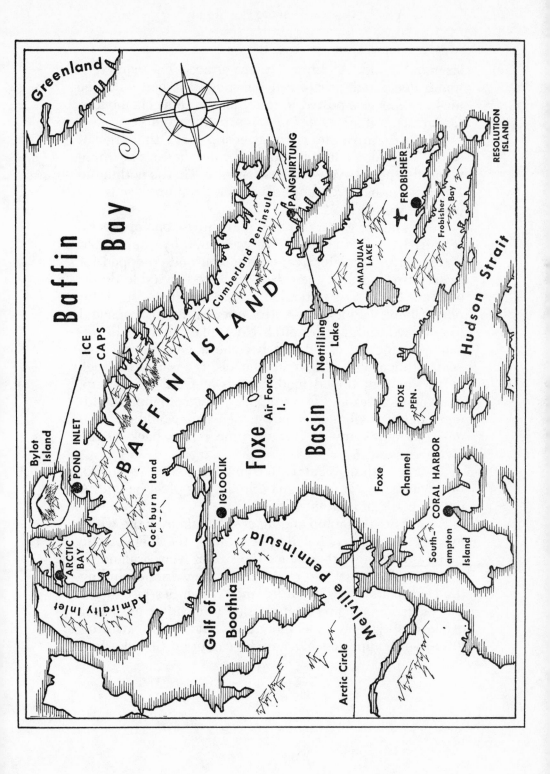

six months old. A chipped piano graced one corner. A guitar decorated a wall. But the musicians had left. The air-force men are posted to the island for only six months. Department of Transport men must stay a year.

"Most of 'em volunteer for a second year," the sergeant said. "They don't like it too well, but there's one thing about this place—you sure save money. There's nothing to spend it on, not even beer. Even the gambling evens out over the winter."

Coral Harbor was a wartime ghost town, one of several scattered about the north. It was built by the United States during the later years of the war and equipped for twenty-two hundred men. Here lay the inevitable debris of war. Coral was intended as an alternate strip for planes flying wounded to North America from Europe and had its own military hospital. Now, like other towns vacated by the forces, it had become a gigantic garbage heap, strewn with old steam shovels, thousands of truck parts, stacks of tinned food, barrels of Coca-Cola syrup, platoons of Mack and Reo trucks, a village of empty buildings, and a small fleet of power boats. It would cost too much to move any of this wartime refuse back to the civilized world.

"This is nothing," Pat Patterson remarked. "At Chimo, in Ungava, the Yanks left an entire paving plant behind. A paving plant, of all things."

We left Southampton and made off again over the white expanse of the bay, heading for Baffin, the huge Arctic island that is more than twice the size of New Zealand. It is, in fact, the fourth largest island in the world, excluding the continental mass of Greenland, which lies just to the east of it. Three hours later we saw it ahead of us, a vast expanse of jagged blue mountains and broad swirling glaciers—the uplifted block of Precambrian that the Ice-

208

landers of Leif Ericsson's day called Helluland—the country of big flat stones (a phrase that also may have meant Labrador).

Here, on the southern tip of this spectacular, forbidding island, on a foggy July morning in 1576, from an eggshell of a ship, there landed the first explorer to penetrate the Canadian Arctic—a bearded and illiterate naval captain named Martin Frobisher, whose name was to rank with Drake's and Hawkins's.

We ourselves might have been looking at the island through Elizabethan eyes, so little had this section of it changed over the centuries. It rose out of the fog before us: the most spectacular scenery in all eastern North America, though too remote for the eyes of the casual tourist, a wild land of blue and white, its coastline tattered by a thousand fiords, its horizons ragged with a regiment of mountain peaks. The land tongue-and-grooved with the sea as we advanced upon it. Long fingers of frozen ocean cut their way far inland, winding beneath the dark cliffs, and every valley harbored a glacier that, from the air, seemed to be spilling at breakneck speed into the ocean.

The sixteen thousand miles of this crinkled coastline are so intricate that mapping it has taken three centuries of careful exploration, and the charting is not yet done. The shores of Baffin seem, indeed, to have been submerged in the sea, for the mountains and valleys march down to the ocean's margin and then vanish beneath its surface, often to reappear as islands along the coastline. Thus it is sometimes almost impossible to tell where the mainland begins. Actually, Baffin is a drowned land, still heaving itself out of the waters that washed over it when the weight of the Pleistocene glaciers forced it down. Marine deposits can be found six hundred feet and more above the present level of the sea. And the strange stone rings that mark the former dwelling places of the extinct Eskimo culture called the Thule are twenty to thirty feet higher than the present native homes along the shore.

The great island, with its eastern wall rising almost sheer from the sea, has attracted a long procession of explorers since the days of Frobisher and his Elizabethan crew. Their adventures have brought rewards. Those who trekked into Baffin's interior found two great lakes near the southern tip in a drab, swampy land, studded with pools and low granite ridges, where gales blew ceaselessly in the winter. One of these lakes was one hundred miles across. Others came upon hot springs, three acres in size, which froze in the winter to form great blue cones of ice through which the sulphurous waters hissed and bubbled. Some pushed up the east coast, past a land of gorges and chasms where the mountains soared straight into the clouds, and rivers of solid ice poured through the valleys to the water's edge. Some followed the western shoreline past masses of layered limestone, banded in yellow, black, and red, past ancient coral reefs rising seven and eight hundred feet, past bricklike cliffs chiseled by the weather "into various romantic shapes as of broken arches, decayed walls, niches and tunnels . . . [like] the ruins of ancient castles or stately palaces."

Those who ventured farther discovered, at the island's western tip, the world's longest fiord, Admiralty Inlet. There are two hundred and forty miles of it, guarded by a thousand-foot mountain wall christened Giant's Castle, into whose gaudy serrated flanks the wind and the waves have graven great pillars and columns and pointed buttresses, gateways, caves, and giant caldrons. Those who trespassed upon the midriff of the island saw a relic of the Pleistocene age, the Barnes Icecap, ninety miles long, forty miles wide, and a quarter of a mile thick. bestriding the mountain backbone.

Since the bold Frobisher first found himself face to face
with "a mighty deer that seemed to be man-kind" (it was
probably a moose), explorers and scientists have carefully
charted the fauna of the island. Those four ubiquitous
Arctic mammals, the wolf, the caribou, the white fox, and
the lemming, roam the interior plateaus but, curiously,
there is no trace of that shaggy tundra oddity the muskox.
There are snow and blue geese in thousands, and in the
interior goose traps have been found—great corrals of
boulders into which the natives drive the birds to club
them to death. There are insects in myriads. One party
identified two species of bumblebee. One captured speci-
mens of butterflies. Another, seeing smoke rising from
an island in a lake, investigated and found it to be a
dense cloud of midges. Another party happened upon a
colony of fulmars, an intriguing species of polar seafowl
that routs its adversaries by spouting pure oil from its bill.
There were perhaps half a million of these birds, the largest colony yet recorded.

Baffin Island, especially its southern section, has been
more carefully and more extensively explored and investigated than any other part of the Canadian Arctic, but
great wedges of it remain unknown. We were flying now
across the mountain spine that braces the eastern flank of
the island and is a continuation of the mountain range that
borders the Labrador coastline directly southeast. These
mountains are still sketched crudely, without contour
lines, on the aeronautical maps. The altitudes aren't always accurate. Dark cliffs that should have slipped beneath us, according to map and altimeter, towered above
us as we swept down a long, glacier-choked fiord.

Ahead of us, beyond the mountain barrier, the frozen
expanse of Baffin Bay stretched for four hundred miles
into the horizon, beyond whose cold mists lurked the ice
wall of Greenland. The bay was named for William Baffin,

211

a self-taught British navigator of obscure beginnings and unknown background, a "learned-unlearned mariner" who charted these shores with surprising accuracy in 1616 and then returned to England, with his tales of the great bay disbelieved, to die shortly after, fighting for his country in the Persian Gulf. Later geographers, on viewing his discovery, called it "the most magnificent bay in all the world," and it has grown rich in the history of the Arctic.

It was here, through the eyes of a whaling captain, that the world had its final glimpse of the most famous and ill-fated Arctic expedition of all. On a bright July day in 1845 the whaler happened upon two stubby three-masters, painted bright yellow, anchored to the ice pack. These were the *Erebus* and the *Terror*, and their commander was Sir John Franklin, an aging British naval officer of bald pate and plump figure. Franklin was waiting impatiently for the ice to break up so that he could press on in pursuit of his own personal Grail, the legendary Northwest Passage. He was an experienced Arctic adventurer, a veteran of two previous expeditions by land and one by sea, but after the whaling ship departed, no white man again laid eyes on him or his party of one hundred and thirty-odd men.

The man-hunt that followed his disappearance stands to this day as the greatest the Arctic has even seen. Today, a century later, it still goes on. In the decade that followed his loss, the British government alone spent three million dollars seeking Franklin. Private citizens, British, Danish, Norwegian, and American, added hundreds of thousands more. Five years after he vanished, there were twelve sailing ships scouring the Arctic for the missing explorer and his men. Some of the searchers themselves went missing, and new expeditions were outfitted to search for them. Many men died vainly in the quest, of scurvy, exposure, exhaustion, starvation, and drowning.

The man-hunt produced some incredible stories of its own. On one expedition conditions were so cruel that the very dogs lay down in their harness and died of madness and depression brought on by the blackness of the polar night and the bone-chill of the seventy-five-below cold. On another, a party of nineteen men, women, and children found themselves trapped for six dark months aboard a floe that was drifting with the wind and slowly breaking to pieces. Miraculously, all were rescued.

The great hunt opened up the Arctic. Sledge teams trekked across the tundra for one thousand miles or more, and sailing ships plied strange waters, charting new islands, new straits, new bays, and new coastline. In the end, Franklin's mission was accomplished. The Northwest Passage itself was discovered winding between the ragged islands of the great archipelago. And strewn along the banks of the legendary channel lay all that was left of the Franklin expedition, graves and corpses, broken boats and bleached bones, books and Bibles and a clutter of naval bric-a-brac—everything, indeed, but Franklin himself. His bones have not been found and his resting place, like Hudson's, remains an Arctic mystery that defies solution.

3 | The Treeless Beach

We had reached the very northeast tip of Baffin and now, as we swept around a long, mountain-bordered arm of the sea, a tiny pinprick of civilization appeared. This was our destination, Pond Inlet, one of thirty Hudson's Bay post settlements scattered, one or two hundred miles apart, along the eastern Arctic coastline. Pond turned out to be a skimpy line of square buildings and tents straggling along a frozen beach on about the same parallel of latitude as the North Magnetic Pole. Behind it there stretched a monotonous low tundra, broken by low valleys, frozen swamps, and hard little lakes. It was an ashen land, streaked with the remnants of the winter's snows and covered by an uninviting crust of lichen.

Pat Patterson banked the plane, preparing to set its wheels on the frozen ocean. The snow that we had seen on the weather map at Churchill was swirling about us. The visibility had dropped alarmingly. We could just make out a wavering landing strip below, marked with oil drums and gunny sacks. Patterson found it, then lost it again—found it and lost it. Landing on white ice is always difficult, especially with poor visibility, because the pilot is never quite sure exactly how far he is from the surface. We hit with a hard jolt, rumbled down the ice, and finally shuddered to a stop.

Once again the silence of the north engulfed us. We clambered out of the plane and onto the ice, shocked at the sound of our voices, so out of place in the hush of the

Arctic evening. A mile or so away, on the low shoreline, we could just make out the buildings of the settlement. They, too, seemed still—as still as the mountains of Bylot Island, across the inlet to the north. But there was movement after all, for looking again, we could make out a thin line of Eskimos and dogs advancing toward us.

Soon they were upon us—a hundred or so Eskimos, mainly children, and as many animals. They came racing out on long wooden sleighs, each sleigh pulled by a dozen dogs fanning out in a wide arc, their lines inextricably tangled and confused. The sleighs were jammed with parka-clad passengers of all shapes and sizes, and each passenger wore a broad smile painted on his face. This was only the sixth aircraft to land at Pond Inlet, and they were making the most of it.

From this swirling, laughing throng, the three inevitable symbols of the white man's north detached themselves: the priest, the trader, and the policeman. Father Danielo, of the Oblates, a cheerful, bearded gnome in a ragged cassock—nineteen years here at Pond Inlet, with only one vacation in all that time; Pete Murdoch of the Hudson's Bay Company, a dark, intense Newfoundlander in sealskin boots and windbreaker, with eight years' experience in the north; Constable James Cooley of the RCMP, neat as a pin in a sealskin jacket and the familiar yellow-striped breeches, his hair newly crew-cut, his face freshly shaved. As Roald Amundsen remarked of a similar scene in 1906: "A policeman looks very peculiar here."

I looked around at the chattering, cheerful Eskimos. This was my first glimpse of them and I inspected them with much more curiosity than they inspected me. Of these people—there are between nine and ten thousand of them in Canada—millions of words have been written by physiologists, anthropologists, medical men, explorers, tourists, casual visitors, professionals and amateurs of all

kind. Yet few people know them, and it is doubtful if many
of that handful of people know them well. But if there is
one opinion on which almost all agree, it is that the impact
upon them of the white man's civilization has been something less than fortunate.

I recalled a luncheon I had had three days earlier in
Toronto with a dedicated young man who perhaps knows
as much about the Eskimo as anyone, yet admits he knows
very little. His name is Doug Wilkinson, and he is a onetime traveling salesman turned movie-producer. While
he was making an award-winning film in the Arctic, Wilkinson became interested in the Eskimo. The Eskimo's
great problem is that his economy is now tied to the price
of the white fox (a hitherto useless animal to him), which
is the only product he can trade for the white man's food,
utensils, and equipment. Because of the fox's four-year
cycle, the Eskimo economy suffers savage ups and downs.
Only one year of every four is a good white-fox year. In
one region of Baffin Island alone, the annual take dropped
in one year from four thousand pelts to a trickle of two
hundred.

Wilkinson, who liked the Eskimos he met, decided to
take a bold and imaginative step. In order to understand
them he would become an Eskimo himself. And so he did.
He was taken in as if he were a son by an Eskimo family,
and for thirteen months he lived with an Eskimo mother
and father and nine brothers and sisters in a drafty tent in
summer and a snow igloo in winter. He existed entirely by
hunting and trapping. He wore clothes made of sealskin
and caribou hide, and he lived on seal, walrus, polar bear,
and whale, most of the meat scorched over a seal-oil lamp
or devoured raw.

Did Wilkinson feel that he had actually become an Eskimo? Physically, yes; psychologically, no.

"I couldn't accept many of the Eskimo ways of living,"

he told me, and went on to explain that the great barrier was the Eskimo's completely fatalistic acceptance of the harshness of his life, and his inability to think of or worry about the future.

Wilkinson's idea is that Eskimos can probably be trained to perform many northern tasks now reluctantly carried out by white men. Properly directed, they might be taught to work in mines, missions, military establishments, airfields, and trading posts. But first, he says, more white men must go out, as he did, to live with the Eskimos and learn to understand them. Wilkinson himself has gone to work for the new Canadian Department of Northern Affairs, which hopes to help the Eskimo in much this manner.

"The Department doesn't know exactly what it should do about the Eskimo," I remember Wilkinson's telling me. "But it *knows* it doesn't know, and that's a big step forward."

I was recalled to the present when Pete Murdoch of the Hudson's Bay brought forward a small, middle-aged native who wore a blue beret and gold-rimmed glasses and smoked a curved pipe.

"This is Idlouk," he said.

We shook hands gravely and then I realized who Idlouk was. He was the man who had been Doug Wilkinson's Eskimo father, and it was in this area that Wilkinson had lived as a native the year before.

Pinned to the breast of Idlouk's white parka was the Queen's Coronation Medal given for exceptional service. Twenty Eskimos across the Arctic wear this decoration. Idlouk had won his because of his hunting, trapping, and leadership abilities. I remembered that Wilkinson had called Idlouk one of the most astute Eskimos he'd known.

Dr. Drury was staring across the white expanse of ice to the blue tusks of Bylot Island's mountains, where his party planned to spend the next six weeks. It was now seven in the evening, but the sun was high in the sky and it could easily have been noon.

"I figure if we could get sleds we might truck our gear over there tonight before bedtime, so's to make an early start in the morning," he said.

"It's a good eighteen miles across to Bylot," said Constable Cooley quietly.

"You're kidding!" Drury exclaimed.

"Nope," said the Mountie. "Some days it seems you could walk over in an hour, it looks so close. But those big blue mountains are six thousand feet high. It's a good day's journey. Better wait here till morning. We'll put you up."

We all stared curiously at Bylot's mountains. The scientists were to live in their shadow for six weeks, and I could not help wishing that I could remain with them. We were looking directly at the Castle Gables, a high alpine area capped by glaciers and cut by deep ravines. Except for a coastal plain in the southwest corner where the rivers bite deeply into the soil, Bylot is a land of mountains and glaciers. Among the loon-haunted cliffs of the northern coast one explorer counted twenty-four great ice-rivers, one of them six miles wide. The mountains on the north rise like tall needles out of the ice, and their peaks are so sharp and steep that no snow remains on the slopes. The highest of all, Mount Thule, rises sixty-five hundred feet into the clouds. Like the other tall mountains, its upper flanks bear no glacial scars, which means that the prehistoric icecap did not entirely cover it.

Far less is known about little Bylot Island (named after a survivor of Henry Hudson's mutinous crew) than about its huge neighbor, Baffin. Few explorers have invaded its wild interior, and the northern coast wasn't properly mapped until 1939. Thus it offers intriguing puzzles for the scientist: a whale's skeleton found five hundred feet above the high-water mark, a narwhal bone discovered a quarter of a mile up a mountainside, and, on this treeless island, a well-preserved section of an ancient tree lying in a bed of rich soil.

"Let's go!" somebody shouted; "the taxis are waiting!" We turned from our contemplation of the island mountains and rode the Eskimo sleds over the bumpy ice. I spent the next seven hours visiting at Pond Inlet.

"There are two beds in my place," Pete Murdoch said. "The ladies can have them."

"But where are you going to sleep?" Mrs. Rosin asked him.

"I just got up," he told her. "I probably won't go to bed again until the day after tomorrow. Everybody keeps pretty casual hours here. In the summer it never gets dark; in the winter it's almost always pitch-black. It's pretty hard to stick to any regular schedule. We sleep and eat pretty much when we feel like it. I've just had fourteen hours."

The light scarcely dimmed during the evening, right through the midnight hour. Outside, Eskimo children laughed and played as if it were high noon. At two in the morning, before we took off again, I checked the light-meter of my camera. It showed almost the same reading as it had when we landed.

We ate pie with the police. There are two constables at Pond—and two Hudson's Bay men, two Oblate priests, and an Anglican missionary. Two hundred and twenty-seven Eskimos are scattered about the general area.

Constable Doug Moodie, a good-looking Montrealer, produced two pies he had baked himself. Like so many men before him, he had been captured by the Arctic. He had just completed one three-year tour of duty and had quickly signed on for a second. His ambition was to push farther north, as close to the pole as land would take him,

219

to Ellesmere Island. Meanwhile he was here, with his cabin mate on this lonely, treeless beach, a policeman in a land that knows no crime.

Moodie's main task was a prosaic one: to administer the government's family allowance to Eskimo mothers. Like every Canadian mother, each Eskimo woman gets between five and eight dollars for every child under sixteen, up to a maximum of six children. In the Arctic the allowance is given in the form of a draft on the trading post for specified groceries. As a result, Pablum has become a staple food for Eskimos—men, women, and children.

These allowances are one of several governmental devices (free chest X-rays for TB are even more important) that have had a tremendous impact on the Eskimo civilization. Critics of the scheme, including some notable scientists, feel that this touch of the welfare state has stultified the Eskimo's enterprise, tying him to the white settlements and dulling his energies. On the other hand, it has brought him his first real measure of security. The allowances, begun in 1944, are cited as one reason for the current increase in the Eskimo population, which had dwindled sharply after the white man came. Certainly more Eskimo children survive now. At Pond, in 1953, for example, there were sixteen births and only eight deaths among the natives. The population in this area has been growing for twenty-five years at an average rate of two per cent a year.

A second task now facing the police represents another aspect of the welfare state. The Eskimo at seventy is eligible for the old-age pension, and receives it in cash from the Mounties. For the first time the native will have no need to carry out the terrible and heartbreaking tradition of killing his parents when they can no longer provide for themselves.

It was of these matters that we talked in the Mountie's cabin, and of the long winter patrols that each constable makes in the depth of the endless night. The previous winter Doug Moodie had traveled a thousand miles across the angry face of Baffin. His journey had taken him south across the high plateau of Cockburn Land, and thence out across the frozen surface of Foxe Basin to Igloolik, an Eskimo settlement off the tip of Melville Peninsula. Then he had pushed north again over the sea to Arctic Bay, a straggle of huts set among the ravines and glaciers of Admiralty Inlet; then home again across mountain and icecap and frozen sea.

He took two komatiks—Eskimo sleds—pulled by dogs. He had two Eskimo helpers, but often enough it was the policeman who became the helper and the Eskimos who gave the orders. The patrol lasted fifty days, and the three men slept each night in a new igloo, built where they halted. The Eskimos did the actual building while the policeman obediently lugged the snow blocks for them. When the patrol was over, Moodie sat down and figured out that altogether he had carried sixty tons of snow for the Eskimos.

"And all the time, of course, I had to continue to pay board to the government," he said.

Moodie and his partner, Jim Cooley, are two of the hundred and forty Mounted Policemen in forty-three outposts scattered across the north. These are no ordinary policemen: each man is postmaster, mining recorder, fishery officer, game warden, customs-collector, aircraft inspector, magistrate, jailer, sheriff, coroner, tax-collector, midwife, nurse, and doctor all rolled into one. They live in small frame buildings with pink gable roofs, always topped with a flapping Union Jack, and they sew, wash, and iron their own clothes, hunt and fish for their dog food, and cook all their own meals. Each winter they set off on the world's toughest police beat across hundreds and thousands of miles of empty, trackless land, accompanied only by a native or two and a team of dogs. Moodie's predecessor, Clifford Delisle, made a memorable patrol of 3,350 miles out of Pond Inlet during the winter of 1942. He was away more than three months, during which time he interviewed seven hundred and fifty Eskimos, recorded fifty births and as many deaths, and officiated at two marriages. On the face of it, the rewards of this harsh and lonely life are meager enough. A constable's starting pay has increased greatly in the past decade, but it is still only $203 a month. And each man risks the final reward accorded to Inspector Alfred Joy, who, at the age of forty-five, finally left the north to be married and died on the eve of his wedding, exhausted by his Arctic travels. Yet there is a lengthy waiting-list of Mounties who have applied for northern service.

While we talked, there was a rap on the door and Moodie answered it. He returned with a parcel in his hand. "This must have come off the plane," he said, his face lighting up. "It's addressed to me. I didn't know you guys brought any mail."

We hadn't. He opened the parcel. It was full of rocks.

"It's the Eskimos," Moodie said, grinning. "They love practical jokes."

Somewhere in the background came a ripple of gleeful laughter, as of small children, chuckling over a prank.

In the corner all this while, smiling and sipping his coffee but saying little, squatted Father Danielo, the bearded gnome in black cassock and beret. A younger priest with piercing blue eyes and the beginnings of a ragged red beard sat beside him. Danielo is a gentle, unworldly man, as one might expect of a priest who has been walled off from the world for a generation. He has little hope of making conversions at Pond Inlet, where only two of the families are Roman Catholic. The remainder belong to the Church of England, whose ministers, usually married, come and go far more frequently than the Oblates. Both churches arrived at Pond in the same year, 1929, but the Church of England has always controlled about eighty per cent of the Eskimos. Danielo and his companion are like men manning a lighthouse. They are here, the two of them, ministering to a tiny handful of natives, because their Church must maintain its outpost on the tip of Baffin. Danielo is the perfect man for the job. He is quite content to stay here and pursue his studies of theology, geology, anthropology, and archæology, traveling on furlough once in ten years to his native Brittany, and then returning to the tiny community in the Arctic. This is the way it has always been. This is the way it will always be until he is a very old man. And this is the way it will be with the younger priest, too.

They both belong to the Oblates of Mary Immaculate, a remarkable order of priests whose most northerly missions lie in the shadow of the pole. Most of them—more than three fifths—come straight from France to the Canadian north, where they must learn at once two new languages, English and the dialect of the Eskimo or Indian tribe to which they have been assigned.

There are sixty of these priests in the north. They are scattered in twenty-six missions all the way from Uranium City in northern Saskatchewan to King William Island, a remote and rocky no-man's land close to the northern limits of the Eskimo. At Uranium City, Father Bernard Brown, a curly-haired and handsome former art student from New York City, is in charge; on King William Island lives the most famous Oblate of all, Father Peter Henry. It was Henry who started a memorable mission at Pelly Bay on the mainland four hundred miles southwest of Pond. This bay is so inaccessible that sailing ships couldn't get within a hundred miles of it because the ice never thawed. For years it was out of the economic range of aircraft. Until the first plane arrived in 1945 with a load of lumber to build a cabin, the priest lived first in a cave and then in a hut made of stones. Sometimes even dog teams couldn't get through and he was forced like an Eskimo to exist off the land.

The Oblates have been in the north for a century, moving slowly ahead of the wall of civilization as it presses toward the tree line. Their history is illuminated by some vivid and tragic scenes. There is the picture of Bishop Grandin, in the days before the airplane, mushing three thousand miles by dog team through Arctic blizzards from Alberta to the Circle and back again. There is the picture of a later prelate, Breynat, the Flying Bishop, scion of a noble French family, gritting his teeth while a fellow priest cut off his frozen toes with a penknife. There is the picture of two early Oblate martyrs, Rouvier and LeRoux, struck down by Eskimos near Coppermine in 1912 and left to rot on the tundra. And there is the picture of another dying priest, Grollier, succumbing to fatigue and pain on the Arctic Circle and crying out in his agony: "My Jesus, I die happy now that I have seen the standards of your Cross raised here on the frontiers of the world."

I left the priests and the Mounties and walked down to the Hudson's Bay house, where Pete Murdoch was ready with more coffee, brewed in a completely modern kitchen, almost identical with two hundred other kitchens in Hudson's Bay trading posts scattered all across the country. "The Bay" mass-produces these homes (the prototype cost twelve thousand dollars) and furnishes them with twenty-seven hundred items, ranging from soupspoons to nutcrackers. (The home-furnisher in Winnipeg is reputed to know the color of every chesterfield, rug, and set of draperies from Pond to Aklavik.) The company stocks each house with a library, adding new books annually, supplies light, fuel, and food at a fraction of the cost, arranges correspondence-school courses for children in isolated posts, and helps send them to Outside schools after they reach ten years. It installs a radio station in each post, hires botanists to encourage home gardening, and nutritionists to check the vitamin and calorie content of the food it supplies, and gives each post manager free medical advice and a medical chest that includes both dental and surgical instruments.

In many ways, indeed, the great company *is* the north. Its red-roofed buildings form the nucleus of scores of Arctic settlements as they do at Pond. The company runs the world's oldest chain-store system, and for three centuries it has faced a staggering problem in logistics. It takes fifty tons of material to complete a post, and most of that material—usually all of it—must be flown or shipped in. The company's planes carry more than one million pounds of cargo a year, and its fleet of polar vessels sails some sixty thousand miles each season, supplying the tiny communities along the Arctic.

Next door to Pete Murdoch's house was the trading post. Canadians, accustomed to the big Hudson's Bay department stores with their escalators and perfume counters, their floorwalkers and their mannequins, forget that the company's operations still revolve to a large extent around these square, barrack-like buildings not even heated by a stove. Here the ancient barter system still has its place, for the trading is done in tokens rather than in cash. The company no longer rules half of Canada in an iron dictatorship. It can no longer marry a man or hang him, levy taxes, declare war, raise an army, fight naval battles, or issue its own money, as it once could. But its *raison d'être* is still the fur trade, as it was in 1670 when that gilded prince of the realm, Rupert, formed the Company of Adventurers and took absolute title to all lands drained by all the waters flowing into Hudson Bay.

In the post, some of the plane crew were purchasing narwhal tusks. The narwhal is another northern puzzle. It is a mammal with only two teeth in the upper jaw. In the male one of these teeth erupts and grows into a corkscrew horn, which runs between four and eight feet and can weigh up to fourteen pounds. Nobody knows what the tusk is for, but it is thought it may be used as a sort of sword. The original fable of the unicorn may well have stemmed from the narwhal, and in fact the early Arctic explorers often called them "unicorns." Certainly the three long tusks in the trading post, each as straight as a die and neatly spiraled, seemed to spring right from a Tenniel illustration in Lewis Carroll.

The flight engineer on the aircraft was standing outside the post in a crowd of Eskimos, talking to an enormous man in a wool sweater and red toque. At first I took him to be a native, but he turned out to be the Reverend Donald Whitbread, the Anglican missionary at Pond.

"I had to come all the way to Baffin Island to find a chap from my own home town in England," the engineer said when he introduced the missionary.

Whitbread had just finished building a new mission house for his Church at Pond. The following winter, he said, he planned to travel over three thousand miles of his parish by dog team. The trip would include a crossing of the hundred-mile ocean gap between Baffin Island and Boothia Peninsula to the west, a feat performed by camping on a floe and letting the wind blow it across the waters. There are twenty Anglican parishes like this in the Arctic, and each parish covers more territory than the British Isles.

The Eskimo children were still swirling about us, chattering like magpies; other Eskimos stood about in groups, watching us curiously as we talked. One of them had a Brownie camera in his hand, but wisely conserved his film.

In one of these groups stood a handsome, pink-cheeked native who looked unlike the others. This was Kadloo Herodier, half Eskimo, half French. His father had been a scientist with Captain Joseph Bernier, the bluff *Canadien* mariner and explorer who, in a series of voyages during the early part of the century, took possession of the Arctic for Canada. When the elder Herodier died, he left a legacy of eight thousand dollars to each of his Eskimo sons. Kadloo is one of them. He is, in every characteristic except his features, a true Eskimo. He lives in a snow house, speaks no English, and has never seen so much as a photograph of his father.

It was now almost two in the morning and the scientists had all gone to bed.

"Well," said Pat Patterson, a little reluctantly, "I guess it's time we were away."

"Okay," said Pete Murdoch, "I'll call you a taxi."

He whistled and a long sled, pulled by a tangle of dogs, drew up almost immediately. All the Eskimos jumped on the sled at once and began pushing one another gleefully into the snow. I piled on too, with the plane crew, the Mounties, the priests, and the Hudson's Bay men. The dogs strained at their leashes, fanning out in front of the sleigh, and the whole crowded caravan shot off across the ice, dropping Eskimo children in the snow as if they were rubber balls. The children raced behind, clambered on again, and pushed someone else off. An elderly Eskimo woman cheerfully pushed Pete Murdoch off. He jumped on and pushed Idlouk off. Other sleighs joined the procession and soon the bumpy surface of the ocean was alive with dogs and sleds and chattering, laughing, tumbling Eskimos.

We had two passengers to bring out to Churchill with us, two gnarled little women almost blind from eye infections, bound for an Outside hospital. Eskimos don't like to leave their homes, and when the boat that makes the yearly trip to these Arctic outposts each summer stopped at Pond, the two old women were nowhere to be found. Now here they were, quite bewildered and terrified as Pete Murdoch helped them aboard the plane.

He seated them in a corner on some newspapers and gave them a little tobacco to smoke.

"Just a moment," somebody said. "Here's Annie. She wants to say good-by to her mother."

An Eskimo girl clambered into the aircraft and stood in front of one of the women, who had squeezed herself tightly into a corner. They talked for a few moments and then the girl began to cry.

"It's all right, Annie," said Pete Murdoch, putting a gentle arm around her shoulder, "they'll be back soon." He led her away, still crying softly to herself. But the little old women never came back to the Arctic.

And that was my last view of Pond Inlet—a crowd of grinning Eskimos all waving furious good-by's, a swirling mass of dogs and harness, a thin line of buildings on the shore, a broad expanse of ice glinting in the morning sunlight, and a young girl crying for her mother. Thirty hours later I was home again among the blooming iris, and that cold and desolate strip of beach with its swarm of laughing natives and its handful of white men seemed as distant as the mountains of the moon.

4   Airlift to the Arctic

I returned to Baffin the following April, to a scene that contrasted dramatically with the bleak and primitive one I had left the previous summer. The great island had come alive with planes, machines, and men. The feeling of timelessness had vanished and a sense of urgency now prevailed. Bulldozers had replaced Eskimo komatiks, and Coca-Cola flowed like ice water.

The reason for this ferment was the construction of the great Distant Early Warning line of radar stations across the roof of Canada, three thousand miles from Alaska's tip to Greenland's midriff. This immense construction job, fed by the continent's greatest airlift, has had a dynamic impact upon northern economy. It is reckoned that the total bill when the task is completed, in 1957, may be a quarter of a billion dollars. (The "McGill Fence," another radar line farther to the south, cost about one half as much.) The job of air-freighting supplies to the radar sites alone is expected to run close to fifteen millions and will strain the resources of eighteen Canadian airlines and tie up more than sixty of the country's largest aircraft for upward of two years. Many of these lines had been operating on a shoestring; since the DEW line contracts were awarded, they have had to double and treble their staff.

I flew north as a crew member aboard a four-motored York—a civilian version of the Lancaster bomber—operated by Maritime Central Airways, the prime contractors on the eastern section of the DEW line. We took off from

Mont Joli, a French village near the Gulf of St. Lawrence, which has been enjoying a boom since war's end. The airlift that fed construction of the great iron mines on the Ungava-Labrador border had been anchored here; now the town had become the springboard to the Arctic. Its streets were crowded with airmen and construction workers leaving for Baffin Island, Coral Harbor, Churchill, and Melville Peninsula. Its hotel lobbies were jammed with men seeking rooms. Its airport was crowded with planes.

We took off early one morning and flew due north along the sixty-eighth parallel of longitude for eleven hundred miles. Within half an hour we had left civilization completely behind, and the land below us was a waste of rock and snow and frozen water. Until we flew over Fort Chimo near the northern tip of Quebec, we saw no sign to indicate that the hand of man had touched this wilderness. The Precambrian land below us—an ancient mountain country ground down to the roots—looked like a wrinkled plain splotched with the white jigsaw-puzzle shapes of lakes lying across the snow-powdered darkness of the forest. Occasionally a low, eroded mountain range broke the monotony of the terrain, but for the most part this land looked exactly like land a thousand miles away—the lakes and rivers wriggling north like twisted strands of spaghetti, and all radiating in the glacial lines that chart the ancient path of the Labrador icecap.

But this land is not so silent or so untouched as it appears. Up the back of the Labrador Peninsula for six hundred miles to the very tip of Ungava runs a dark rusty smear of sedimentary rocks that geologists call the Labrador Trough. Today small parties of geologists and surveyors are beginning to chart this new Mesabi. Already at its southernmost tip, on the Labrador-Ungava border, the great Iron Ore Company of Canada is mining millions of tons of high-grade ore and shipping it south along a new railway hacked from the rock. Six hundred miles to the north a platoon of companies is probing further deposits along the pathway of the ancient syncline.

The land grew whiter and blended with the frozen expanse of the sea as we flew along the western margin of Ungava Bay. The terrain looked as forbidding and empty as ever, but along this shoreline, at some future date, new ports may spring up to ship iron to the steel mills of Europe, and towns of ten thousand or more may flourish. Already the rival drilling crews of half a dozen companies strung out along the trough are testing the grade of the vast block of iron ore that lies just below the mossy surface of the rocks. One of the largest of the Canadian companies, Consolidated Fenimore, believes it has a billion tons of ore, ninety per cent of it on tidewater or within twenty-five miles of it, and most of it on the surface. But this estimate is dwarfed by that of the Cyrus Eaton Associates, who are reckoned to hold between thirty and sixty billion tons of low-grade ore—probably the largest iron deposit in the world in one area. Eaton's two private companies—International Iron Ores Limited and Tidewater Iron Ores Limited—hold 760 square miles of mineral rights within easy reach of good harbors and hydroelectric power sites.

It is on Cyrus Eaton that the eyes of the mining world are focused, for this soft-spoken Cleveland steel and utility czar has a habit of being right. Born the son of a poor storekeeper in the farming district of Pugwash, Nova Scotia, he is now reputed to be one of the continent's twenty richest men. He is a curious mixture of the pious and the practical: he started out to be a Baptist minister, but became instead a disciple of John D. Rockefeller, whom he still venerates. He works fourteen hours a day, rides to the hounds, swims and skis like a stripling, enjoys the company of scholars, and reads Homer and Spinoza.

He has also been a power in some large and familiar U.S. corporations (United Light and Power, Republic Steel, Goodyear Tire and Rubber, B. F. Goodrich Rubber, and Firestone Tire and Rubber). Today he is best known in Canada for his development of the great iron-ore bodies at Steep Rock in western Ontario—a twenty-million-dollar gamble that involved draining a fifteen-mile-long lake by punching a two-thousand-foot tunnel through solid rock. Now Eaton is gambling again in this gaunt and dismal peninsula, so remote that the world's largest crater, three miles across, lay hidden here from the eyes of man and was visited for the first time in 1950. It was created some four thousand years ago by a meteorite, which gouged out ten billion tons of rock and caused the globe's mightiest blast, equivalent to a thousand Hiroshima atom bombs.

As we reached the mouth of Ungava Bay, a singular spectacle met our eyes. Out of the frozen sea rose the thousand-foot cliffs of Akpatok Island. This flat triangle, thirty miles long and fifteen miles wide, seems to have been heaved out of the ocean, for its sides drop vertically to the edge of the pack ice. There it lay, like a dark, ice-encrusted table, the top quite smooth, the edges perpendicular. There was no sign of life, but polar bears are supposed to roam across its table-top. Looking down on it from the air, we found it hard to understand how any living thing could scale those forbidding cliffs to reach it.

Now we were crossing Hudson Strait, a deep ocean trough gouged out in glacial times by a mile-thick river of ice squeezing out of Hudson Bay to the Atlantic. Shortly after, the low, withered tip of southern Baffin Island crept out into the sea to meet us. The land below us now seemed more ancient than anything I had yet seen. The surface looked like freshly stirred porridge: rocks older than time, scoured, pitted, scratched, and clawed by ice, wind, and water. Off to the east stretched a black canyon that looked more like a fissure, cutting raggedly into the rough surface of the island. And everywhere we could see the swirling tracks of the glacier winding down from the interior toward the sea.

We were crossing the serrated peninsula that Queen Elizabeth I named Meta Incognita, the first land in the Canadian north to be visited by explorers. On the east side lay the frozen expanse of Frobisher Bay, a one-hundred-and-fifty-mile-long neck of the sea stretching inland. To this bay in 1576 in a tiny tossing ship came Martin Frobisher, a onetime pirate and slaver, choleric and passionate, heavy of frame, florid of feature, violent of temper, and "full of strange oaths." This venturesome Elizabethan, who was eventually to become his country's First Sea Lord, sailed into the bay that now bears his name, with the blessings of Queen Bess still ringing in his ears, half believing he had happened upon the mystic land of Cathay with its mountains of gold, its mounds of rubies, and its acres of diamonds. Instead he found a curious black stone that he persisted in believing to contain gold, and a queer race of heathen who seemed, at first glance, to be half fish, but turned out to be Eskimos in kayaks. Five of his men vanished into the hinterland and were not seen again, but Frobisher managed to take a native hostage by hauling him out of his kayak and heaving him aboard ship—"a strange infidel . . . whose like was never seen, read nor heard of before." The unhappy captive bit his tongue in two with chagrin at being made prisoner and soon died of a cold in the head.

With his black stone and his sea-unicorn's tusk—a present for the Queen—and his tales of a frozen domain beyond the ocean's rim, the first explorer soon had the nation believing he had discovered King Solomon's mines. In no time at all he was back again with three ships industriously digging up two hundred tons of glittering but worthless

iron pyrites, which were eventually hoarded under quad-
ruple locks in the Tower of London and Bristol Castle.
Then, after a third voyage, the Arctic bubble burst and
Frobisher was denounced as a madman, a derelict, and a
thief. But a man who could brave floating mountains of
ice in a twenty-ton sailing vessel could not be subdued for
long. Frobisher went on, with his comrades Drake and
Hawkins, to drive the Spanish Armada from his country's
shores and to earn himself a knighthood and a place in
history.

There was a queer sequel to this discovery of Baffin
Island. Two centuries after Frobisher's abortive mining
expedition—when the whole record lay half forgotten in
yellowing journals—an American seacaptain named
Charles F. Hall sailed into the same bay, happened upon
the ancient diggings, and then, to his astonishment, heard
from the lips of the Eskimos a clear account of Frobisher's
arrival, together with the fate of the five missing men who
had lived and died among them. The details had been
handed down from generation to generation, preserved in
the memories of an aboriginal people whose minds, un-
cluttered by the paraphernalia of civilization, are so
crystal-sharp that they can recall to the last nut and bolt
the structure of an outboard motor or a Diesel engine.

Now a minor revolution was taking place in this historic
land. At the head of the long bay, caught between two
rocky ridges, lay a bright rectangle of civilization. Most of
Baffin remains much as it was when the first white men
sailed up these waters. But Martin Frobisher would lose
some of his Elizabethan aplomb if he saw the great airbase
that has borrowed his name. The York clattered down a
hard runway and now, after crossing a thousand miles of
dead and empty land, we stepped out into the twentieth
century.

234

The airbase of Frobisher Bay is imprinted in my mind as a confused mosaic of men and machinery:

Twenty-one aircraft parked along the runways, some of them among the largest flying machines in the world: Yorks, DC-3's on skis, Canso flying boats, plump C-46's, big bellied, red-snouted Flying Boxcars, and immense triple-decked Globemaster troop-carriers whose yawning maws gulped twenty-five-ton D-8 tractors . . .

American pilots of all shapes and sizes in blue parkas; bearded *Canadien* laborers with sheath knives at their belts; an Eskimo looking out of place in dungarees; cooks in white, weathermen, radiomen, clerks, and mechanics; and a lone civilian complete with briefcase, brown fedora, and rubbers . . .

Coca-Cola, T-bone steaks, Irish stew, dumplings, grapefruit, pickles, ham and eggs, apple pie, and ketchup, ketchup, ketchup . . .

A soiled husky pup sleeping in the middle of the runway . . .

A blue bus stuttering along a surfaced road between mountains of filthy decaying snow . . .

The beehive of a radar station silhouetted on a gnarled rock ridge; the whirling antennæ of the Ground Control Approach system on a yellow truck parked on the runway's edge; a small thicket of radio towers; a platoon of crimson oil tanks crouched under the dark Precambrian hills; and an Eskimo settlement far away, sprinkled along the flank of a distant valley . . .

Water running, snow melting, planes zooming in and out, and a cold, bitter wind whipping along the runways . . .

Maps, maps, maps: maps of the Arctic, maps of Baffin, maps of the radar chain; sea maps and air maps; and, from a humming little fascimile machine, a new weather map unrolling slowly, prepared only a few moments before by a scientist sitting in a steam-heated office in Montreal, more than a thousand miles away . . .

The clatter of machines: little yellow forklifts shuttling from plane to plane; a powder-blue Chev station wagon hurrying across the runway; baby tractors, giant bulldozers, scarlet jeeps, great towering road-graders, and one enormous oil-tanker squatting like a gross centipede on its eighteen wheels . . .

In short, the paraphernalia of the air age, most of it flown in at great expense and trouble by an airlift that spans half a continent.

This was Frobisher Bay, built originally as a wartime refueling base, left to rot and decay as another postwar ghost town—like Coral Harbor, Canol Camp, Fort Chimo, and Pinchi Lake—then reopened in 1951 when the first radar stations were built. Now it was manned by two hundred airmen, mainly Americans, and another hundred construction workers, building the DEW line.

Here a new northern community was being planned—the largest north of the Arctic Circle. When it is complete it will hold one thousand people and act as administrative center for the eastern Arctic, the hub of the great frozen wilderness now rapidly assuming strategic importance and the anchor point for the new chain of weather and radar stations. The mayor and manager would be Doug Wilkinson, the man who had lived with the Eskimos at Pond Inlet. The town itself was being planned as a test city, the first where whites and Eskimos would have an equal share in running the local government and managing their town affairs.

John Morden, our pilot, was up in the briefing-room, looking at the great wall chart that listed landing conditions at the various radar sites in the eastern Arctic ("very rough . . . snowdrifts, hard compacted . . . no runway . . . approach from north or south . . . watch out for ridges . . . four inches slush"). There are close to fifty of these sites, and in this April of 1955 they were little more than scratches on the white surface of the Arctic. The DEW line was only two months old and the handful of construction workers on the scene had scarcely had time to level out runways for the big planes bringing in supplies, oil, food, and equipment, to build each station.

The first planes to arrive had been DC-3's on ski-wheels, and they had landed with no runway at all on bumpy sea or lake ice in the vicinity of each proposed station. Usually they flew in tandem, the first plane carrying a wooden ramp and the second a baby bulldozer. The bulldozer was unloaded on the ramp and put to work clearing a small strip so that larger planes could land with larger bull-dozers—and with the thousands of gallons of fuel oil, the fabric huts, the steel for radio towers, the crates and sup-plies and the machinery needed to push the job toward completion. The fat Globemasters, unable to land on the short strips, flew overhead and dropped fifty-thousand-pound bulldozers from their bellies by triple parachute. On one occasion the parachutes failed to open and a huge yellow machine tore its way through fifty-eight inches of solid ice.

Our York had three loads to take north to the radar sites before it would fly back to Mont Joli for another long haul. The airbase at Frobisher was really an enormous supply depot. Planes from the United States and Canada dumped their freight here. After it was sorted, other planes relayed it north to the DEW line. There are similar supply depots all across northern Canada. Coral Harbor, the bleak war-time ghost town I had visited the summer before, was another one; it, too, was now alive again with men and machinery.

We had brought tractors from Mont Joli to Frobisher

Bay. We were to take oil north, as well as a prefabricated Atwell hut—a new device, half wood paneling and half insulated fabric, which is light and maneuverable and surprisingly warm. A group of bearded workmen in shapeless parkas began to switch cargoes at top speed. It was already well past six o'clock in the evening, our destination was two hours distant, the sun was due to sink at nine p.m., and there were no lights on the makeshift runway on which we were to land.

The sense of pressure increased as the evening wore on and as more and more planes zoomed in for reloading. In the early days of the airlift, when daylight was scanty, the pilots would turn out in the darkness and take off on Frobisher Bay's lighted runway so as to be able to land at each radar site by sunrise. By split-second timing they could manage two ferrying jobs a day, taking off from the site on the final trip at sunset and landing at Frobisher in the dark. Now, with more light, the daily trips were more frequent. The airlift was being operated against time, for by June the ice would no longer be safe for landing, and it was important to get as much material as possible to the sites before warm weather stopped the airlift.

Morden, the pilot, looked at his watch as the sun dropped toward the horizon. "Kinda close," he said.

"Pretty goddam close, I'm telling you," the co-pilot said.

Two little yellow tractors chugged up, hauling the sections of the Atwell hut on a sled. The snow had been swept from the runway, and the runners grated harshly on the resistant surface.

"You think you got troubles?" the foreman of the crew shouted as Morden looked at his watch again. "Listen, I'm four men short and there's two more planes landed want to be loaded up immediately."

Planes seemed to be arriving by the minute now, each trying to get one last cargo before the light failed.

238

Finally the load was on and the doors jammed closed, and once again we were over the white gruel-like surface of the great island.

The land below us now was a terrifying monochrome of white, so flat, so barren, and so thick with snow that land, ocean, lake, rock, river, and sky all blended into one, with only the occasional razorback of a glacial ridge snaking across the empty expanse to chart our way. The sun was an orange ball on the horizon, and as it slowly dropped, the whole land became veiled in blue shadows that further obscured the landmarks.

Thus we flew north for two hours up the blank and empty Nettilling Valley of southern Baffin Island. Suddenly a rugged scarp appeared ahead of us. We skimmed over it and there, on a frozen lake, we saw once again the tracks of man: the snow had been shorn from the ice, which gleamed in a neat rectangle a mile and a half in length. Around this airstrip clustered the tiny figures of men, some little yellow tractors, a big silver plane, a huddle of Atwell huts, and the thin spire of a radio tower, all strangely out of place among the huge boulders, the "big, flat stones" of the Icelanders, that lay strewn about like enormous marbles.

The plane below us took off, and a moment later we bumped down the shiny runway. Up rattled a fifteen-hundredweight truck followed by a little tractor, a dark-blue snowmobile, and a gang of men dragging a heavy steel and timber sledge. With hardly a word they began to unload the aircraft at top speed.

"C'mon up for coffee," sang out a voice from within the snowmobile. It belonged to a cook in white ducks and a checkered windbreaker. We were hardly aboard before the curious machine with its front-end skis and its rear-end rubber treads charged off across the tundra toward the group of huts under the ridge.

"Drove this thing right across Baffin Island," the cook said as he rattled over the rocks and ice at a twenty-five-mile-an-hour clip. "Never thought you could drive across the Arctic, I bet, eh? Well, it was easy as pie."

He pulled up at one of the Atwell huts and we all scurried inside, out of the zero weather. The interior was a small furnace, heated by a great square cookstove and crammed with food—everything from fresh turkeys in Cellophane bags to small mounds of Melba toast.

"C'mon and eat up," the cook cried. "Here, have some of this caramel! Have some cake! Have some of these shortbread biscuits just baked today!"

"You like this better than Frobisher?" somebody asked him.

"Sure," said the cook with a great wink. "The grub is better and so are the women." He began to do a little dance around the stove, singing, off-key: "Those wedding bells are breaking up that old gang of mine." He was a plump youth with pink cheeks and curly hair, and he seemed supremely happy.

"Come on," said Morden, the pilot, gulping his coffee hastily. "Look at the light."

Back to the plane we clattered in the snowmobile. The last of the oil barrels was being rolled out of the door and onto the heavy sledge.

"How long will it take before you get all your stuff?" Morden asked the foreman, a great wrinkled man with a matted beard.

"Can't say. I asked for four thousand barrels fuel oil. So far I only got a thousand."

"Where'll the permanent airstrip be?"

"A little bit down the lake. There's a flat area there."

"Gravel?"

"Don't know. If not, we'll have them fly in a rock crusher and make our own."

240

We took off in the blue twilight, which lasts for an hour and a half this time of year. The hills stood out as somber bulks against the orange sky, the black stones on their crests silhouetted like ungainly graven images. The oil flares along the airstrip made their own small sunsets against the blue of the snow. By the time we reached Frobisher, the black shroud of night had engulfed the island, and the red lights of the radio towers mingled with the pinpoints of the stars.

It was past midnight. We made our way between the shadowy mountains of snow and found a clump of Atwell huts bunkered among them. We entered one of these dark caves, full of snoring men, and in the pale glow of a flashlight picked out four empty bunks. Here we unrolled our sleeping-bags and snatched five hours' sleep.

We were up before six that morning, for Morden had two more trips to make before returning to Mont Joli. The stillness of the Arctic was splintered by the roar of the air transports warming up for take-off. We were off with the dawn, up the eastern flank of the island, this time, where the mountains that line the northern coast have their beginnings. Once again, out of a white nowhere, we spotted the tiny airstrip, the little yellow tractor, and the huddle of men that marked the start of another radar site. Once again the cargo was hastily unloaded, and then we flew back to the airbase for another load.

While the York was being reloaded, Morden climbed the stairs to the operations room to learn his destination. We were to fly along the west coast this time.

"How's the runway?" Morden asked.

"It's five hundred feet longer than the last time a York landed on it," he was told.

"It still doesn't look very good to me," Morden said, looking at the big chart. It read: "Sea ice; four inches loose snow."

"Well, take a chance on it anyway. If it looks too hazardous, go on to number 35 and change your manifest."

"Okay," Morden said, "we'll have a bash."

Off we flew again across the white world. Where was the sea? It seemed to melt into the land with no perceptible line to mark its margin. Somewhere below us, so the maps told us, lay Air Force Island, so flat and so close to the water that it had not been identified as a land mass until 1948.

But we found the airstrip, hacked out of the frozen ocean, made a shaky landing in the slush, disgorged our cargo, and then headed back empty. I had one final glimpse of Frobisher Bay, with its huge machines and its men scurrying against time, and then once again we were drifting over the bleak expanse of the iron country. Now the sense of urgency and pressure left us. For the next five hours we left the twentieth century behind and seemed to hang suspended over forests primeval and lands forlorn.

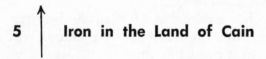

5   Iron in the Land of Cain

A month later I was back in the heart of the iron country, deep in the gloomy interior of the Labrador Peninsula, whose somber cliffland, rising from the chill ocean

The LABRADOR PENINSULA

BAFFIN

FROBISHER

Atlantic

Hudson Strait

Chubb Crater

RESOLUTION ISLAND

CYRUS EATON CONCESSION

Payne R.

Akpatok Island

Ungava Bay

Torngat Mts.

N

Low Grade Iron

Leaf R.

George R.

Ocean

U N G A V A

Koksoak R.

FORT CHIMO

Whale R.

I R O N   T R O U G H

Fort George

R.

KNOB LAKE

(Iron Mines)

Hamilton Falls
(4 Million H.P.)

GOOSE BAY

QUEBEC

Hamilton R.

L A B R A D O R

Moise R.

SCARP

LAURENTIAN

SEVEN ISLANDS

MONT JOLI

NFLD.

Gulf of
St. Lawrence

QUEBEC

N. B.

mists, cast a pall on Jacques Cartier, the Breton explorer. The discoverer of the St. Lawrence stared up at the forbidding shoreline and called it "the land God gave to Cain," then passed on upriver in a vain search for the jeweled mountains of Cathay. In the four centuries that have passed since that day, the great peninsula has resisted those who followed in Cartier's wake, to remain an inaccessible and rarely traveled wasteland of rock and muskeg. Only in the days since World War II has it begun to yield up its secret treasures; but these are easily as rich as all of Cathay's legendary gems.

I started out from the little port of Seven Islands, on the north shore of the Gulf of St. Lawrence, across the water from Mont Joli. The iron country lay four hundred miles due north, and because of its development the tiny town of six hundred persons, which had slumbered for three centuries among the Laurentian rocks, was now a booming seaport of six thousand, where lots had jumped to as high as thirteen thousand dollars apiece and freighters, each capable of loading thirty-two thousand tons of ore, lay moored against the new docks. The streets were only now being paved, the sewers only now being laid, but the Cadillacs and the cocktail bars and the bright new company homes told the story of Seven Islands' sudden prosperity.

At seven o'clock one morning I boarded one of the little passenger cars of Canada's newest railway, the Quebec North Shore and Labrador, a three-hundred-and-sixty-mile line that knifes across the Precambrian plateau to connect the iron country with the sea. Completed in 1954, it represents a prodigious feat of engineering. We had traveled hardly a dozen miles across the gray expanse of muskeg and stunted spruce before we reached the outer edges of the great Laurentian Scarp, a granite barrier three thousand feet high, which walls off the interior of the peninsula from the outside world and defied the rail-way-builders. Bored into the face of this natural bastion was a tunnel, dripping with water, through which the train plunged. Half a mile farther on, a pinpoint of light appeared and we burst from the bowels of the mountain to find ourselves suspended in mid-air seven hundred feet above the canyon of the Moisie River. The train snorted across the slender orange trestle and then clung to the dynamited flanks of the sheer rock cliffs, climbing wearily for mile after mile toward the plateau of iron.

We had entered an unearthly world, half fairyland, half purgatory. Here were boiling rivers, harsh canyons, piles of granite rubble blasted from the hills, and camel-backed mountains with sheer faces that seemed to have been split in twain by a giant cleaver. Here among the spiky black spruce were thin mists of deciduous green where the birch and larches heralded the onset of spring. And from the rocky heights above, a thousand waterfalls dropped in lacy cascades. Indeed, there was water everywhere. The black cliffs were wet with it; the forests gurgled with it. Foaming torrents poured under the railway culverts and tumbled on down the steep slopes. Falls, still imprisoned in the grip of a dying winter, hung like enormous icicles from the granite scarps. And far below, the river hissed and roared as it cut its way through the mountain barrier.

The track clung to the cliff edge. Only the riches of the Labrador-Ungava iron country could force as ambitious an engineering venture as this one: a quarter of a mile of docks, thirteen airfields, two hydroelectric plants, a new city, and this spectacular line of track. The total bill came to $235,000,000, and the Iron Ore Company of Canada, which controls it all, had to have forty years of ore produc-tion in sight before the scheme was feasible. Before the trains began to move, everything from bolts to bulldozers was flown into this country by air, so that the mining com-

pany found itself operating one of Canada's largest airlines, shifting as much as three hundred tons of goods a
day north to the land of Cain. At the peak of its operation
the airline had seventy-five pilots in its employ, and sometimes its planes were taking off at the rate of one every
five minutes to supply the railway-builders.

Slowly the train heaved itself out of the gorge and river
country and we found ourselves sliding across the table-
top of the great Labrador plateau in a monotonous land of
lakes and muskeg, moss and lichen, harsh brown sand,
soiled patches of snow, and a single variety of tree: the
black, stunted spruce, whose twisted body seems racked
continually by some inner torture. The Labrador Peninsula, which takes in most of the province of Quebec and
all of the territory of Labrador (part of Newfoundland),
is more than half a million square miles in size and most of
it looks like this. It is, indeed, a great rigid block of Precambrian rock, unmarked by hills, except for the spectacular mountain ranges along its eastern and southern
coastlines. Its surface is carpeted in a foot-thick blanket of
moss and lichen and a fragrant shrub called Labrador tea,
which turns bright orange in the fall. From this spongy
floor the gaunt trees protrude like posts, many of them
almost devoid of leaves or needles, growing so slowly that
it takes them almost a century to reach their full height.
Through the rock the rivers cut in dizzy gorges, many of
them one thousand feet deep, for this continental corner-
post has slowly been rising over the ages as the rivers
worked their way down.

It is this downward erosive action that has produced the
bare jagged peaks of the Torngat Mountain range at the
northeastern tip of the peninsula. "Torngat" is an Eskimo
word meaning "evil spirits," and evil spirits they seem to
be, horn-shaped and saw-toothed, many of them five thousand feet in height. They spring abruptly from the fiords

or the ocean, the most rugged mountain range on the east coast of the continent, rivaling the Alps of Switzerland and the Selkirks of British Columbia, stretching in a long gap-toothed line for one hundred and fifty miles, bejeweled with ice cornices, decked with green lakes, and gouged by immense glacial gulleys.

Farther to the south lies another mountain range, equally terrible, equally majestic. They are really mountain stubs, created by molten rock surging up from the bowels of the earth within the body of earlier mountains. The outer flesh of crystalline rock has long since been torn away by the elements so that only the ebony core remains, bare of vegetation. This rock, called *gabbro*, contains a feldspar of great beauty known as "labradorite," whose glassy surface, prism-fashion, breaks up white light into its colored components so that it seems to flash with purples, violets, blues, and occasionally yellows, oranges, and reds. It is undoubtedly this phenomenon that has caused the Montegnais Indians of the coast to talk of flashing fire rocks and the Nascopies of the interior of fire mountains along the height of land. One explorer tried to market the labradorite as a precious gem, but Tiffany's found it too brittle to work with. It occurs in various places throughout the plateau.

All around us as we crossed the tableland were the shapes of the lakes that lie in the hollows of the rocks. There are parts of Labrador that are almost three-quarters water, for this is old glacier country, and the dikes of glacial rubble have dammed up the old watercourses so that there is no recognizable pattern of drainage. Thus the rivers seem to run in all directions, twisting and corkscrewing around the obstacles left in the wake of the receding ice sheets. Vast sections of the peninsula, especially toward the southeast, are pocked with *kames* and *kettles*. The kames are round little knolls of glacial till; the kettles are small bowls in the earth that mark the last resting-place of scattered ice-blocks—remnants of the great glacier. Because these hummocks and hollows are scarcely marked by erosion, many geographers believe that this was the final domain of the Labrador icecap. Some think, indeed, that it is only a brief two thousand years since the glacier vanished from this corner of the peninsula.

As the train rattled north, long fingers of ice began to appear on the lakes, and the patches of snow, caught in the hollows of the hills, increased in number. It was June, but spring had scarcely arrived. Labrador is no closer to the Arctic than northern Saskatchewan or the warm valleys of British Columbia, or the entire cultivable portion of the U.S.S.R. and yet in its temperature it is wholly Arctic or sub-Arctic. With the possible exception of eastern Siberia, no other region of Arctic climate extends so far south. It has only one frost-free month, July, though the latitude of its heartland corresponds with that of Dublin, Liverpool, Hamburg, and Berlin. For the great peninsula is caught between two natural refrigerators. A river of ice, the Labrador Current, pours down from the Arctic to cool the eastern coastline. A stream of polar air sweeps across from northwest Canada, growing colder over the frigid surface of Hudson Bay to chill the Labrador interior. The plateau itself, two thousand feet above the sea and almost devoid of obstacles, is swept by icy winds that often reach one hundred miles an hour. (At the iron mines in Knob Lake the winds averaged sixty miles an hour for twenty-four hours on one winter's day in 1955.) F. K. Hutton, an old Labrador hand, has written of the howling northwest wind, the *attuarnek* of the Eskimos, which "storms along with a ceaseless roar over the frozen plains and valleys and fills the air with powdered snow as thick as a London fog. No living thing can face it, buildings shake, snow huts are worn thin. When the snow drift is thick one can scarcely see anything half a dozen yards away. On some days one cannot see the dogs. One is lost somewhere in Labrador."

Indeed, since Cartier's day, travelers, explorers, writers, and scientists have strained for imaginative phrases to describe the harshness of Cain's land. The Labrador Peninsula is one of the world's three largest outcroppings of continental land, and like the other two, Alaska and Arabia, it has been regarded until recently as virtually sterile. Cartier remarked with a sneer that "there was not one cartful of earth in the whole of it." Hesketh Prichard, a traveler at the turn of the century, called it "a menacing wilderness" and added that "a desolation more appalling cannot be conceived." Two of his predecessors were equally emphatic. "A country formed of frightful mountains and unfruitful valleys . . . a prodigious heap of barren rock," wrote Lieutenant Roger Curtis. "God created this country last of all and threw together there the refuse of his materials as of no use to mankind," wrote Captain George Cartwright, who spent sixteen years on the Labrador coast. Elliott Coues, a naturalist from the semi-tropics, set down his own equally graphic impressions of the peninsula:

"Fog hangs low and heavy over rock-girdled Labrador. Angry waves, paled with rage, exhaust themselves to encroach up her stern shores, and, baffled, sink back howling into the depths. Winds shriek as they course from crag to crag in a mad career, and the humble mosses that clothe the rocks crouch lower still in fear."

The land has lived up to its billing. One famous American naturalist, Alpheus S. Packard, came to the tableland to study insect life, but the insects were so fierce they drove him from the country. One explorer of note, Leonidas Hubbard, Jr., who tried to make his way northwest across the peninsula from Hamilton Inlet on the east coast to Ungava Bay in the north, starved to death by inches in the valley of the Susan. Hubbard, who died in October 1903, a march or two from safety, waiting for his two comrades to bring help, left a diary, which graphically describes the hardships that face the unwary wanderer in the Labrador wasteland. The final item was written after Hubbard had gnawed on a caribou-skin moccasin to give him strength to scribble it down:

"Tonight or tomorrow perhaps the weather will improve so I can build a fire, eat the rest of my moccasins and have some more bone broth. Then I can boil my belt and oil-tanned moccasins and a pair of cowhide mittens. They ought to help some. I am not suffering. The acute pangs of hunger have given way to indifference. I'm sleepy. I think death from starvation is not so bad. . . ."

Undaunted by her husband's death, Hubbard's slender and handsome widow, who had waited for him at home, decided to complete the journey that he had attempted. Alone, except for two Indian guides, heavy-skirted and bloomered, with a revolver on her hip and a knife at her belt, this remarkable young woman trekked through almost a thousand miles of river, bush, rock, and tundra successfully to attain her objective and meet the challenge of the peninsula.

Now, half a century later, others are meeting the same challenge. For, paradoxically, the very factors that have given Labrador its reputation for bleakness and unfriendliness are now proving to be its greatest asset.

—The harsh climate causes trees to grow with maddening slowness so that the growth rings are so close they are hard to distinguish one from another. Yet this very phenomenon is the reason for the long fiber in the pulpwood the papermakers cherish. There are enormous stands of these dense spruces across the rockland of Labrador, and there is little doubt now that they will soon be harvested.

—The fierce, impassable rivers that make the peninsula

so difficult to navigate by canoe are now proving to be the source of a vast hydroelectric potential. The myriad lakes, dammed up by the glaciers of old, hold an enormous storage of fresh water waiting to be tapped. There may be as much as twelve million horsepower in Labrador, or about five times as much as is produced by the Grand Coulee Dam.

—The naked ocean of rocks that looked so barren to Cartier hold, locked within them, a fortune in iron ore, not to mention copper and other base metals.

Already a huge company, the British Newfoundland Corporation, backed by Rothschild millions, is exploring a fifty-thousand-mile tract of Labrador under an arrangement with the province of Newfoundland. The company's objectives include a search for metals and pulpwood, but its main energies are focused on the spectacular Grand Falls of the Hamilton River, where, it is believed, four million horsepower can be developed at low rates. This enormous cataract is reckoned between 245 and 305 feet high; it defies proper measurement because the tall column of spray, visible for fifty miles, obscures its lower portions. The river, frustrated in its former course by glacial dikes, has cut its way down through the soft alluvial rubble in a writhing pathway that leads it eventually to the preglacial stream bed. In a dozen miles of this tortuous journey the level drops seven hundred feet, and it is this section of the river, as swift as a millrace, that the engineers hope to develop.

Our train stopped at Mile 224, where a roadway to the Grand Falls is already being surveyed, and here a group of men disembarked heading for the Hamilton River. Then the train rumbled on into a dead gray world—a burned land where the very lichens had been charred from the rocks, and the trees were ashen poles rising from the lifeless terrain. There are thousands of square miles of this burned country on the Labrador Peninsula—more perhaps than anywhere else in the north, for it takes close to a century to renew it. Burned areas reported by geologists in 1892 were still unforested in 1955. In the middle of the last century an observant explorer, Henry Youle Hind, came upon an enormous desert of this burned country in the tableland above the Moisie River—the same country through which the railroad now cuts. Appalled at the hundreds of miles of ruined forest, he suddenly recalled the queer "dark days" that had fallen over eastern Canada fifty and sixty years before. The darkness had extended from Montreal to Fredericton, New Brunswick. It was so dark on some days that it was impossible to read a newspaper at ten in the morning. Eyewitnesses wrote that the darkness seemed to come out of Labrador. At Seven Islands the atmosphere had gone red and fiery, and the sea water became black as ink. The scientists of the day blamed a volcano, somewhere in the unexplored midriff of the peninsula, but later research has uncovered no volcanic evidence. Hind reasoned, probably correctly, that the real explanation lay in these vast acres of smoldering caribou moss, ignited by spontaneous combustion, sending up clouds of ashes and wood smoke.

A long train speeding south rattled by us, each of its open cars piled with the red-brown iron ore. In the fourteen-hour trip between Seven Islands and Knob Lake we passed six of these trains. Each pulled one hundred and five cars; each car held one hundred tons of iron ore. We were entering the iron country. Around us, as we moved north, the trees were growing sparser and more stunted; the ice was growing thicker on the lakes; and the soil was growing redder.

It was this red soil that told us we had entered the great Labrador Trough, the geological key to the development

of the entire peninsula. Here is the promise of the land of
Cain, a king's ransom in iron that has lain undisturbed for
half a billion years. From the air, or on the map, the trough
is easily recognizable, for the lakes run north and south in
long, parallel shreds for almost six hundred miles.

The trough represents an ancient arm of the sea—a shallow inlet a hundred miles in width that invaded the Precambrian rockland in Proterozoic times, before life existed
on the face of the earth. The sea swept down from Ungava
almost splitting the peninsula in two, and there it lay for
millions of years eroding the soft sandstones and muds
that flanked it. These sediments formed an enormous
weighty layer thousands of feet thick. The top eight hundred feet consisted of iron and silica in bands of varying
width. How these iron deposits were formed is still something of a mystery to scientists; all that is known is that at
this period, all over the world, a set of conditions existed
which allowed iron and silica to be deposited in this manner. In South America, in India, in the United States
(where the Mesabi Range was building), and along the
shores of Lake Superior, where the great Steep Rock mine
has been developed, iron oxides were being laid down in
this way.

New forces came into play. The ocean retreated and the
sediments, being weaker than the surrounding granite,
were caught as in a vise between the teeth of the Canadian
shield. As the earth's crust cooled and wrinkled, enormous
pressures from the northeast squeezed the softer rock
against the unyielding buttress to the south. Caught in
these natural forceps, the floor of the trough warped and
buckled and split until it was forced up into a mountain
range. Over the ages the mountains were gnawed away by
the tooth of time until the land was again as flat as a
billiard table. But the ceaseless rains, washing through

the crevices in the soft rocks, had leached away the surface silica, leaving almost pure iron behind. Without this historic washing action, the iron of Labrador would be scarcely worth mining, for, mixed with vast quantities of silica, the ore would not be rich enough to freight south. But wherever the water could get at the rock, there are high-grade deposits. The very process that produced the ore makes it easy to mine: because the water action took place in pockets and fissures near the surface, the ore can be dug without tunneling, by an open-cut process. Because the silica has been removed, the ore is porous—like a cheese full of holes—which means it crumbles and digs easily.

Exploration parties in the vicinity of Ungava Bay, far to the north of the richest iron deposits, are now beginning to suspect that the geological upheaval that shaped the land brought more than iron. In the days when the mountains were heaved up, great faults split the rock on the northeast side of the trough, in the area where the pressure was the greatest. It was as if the lid had been removed from a bubbling caldron. Up through these crevices from the molten womb of the world, in the form of hot solutions and steaming vapors, came various metals, notably copper. Concentrated in tiny fractures in the rocks, they cooled and formed deposits. These deposits are now slowly coming to light in the area of Chimo, the old Hudson's Bay Company fort on Ungava Bay.

The first man to outline the shape of the trough and to suspect the presence of iron in the land of Cain was a remarkable Canadian government geologist, A. P. Low, a hefty scientist whose curiosity was as prodigious as his physical stamina. Low stands today as the only man who has trekked across Labrador from north to south and from east to west. He traversed seven thousand miles of country by foot, canoe, and snowshoe, living off the country and scribbling ceaselessly in his notebook. One year he and a fellow surveyor probed deep into the heart of the peninsula and then fell to arguing about who was the proper leader of the expedition. Finally Low decided to settle the quarrel. "I'll walk to Ottawa and find out," he said. And he did—in three weeks. On his journeys through Labrador, Low produced complete notes on mineral wealth, power sites (including the Grand Falls), topography, fish, flowers, birds, and mammals. And in 1893 he noted the presence of an iron formation along the length of the great trough.

But it was more than half a century before anyone bothered about the iron that Low reported. Other geologists, most of them looking for gold, found more definite showings, but there was little reaction. One of the areas now being mined by the Iron Ore Company was actually discovered by two Montreal geologists in 1929. Their company soon ran out of funds. Then in 1936 there was the familiar touch of romance that seems to precede all great northern mining developments. A gnarled old Indian chief of the Montegnais emerged from the heart of the peninsula with a piece of "pretty rock" and showed it to Dr. Joseph Retty, a geologist who was already exploring the area for a development company. The rock looked very pretty indeed to Retty: it was dark blue in color and it was almost solid iron. It came from a spot not very far from the area that the Montreal men had found years before. Retty's company, which owned a huge concession on the Newfoundland side of the Labrador-Quebec border, was taken over during World War II by Hollinger Consolidated, the biggest gold concern on the continent. Retty, who had been exploring the area, recommended that the company also get a concession on the Quebec side, for he reasoned, accurately, that the iron ore lay along the height of land that separates the two territories. The result was that Hollinger, a gold company, found itself with twenty-four thousand square miles of stick forest and some promising iron showings.

It was at this point that a shy, lantern-jawed millionaire with gold-rimmed glasses and a subtle, imaginative mind entered the picture. This was Jules Timmins, the president of Hollinger, and the scion of the most famous mining family in Canada. The name of Timmins is a legend in northern Quebec and Ontario. Jules's father, Henry, a storekeeper from the village of Mattawa, had in 1903 bought a quarter of a share of an unknown silver mine in the Precambrian wilderness of northern Ontario. His friends soon stopped scoffing, for it was this mine that turned Canada into a silver-producer and built the incredible boom town of Cobalt. Henry sold out for a million dollars. Six years later Jules's uncle, Noah, grasped the significance of a gold find made farther to the north by a nineteen-year-old prospector named Benny Hollinger. He bought Hollinger's claim, and the two brothers parlayed it into the most lucrative gold mine on the continent. The town of Timmins, Ontario (population: 27,000), sprang up around it, and the mine itself has produced more than one hundred and fifty million dollars.

Jules Timmins was born with a gold-and-silver spoon in his mouth, but he worked as a mucker in his family's mine and studied geology at university. When Retty talked to him about iron in Labrador, he told him to find out how much there was and what it would cost to get it out. Retty and his crews spent eight years and six million dollars on this task. They proved up four hundred million tons of high-grade iron ore, but by this time Timmins knew it would cost him a quarter of a billion dollars before the first shovelful was mined. A lesser man might have been staggered by the immensity of such a project, but

Timmins set about getting customers for the iron and money to produce it.

He chose a singularly propitious moment. The big steel companies in the United States had been caught napping at the war's end. The expected drop in steel consumption didn't come and, as a result, the great Mesabi Range of Minnesota began to show signs of exhaustion. Led by M. A. Hanna Co. of Cleveland, six large U.S. steel firms joined with Timmins to form Hollinger-Hanna Ltd. and develop Labrador's iron. The new company put up a million dollars; nineteen insurance firms loaned the rest. A small army of subsidiaries, of which the Iron Ore Company is the most important, were formed to build the railway, operate the airlift, open the mines, and produce the ore. Just six years after the first announcements were made, the shovels were munching into the red soil of the trough, and the ore trains were speeding to the sea.

We reached the new town of Knob Lake after dark and the following morning I set out to view the surrounding iron country. The community itself was still in crucible. Bulldozers were everywhere ripping into the soil and leveling out new blocks. Churches and schools were a-building. Telephone poles were going up alongside new three-bedroom homes of cedar siding. Plans were being laid to complete a television station by Christmas—the most northerly TV outlet on the continent. It was being designed to show films, but there was already talk of purchasing cameras and doing local production.

A guide drove me out a few miles through the gray stick forest, and then, suddenly, we entered a world of flaming crimson. We stood on the rim of a blood-red crater gouged out by some of the world's largest steam shovels, and for the first few moments it seemed as if we were on the lip of the inferno itself. But there were no embers here, only a brilliant expanse of high-grade iron ore stretching off almost to the horizon in a multitude of colors—alizarin crimson, burnt orange, deep purple, blue-black, oxblood brown, yellow, and scarlet. What we were looking at, mainly, was an enormous deposit of rust—as if a million steel girders had been allowed to oxidize for a century, and the deposit collected here in a mighty heap. Other deposits, darker red in color, consisted of hematite, which is simply jeweler's rouge.

The land about us was a monochrome of red. The hills in the foreground were red. The water lay in pools as red as blood. The men themselves were red, caked with the red dust that rose in clouds and permeated everything so that clothing, trucks, buildings, and foliage were layered in a thin veneer of crimson. It was a relief to look off beyond the craters at the blue Labrador skyline flecked still with small patches of snow, but even here one could see the red roads winding through the thin forests to the horizon.

Below us the great shovels were gouging into the soft red face of the crater in ten-ton gulps. Enormous Diesel trucks, belching clouds of blue exhaust, strained and groaned up the inclines, each loaded with thirty-five tons of ore. From the moment the shovel scoops it up, this ore scarcely stops moving until it reaches the steel mills of the United States. The trucks dump it into a hopper where it is screened, and from here an endless belt pours it into the waiting ore cars. The cars begin moving almost immediately down the railroad to Seven Islands. Here they are seized in steel jaws and turned turtle into another belt, which carries the ore to a freighter, which, loaded in a few hours, moves off at once up the St. Lawrence to the Lakes, or down-river to the Atlantic coast.

Jutting out into one of the scarlet craters (there are

three large mines in operation in the vicinity of Knob Lake) was a small peninsula of land, and on it the remains of a log city. This was the original iron town of Burnt Creek, originally planned as the community around which the iron mines would be based. But a group of geologists, testing out a new drill on the main street, discovered that Burnt Creek was sitting on a vast hoard of high-grade ore. The town was shifted to the new site of Knob Lake, and now the ore-diggers had eaten their way to within a few feet of the main street. Soon it would all vanish into the scarlet pit.

I spent two more days watching the swift human erosion of this richest section of the Labrador Trough. The ore is moving from the mines at the rate of ten million tons a year, and when the St. Lawrence Seaway is completed, this figure is likely to double. The four hundred million tons of high-grade ore already proved represent only a fraction of the total amount lying under the ashen soil of this bleak land. (There are literally billions of tons of low-grade.) All along the trough, especially on the northern coast, other companies are drilling for ore—and for other metals, too. Labrador's moment in history has arrived. Finally, after four centuries, it begins to look as if the land no longer belongs to Cain.

Postscript

One of the themes of this book is that the Canadian north is a land of boom and bust. Ghost towns litter the landscape. The hosannas that accompany each new mineral discovery are followed by dirges when the mines close and entire communities collapse.

That has been the history of the north since the days of the Klondike stampede, but few northerners absorb the lessons of history. It should be obvious that a vein of gold, iron, lead, or silver is finite; that world markets for minerals are notoriously unstable; that no boom can last forever. But it isn't. When Eldorado Mining pulls out of its company town, the five thousand residents of Uranium City are shocked and embittered. But uranium is not a renewable resource like wheat and hydro power, and the demand is fickle. Several towns have sprung up and died since I wrote this book. Schefferville, Quebec, is one of them.

I visited Schefferville in May 1955 when it was still known as Knob Lake. It was booming then; it is a ghost town today, all in the space of three decades. But the Grand Falls on the Hamilton River, whose potential I described in these pages, have become one of the great continuing sources of long-distance electrical power. The river's name has been changed to the Churchill River and the falls are known as the Churchill Falls. When they were harnessed, between 1966 and 1974, the project was the largest ever undertaken in North America. Since then, the contract that Joe Smallwood signed with Quebec has been the subject of a long, acrimonious, and (from the Newfoundland viewpoint) unsuccessful dispute. Newfoundland got taken when it signed a long-term contract to sell its Labrador power cheaply. Today that power, however, is not so cheap, and Quebec benefits. The contract will eventually run out; fortunately the falls won't.

When I travelled north on the new Labrador railway in May 1955, the development on the Hamilton River was still a dream. The railway had been completed only the year before, and the first carloads of ore had started to move south just the previous July. Between the two editions of this book the boom came and went. Iron prices dropped; markets vanished; the metal became too expensive to mine. Brian Mulroney, then president of the U.S.-owned Iron Ore Company of Canada, was forced to announce that the operations at Schefferville were at an end. The town, which had once held several thousand people, became another empty community like Pine Point, Uranium City, and Port Radium.

There is still iron in Labrador, but at the moment most of it is too expensive to mine. Labrador City, the Iron Ore Company's other boom town, which didn't exist when I wrote this book, has gone into decline; once it was home to fifteen thousand people. And the various projects around Ungava Bay that I so enthusiastically described have come to nothing.

Perhaps the most significant change in the Arctic has nothing to do with boom and bust. The place names are being returned to the native people. Frobisher Bay is once again Iqaluit, "the place where the fish are." This name change, which took effect on January 1, 1987, heralds a new attitude. It is said that as many as ninety thousand place names and geographical features will acquire native names or have their present names changed. In *The Mysterious North* I wrote that the government was planning a new community at Frobisher Bay, the largest north of the Arctic Circle, large enough to hold a thousand people. That prediction has been exceeded. The population of Iqaluit has reached three thousand, half of it Inuit. The town continues to be the anchor point on the DEW line (soon to be replaced by the more ambitious Northern Warning System), complete with a native TV and radio station.

Pond Inlet, at the far end of Baffin Island, is now known as Mittimatalik. With a population of eight hundred it is the largest of the thirty Inuit communities on the great island's east coast. Idlouk, whom I met when I landed on the ice, is dead now, but his family still lives in the community, not in a skin tent but in a government bungalow with electricity and a flush toilet. Appearances, alas, can be deceptive. "The people of the seal," as the early anthropologists called them, are faced with the extinction of their traditional culture. The villains of the piece are the foolish and unthinking activists of the animal rights movement, who apparently care more for the welfare of animals than that of human beings.

The adult ringed seal is at the core of the Inuit way of life on Baffin. The banning of the white pelts of the Canadian harp seal pups in Europe in 1983 and the popular disapproval of seal hunting in general caused a collapse of the European sealskin market. Yet the seal has been traditionally the mainstay of life for the Inuit families. The fat provides cooking and heating fuel in a treeless land. The meat, rich in vitamins, has long been their main source of nutrition (and the chief reason why the Inuit do not suffer from the scurvy that plagued the Arctic explorers). The hide is turned into boots, mittens, trousers, and parkas. More important, the sale of seal pelts provided the native families with a stable economy, allowing them to purchase flour, rifles, ammunition, and outboard motors.

The economic power that helped the Inuit move into a twentieth-century world has dwindled. In just a decade their total annual income from the sale of seal pelts has dropped from $586,000 to a dismal $76,000.

The people of the seal still eat the meat, but the skins now largely go to waste. The hunt has diminished; there is less reason for it. With nothing to do, the hunters sit idly in their houses, their sense of worth dwindling. The future is predictable. When the culture goes, when the traditional way of life vanishes, alcohol and drugs take over; murder, suicide, and child neglect follow.

That is why I have no patience with Brigitte Bardot and her supporters in the animal rights movement. The ringed seal is not an endangered species. The Inuit of the Baffin coastline most certainly are.

Part **V**

THE LAND OF FEAST AND FAMINE

1 | Fur Country

It was a hot evening in early August 1954—the sun was still high in the heavens and the temperature in the humid eighties—and I was flying north down the Mackenzie Valley to Aklavik, perhaps the greatest fur-trading post in the world. I had left Toronto the previous afternoon. Now I was thirty-five hundred miles away, far north of the Circle, high above the delta of the continent's second largest river, on the very edge of the Arctic.

Once again I found myself crammed into a tiny Canadian Pacific Airlines plane, this time in company with a schoolteacher, two army dentists, and an Indian mother. How many miles, I thought to myself, had I flown through the north with CPA? This was the line's longest domestic hop. We had come 1,154 miles northwest from Edmonton and now, in the sticky, almost tropical heat of an Arctic summer evening, we were nearing the end of the flight.

Out of the ooze of the Mackenzie delta, the frame and log buildings of the little town rose up to meet us, poking their heads above a soggy peninsula that juts out into the Pokiak Channel, one of dozens into which the great river splits as it reaches the ocean. The town is imprisoned by this channel. The muddy waters embrace it on three sides. An undrainable swamp blocks its rear. Each year the channel gnaws deeper into the wet silt of the main street, pushing closer and closer to the row of frontier buildings that lines the banks. No wonder the residents sometimes call Aklavik The Mudtropolis of the North.

Aklavik is so far from civilization that it costs the eastern department stores almost seven dollars to fly a mail-order catalogue in. Beef is too expensive to import, and the seven hundred permanent residents exist largely on reindeer meat. Half of the people are Loucheaux Indian or Eskimo. The three hundred and fifty whites are a varied lot. They include a self-educated trapper who makes a yearly trip to Seattle expressly to purchase one hundred dollars' worth of second-hand books (Hemingway to Einstein), and a motherly-looking woman who claims to be the daughter of Jenny Lind, the Swedish Nightingale. Most of the natives depend on the fur trade for their livelihood.

The little plane's floats touched water and we skimmed along beside the strip of beach. There was a confused impression of Indian shacks and decaying fishing boats. Then we came to rest, and there, up on the bank, were the ubiquitous buildings of the Hudson's Bay Company, surrounded by their neat picket fences, with the familiar sign over the main doorway, proclaiming in Old English lettering the company's proud boast that it was founded in 1670. Henry Hudson's bay was thirteen hundred air miles to the southeast, but the Company of Adventurers were here, as everywhere. Without them there would be no Aklavik. It was a Hudson's Bay man who, in 1912, trudged through the stick forest from the Peel River in the Yukon to set up this outpost and trade with the Eskimos of the delta. As always, priests, parsons, and police followed, and Aklavik became the biggest fur-trading post of them all.

The town is built around the big Hudson's Bay store, whose merchandise ranges from polar-bear skins to Mickey Spillane novels. As in almost every fur community, the Bay dominates the settlement, physically and economically. The first man I met as I climbed the bank and walked along the wooden sidewalk was Herbert Figgures,

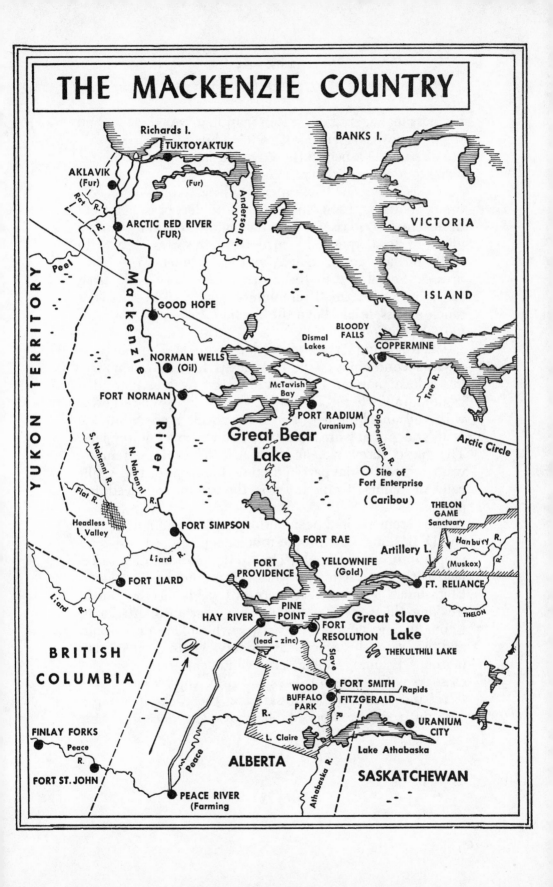

THE MACKENZIE COUNTRY

Richards I.
BANKS I.
TUKTOYAKTUK
AKLAVIK (Fur)
(Fur)
VICTORIA
Anderson R.
Rat R.
Peel R.
ARCTIC RED RIVER (FUR)
ISLAND
YUKON TERRITORY
Mackenzie
GOOD HOPE
BLOODY FALLS
Dismal Lakes
COPPERMINE
NORMAN WELLS (Oil)
River
McTavish Bay
Tree R.
FORT NORMAN
PORT RADIUM (uranium)
Coppermine R.
Arctic Circle
S. Nahanni R.
N. Nahanni
Great Bear Lake
Site of Fort Enterprise
(Caribou)
Flat R.
R.
THELON GAME Sanctuary
Hanbury R.
Headless Valley
FORT SIMPSON
R.
(Muskox)
Liard R.
FORT RAE
Artillery L.
THELON
FORT PROVIDENCE
YELLOWNIFE (Gold)
FORT LIARD
FT. RELIANCE
Liard R.
PINE POINT
HAY RIVER
FORT RESOLUTION
Great Slave Lake
BRITISH COLUMBIA
(lead - zinc)
Slave R.
THEKULTHILI LAKE
FORT SMITH
WOOD BUFFALO PARK
FITZGERALD
Rapids
URANIUM CITY
FINLAY FORKS
Peace R.
R.
L. Claire
Athabaska R.
ALBERTA
Lake Athabaska
SASKATCHEWAN
FORT ST. JOHN
Peace
PEACE RIVER (Farming

the post manager, a dark, lean man in a tweed jacket and slacks, who has spent most of his adult life in the north. He offered me a bed in the Bay staff house, then took me along to a cocktail party.

It was very much like a cocktail party anywhere. We drank Scotch and soda in highball tumblers or punch from thin-stemmed glasses. We munched the usual stuffed olives and canapés. The men wore business suits with white pocket handkerchiefs, and the women wore party dresses. Social life in the north differs very little from social life in any small community, and a white shirt is as much an essential above the Arctic Circle as a bottle of mosquito lotion.

The following day I attended a wedding. The daughter of the second chief of the Loucheaux Indians was marrying a local native. The wedding, too, was similar to a wedding anywhere. The bride wore a long white gown, with veil and bouquet. The bridesmaids wore white, as well. The groom wore a blue serge suit with a boutonniere. The guests threw rice and confetti. When the ceremony was over, the bridal party posed on the steps of the Anglican All Saints' Cathedral for the traditional wedding photo.

The ceremony had been performed by the Right Reverend D. B. Marsh, the purple-robed Anglican bishop whose proper imprint is "Donald, The Arctic," and whose mission field is the largest in the world. This round-faced, jovial Englishman has spent twenty-five years in the north, trekking thirteen thousand miles a year from Alaska to Labrador and commuting between his office in Toronto and the seat of his diocese at Aklavik, where each Sunday morning Eskimo, Indian, and white children in scarlet cassocks with white surplices and ruffs sing hymns.

Yet the white bridal dresses and the cocktail canapés and the scarlet-cassocked choirboys are deceptive, for

Aklavik, in spite of its thick varnish of civilization, is not at all like other towns. In the *Muskrat,* the mimeographed newspaper of All Saints' School, some brief but graphic essays by small Indian and Eskimo children tell of a quite different existence on the shores of the Arctic.

Here is a twelve-year-old Eskimo boy describing his life with his parents:

"This is my story of whaling in the Arctic Ocean. My father and the other men go out in their boats to get whale. We see whales jumping in the air and diving in the water. The little ones are grey and they jump the most. The mothers just come up to have air and to breathe. Once we went whaling. My father was shooting the whale. It was shot in the head twice. It started to go mad. It went under the boat and started to hit the front of the boat. My father shot it in the back. It sank to the bottom. The water was shallow. We looked for an hour. Finally we found it and my father threw the harpoon into it. We stopped for a meal. On our way back home my father let me take the wheel. After my father took the wheel and I went to sleep. When I woke up we were at the shore and the whale was pulled up. When the women finished their dinner they started to cut the whale into big pieces. The whale is used for food. Oil is taken from the blubber and put into barrels. The meat is stripped off and hung up to dry. The whale has a tiny ear. The skin is also used for shoes."

Here is an Indian boy of fourteen describing a reindeer roundup:

"The roundup begins about July 25. The herders bring the herd near the corrals and when all is ready they are driven into the first corral. Then the herders go and get their meals.

"Before the checking begins the herders decide who will go into the first pen and who will go into the second

pen. The herders start putting the deer through the pens and count them. There are different classes of reindeer such as yearling bulls, adult bulls, adult females, yearling steers or one year female fawns. The deer are frightened animals so you must not make much noise or throw stones at them. There is much fun in catching the fawns. When the man who is counting the deer tells us to catch them we try to do so. They kick and wrestle to try to free themselves. The fawns have to have their ears cut with a mark something like a V. Sometimes the big deer have to be castrated. When the work on a reindeer is finished it is let out into the end corral where the other finished deer are to be let go when the corral gate is opened.

"Some of the big deer have to be vaccinated. I can remember one time I had to bring one fawn to one of the separate pens where they do the first aid work. This one that I brought was a strong one. It kicked and kicked. I was kicked in the knee but it did not hurt. Some of the fawns have to be tagged. The tag is a strip of copper with some writing on it. It is tagged on the ear."

Here is a fourteen-year-old Eskimo girl telling how she traps muskrats:

"The ratting season opens March first. We do not start until the beginning of April when it is warmer. We went across the river to our ratting area. It is nice to walk along in the soft snow. We went to one lake and looked for rat push-ups. They were frozen so we went to a narrow lake which was no better. On the way to a third lake through the willows we saw ptarmigan tracks. They have three toe nails. When we reached the lake Joanne and Jessie were setting traps. I found a rat house. I took some snow off and opened the house. I put in my hand and felt something inside. I screamed and ran. I

*thought it was a live rat. The others laughed at me.
Emma chopped the snow away and we saw a dead rat.
You have to be careful with a live muskrat for they bite.
We kill them with a stick. We set a trap on the muskrat's bed. When they come up through the hole in the
ice to eat they get caught in the trap. When the trap is
set we repair the opening made in the house and cover
it well. The hole might freeze and we could not use it
again. While we were setting the trap bubbles came up
and a muskrat put his head right out of the house. After
supper the children who have caught rats skin and
stretch them. We give the meat to Mrs. Cooper to cook
for our dinner."*

Here is a twelve-year-old Indian boy writing of an encounter with a lynx:

*"A long time ago, before I came to school, I used to
set traps with my brother. He set traps on the bank of
the creek. Once he told me to go with him to his traps.
A lynx was caught in a trap. It dragged it through the
creek a little way. It was caught by one of its hind legs
and was alive. We had no gun so my brother went back
to the sled to get some wire. I was scared and followed
him everywhere he went. After he had the wire he cut a
willow. He put the wire on the end of the willow and
made it round like a rabbit snare. Then he went to the
lynx and he held the wire near its head. It jumped and
its head went in the loop and the wire was around its
neck. He went to the bush. The lynx could not go after
him because the chain which held the trap was tied to
a big willow. He pulled the wire and the lynx couldn't
breathe so it choked."*

Indian children who help castrate reindeer and trap
lynxes before they are twelve, then wear white wedding
veils when they marry, form only one of Aklavik's several
paradoxes. Another anomaly is the settlement's apparent

wealth and actual poverty. At first glance, it looked to me like a boom town. The *Toronto Star Weekly*, the month before I arrived, had called it just that. "Aklavik is a boom town which has doubled in size since the war and may well double in the next five to ten years," a staff writer reported. The fresh piles of lumber in the streets seemed to confirm his view. There was new building everywhere. The Roman Catholic mission was planning a new hospital. The Anglican mission was planning a new school. (There are three schools in town, Catholic and Anglican residential schools, and a nondenominational government day school.) Plans were drawn for a teacher's home, a principal's house, a mammalogist's laboratory, and a military barracks.

Yet the hard fact was that in this humid summer of 1954 Aklavik was grappling with a depression as black as the one that hit the outside world in the thirties. For fur is its only commodity, and it is a sad but evident truth that the decision of a few Paris *couturiers* can affect the lives of hundreds of families on the Mackenzie delta.

Aklavik lies in the heart of the greatest muskrat trapping grounds in the world. In the million pools that pockmark the moist delta land, the animals breed and die by the hundreds of thousands. Even the little boys at the mission school have traplines on the edge of town. In 1950, three hundred thousand muskrat pelts poured through Aklavik. Each sold for an average of two dollars. But by 1954 the caprices of fashion had forced the price down to fifty cents. At the same time the muskrat's mysterious life cycle had reached its ebb and only half as many were trapped. Aklavik's income had dropped by seven eights in just four years.

This was only half the story of Aklavik's dilemma: the rest was more ironic. All the building planned for the town was government construction work—either out-and-out government buildings, or government-subsidized buildings such as the schools and hospitals. It was absolutely necessary to build them, because the native population is increasing so swiftly. The old people are living longer, more babies are surviving, tuberculosis has been controlled by free chest X-rays and improved medical service, mothers are getting better prenatal care, family allowances are encouraging bigger and healthier families, and old-age pensions have made grandparents a blessing instead of a burden.

This great fundamental change in the north has become evident only in the past few years. It is strange that a land so empty of people as this should suffer from a population problem of the same kind that haunts the teeming East; yet this is precisely what is happening. All up and down the Mackenzie the native peoples are on the increase. In the Fort Simpson area in 1953, to cite a dramatic example, there were fifty births and only one death. In the old days the death rate there from TB alone was twenty-five a year. The Aklavik school enrollment has become the largest in the Northwest Territories. There are nine hundred children in the town's three schools. It is quite evident that the two so-called "dying races," the Eskimos and the Athapascan Indians, are now on the increase, and the census figures prove it. They show, for example, that the Eskimo race alone has increased by approximately one seventh in a decade.

This, then, is the plight of Aklavik, the greatest Eskimo shopping center in the Arctic. There are more natives than ever before. There is less income for them. And it is on the natives that the economy of the fur country rests. Police, traders, missionaries, and civil servants are here solely because of them. Only natives can now secure trapping licenses under a new law enacted in the Northwest Territories before World War II. If the native goes broke, the country goes broke, as an Edmonton produce company discovered the year I visited Aklavik: it had been forced to cut its shipment of vegetables to the Mackenzie River ports by a third. The previous season the tiny little settlement of Fort Good Hope had returned sixty-five C.O.D. parcels to the big eastern department stores. The natives simply didn't have the money to pay for what they'd ordered. Traders were packing up because they couldn't afford to stay in business. Just the previous year one of them had reluctantly closed his post and left town. He had lost money two years in a row. In front of the Hudson's Bay store I ran into a worried little trapper, a Finn named Earl Moranda. He, too, was planning on leaving. There wasn't enough money in trapping to pay for his annual grubstake. Moranda is a carpenter and he can get work Outside. But for the native, who knows no other life, there is no escape.

I found that up and down the river, for almost two thousand miles, this unhappy situation prevailed. The price of marten skins had been cut almost three quarters; many trappers no longer considered them worth taking. Beaver was down to a third of its wartime peak. At Fort Smith, a thousand air miles to the southeast, a single trader had once bought five thousand skins in a year. Now three traders could scarcely buy eight hundred. It is quite clear that a basic change is taking place in the economy of the fur country. Since the days of Alexander Mackenzie, the first man to paddle down the river, one industry and one industry alone has kept the fur country thriving. It can no longer do so.

The situation is complicated because over the years, in boom times of the past, the Indians and the Eskimos approached a Coca-Cola standard of living. "My sincerest wish for our friends the Eskimo is that civilization may *never* reach them," the explorer Roald Amundsen once wrote. But even Amundsen must have known that this could not be. The Eastern Arctic Eskimos, such as those I met at Pond Inlet, are still comparatively—though by no means completely—free of white influence. The Western Arctic Eskimo is a different creature. His facial bones have been warped by the tincture of Caucasian blood that runs in his veins—from whalers, trappers, traders, explorers, and even missionaries. The course of his life has been re-channeled by the white man's fancy for the pelts of mammals that were once useless to him. But it is the white man's manner of life and standard of living that he hungers for, yet cannot attain. Like Tantalus of old, he strains for the coveted fruit, but it eludes him, and this is the quandary in which the fur country finds itself.

I met only one native on the delta who lived like a white man. His name was Fred Carpenter, and it was a paradox that this Eskimo with the English name should be the wealthiest man in Aklavik at a time when most of his fellows were facing privation. I walked down to the water-front one afternoon to visit him, and an odd experience it was. Carpenter is another Canadian Eskimo who wears the Queen's Coronation Medal. There his resemblance to Idlouk of Baffin Island ends. He greeted me from the deck of his twenty-eight-thousand-dollar schooner, which is more like a yacht. His sister, in a bright print dress, was doing the family washing in a new gasoline-powered machine. (His wife was in the hospital suffering from TB.) His children ran about, dressed in neat little suits. Carpenter, a long-nosed freckled-faced man in a new plaid shirt and pressed slacks, looked about as much like the traditional grinning, parka-clad Eskimo as Anthony Eden. We sat on the antiseptic deck and discussed basic economics.

Carpenter's father was a white whaler, but he himself was brought up without schooling in a snow house and a skin tent. Now besides his other assets, which were impressive, he had fifteen thousand dollars in the bank and was perhaps the world's richest Eskimo.

He lives on Banks Island, a storied rectangle of tundra rising out of the ocean to the northeast of the delta and prominent in the journals of the early explorers. Here he is the nearest thing to a king, in the old-fashioned sense, that remains.

"I got another washing-machine just like this one up there, and a sewing-machine too, of course, and I got three radios altogether, one here in the cabin, one on Banks, and another at my place on Tuk," he said in a flat, matter-of-fact, almost sheepish voice.

On his Arctic desert island the king had erected a palace, lit by electricity, laid with linoleum, and furnished with chesterfield suites bought by mail order. His children do not eat raw seal meat; they have cornflakes for breakfast. His two eldest sons are each worth ten thousand dollars. The king wanted to buy an airplane for one of them and make a pilot of him, but discovered to his chagrin that the boy did not have the necessary qualifications.

The collapse of the fur market hit Fred Carpenter, the provident Eskimo, as it hit everybody. But he is a man who saves his money or reinvests it in equipment. He earns an income from his boat and sells his furs for top prices at Outside auctions. When white foxes sold at forty dollars a pelt, Carpenter brought in nine hundred of them in a single year.

There have been times when other natives lived almost as well. In the days of good muskrat prices Eskimo mothers used to send their children to the Hudson's Bay stores with twenty-dollar bills to buy cigarettes and candy. Eskimo babies played in the streets with fifty-cent pieces for toys. Some Eskimo trappers earned as much as sixty-five hundred dollars a year, and one took his wife to California for a holiday, returning with ten trunkloads of clothes, including four tuxedos.

But now the schooners sat on the Aklavik beach, the paint peeling from their hulls, and the natives went hungry. All of them found it painful and bitter to revert to the primitive standards of living.

This was one of the knotty problems facing the new Canadian Department of Northern Affairs and its handsome young Minister, Jean Lesage, who arrived in Aklavik with an official party a few hours before I did. It was more than a decade since a minister of the Crown had visited the Mackenzie delta. Lesage and his party had been traveling all through the Canadian north, and this in itself is a measure of the new interest that the Canadian government is taking in the land north of sixty. As a gesture toward the Minister, the town fathers had dragged some of the dirtier and more dilapidated of the native shacks off the beach and into the protective cover of a copse of willows.

Aklavik was making news. The government had announced its intention of moving the entire settlement out of the muddy peninsula into which, the newspapers said, it was slowly sinking. This was perhaps the most intriguing tale to come out of the delta since that cold January, more than a generation before, when the mystery of a surly figure who called himself Albert Johnson had tantalized the continent. Who he was and where he came from no one will ever know, but they called him the Mad Trapper of Rat River and he was the object of the greatest manhunt the north has ever seen. On New Year's Eve 1931, holed up in an unassailable log fort that he had built himself on a vantage point above the twisting Rat, he had shot an investigating Mountie just below the heart. A fellow policeman rushed his wounded colleague eighty miles to Aklavik, where the town doctor saved his life, but the blood of the force was up. There followed a six-week siege and chase across the top of the continent in the dark, bald land of the Loucheaux. They tried to blast the Mad Trapper from his fort with dynamite, but the walls held. They tried to starve him out, but his cabin was crammed with grub. When they returned to resume battle, the trapper had fled to the crusted, wind-blown slopes of the mountains. They called in reinforcements—more dogs, more men with rifles—and the chase went on. They cornered him in a tangle of willows on the riverbank, but he shot a Mountie through the heart and escaped into the snows. All that month and most of the next the hue and cry went on in the shadow of the great mountain divide that separates the Yukon watershed from the Mackenzie. North from Edmonton flew Wop May, the bush pilot, to track the Mad Trapper from the air. May, in his tiny plane, spotted Johnson's snowshoe tracks crossing the 2,500-foot divide and leading down the other side toward the Alaska border. There the trapper was finally trapped on the banks of the Eagle River, and there, with the plane circling slowly above him, he fought it out with his pursuers from a bunker in the snows and died. They brought his bullet-ridden, half-starved body back to Aklavik, and there it rests under a tree into which the initials "A. J." have been hacked. But that was not really the end of Albert Johnson at all, for, whoever he was, he has become one of the north's most indestructible legends.

Now some of the men who helped track Albert Johnson through the snows were meeting in the white little federal school with their fellow citizens to hear the news of Aklavik's fate. This encounter between the new Cabinet Minister and the people of the north was a singularly dramatic affair. Here were the Eskimos in their summer parkas, and the Indians in their denims, and the breeds in their bush shirts, listening to the youngest Canadian Cabinet Minister, fit and forty, blond and handsome in his freshly pressed double-breasted suit and white pocket handkerchief.

Most of Aklavik was here. In the second row sat the old Loucheaux halfbreed whose father had established the town at "the crossing of the bear." He was a wiry, wizened, brown little man, so tough that the last time he needed a doctor he walked thirty miles through the snow to find one. A few nights later I watched him nimbly dancing the rabbit dance at exhaustive length, on and on through the night until four a.m., capering to the singsong music of a fiddle, never missing a beat, never changing expression or uttering a word, with no apparent fatigue though he was seventy-three.

On the other side of the room was big Karl Gardlund, the trapper, who helped shoot down Albert Johnson. There at the back sat the town dentist, looking every inch an Englishman in a blue blazer and white silk scarf, and the town doctor, a Dane, who spent twenty-eight years in Greenland and came to Aklavik to retire, only to find himself at work again. There was the man from the U.S. Wildlife Service who comes to Aklavik every summer to count ducks, and the flying evangelist whose Bible-thumping sermons are wooing the natives away from the established churches, and the Loucheaux Indian deacon who preaches each Sunday in All Saints' Cathedral in three languages, and the bearded young government scientist whom the townspeople had dubbed Johnny Permafrost.

All of them listened patiently while the Minister of Northern Affairs, a lawyer from the province of Quebec, unable to resist a few opening oratorical flourishes, told them in his liquid accent that he had always heard that northerners were a grand people and that in his opinion the people of Aklavik were "*grander* than grand."

Silence from the natives. A murmur of applause from

the whites. Then the Minister got down to business. The town was built on a sponge and it would have to be moved. Everybody knew the facts of life about Aklavik. The problem of permafrost that plagues the north is insurmountable here. When the moss is stripped from the soil for the foundations of a new building, the frost melts and the soil reverts to mushy silt. As the ground thaws, it contracts and sinks. Excavations become small lakes. As a result, the town has no sewer system because heated pipelines are not possible in a land that turns to gruel whenever it thaws.

The Minister said, simply, that it would be easier and cheaper to trundle the entire town fifty miles away to the river's eastern channel, where the ground is high and hard. Then he mentioned casually what is undoubtedly the main reason for the move: a modern airstrip capable of landing jet planes would soon be built here on the Arctic's rim. The new town would be a long way from most of the trapping lands, but for a few years at least there would be plenty of work for everybody at the airport and in the new town.

And what about the future? Here was the real problem. The Minister talked about the diversification of employment, of vocational training for the natives, of a slow, perhaps painful program that would lead the people of the north away from the fur trade and into new lines of endeavor. Until 1920, furs supplied the sole income for the Northwest Territories. Now, in the words of Father Lesage, the Minister's cousin, an Oblate priest with a generation of experience on the river, "the profession of trapper is becoming obsolete."

For the next few days, as he traveled up and down the delta country and along the Arctic coast and back upriver again, Jean Lesage heard the same tale over and over again from priests in long black robes, from Mounties sweating in unaccustomed scarlet, from Anglican missionaries over cups of tea, from Eskimo leaders, wrinkled and ancient, and Indian sub-chiefs in blue serge suits. And always the problem was the same—the age-old problem of the land of feast and famine.

I went along with him at his invitation. He and his four colleagues were flying about the north in a spanking new Otter aircraft flown by a curly-haired Yellowknife pilot named Max Ward. There was lots of room aboard. The Otter is the newest and the biggest of the northern bush planes (and also the most expensive). Along with its little brother, the de Havilland Beaver, it is slowly making every other type of bush aircraft obsolete. It can carry either a ton of freight or nine passengers and its take-off speed and rate of climb are unbelievable. Johnny Dapp, a diminutive pilot who works for Max Ward, once told me he got this same Otter—unloaded—off the water in just three seconds.

The Otter flew north across the delta, the enormous olive-green sponge that stretches for six thousand square miles between mountain and ocean at the very top of the land mass of North America. From the air it is a land punctured by a million ponds, with a network of muddy brown channels winding lazily from horizon to horizon through the primeval silt—a sight spectacular in its monotony, a labyrinth of water and muskeg that sweeps on for a hundred and twenty-five miles. Below us lay dramatic evidence of the need for moving Aklavik: carved into the yellow muskeg were the faint lines of an airstrip that hadn't worked. One of the bulldozers that tried to scrape it out had been swallowed by the silt when the permafrost melted.

"Naked country," Alexander Mackenzie called it when in 1789 he reached the end of the long river he had hoped would lead to the Northwest Passage. Here, in this maze

of islands and ponds and channels, the first explorer finally
learned the truth he already suspected: the long, mysterious river had taken him not to the Pacific but to the
frozen ocean, a foreign, friendless wasteland of whales
and Eskimos. The long days in the canoe, the wearying
palavers with the reluctant Indians, who complained that
the stubborn Scot was driving them to exhaustion, the
endless arguments with his guide, a strange woodland
creature who called himself the English Chief, the portages and lake storms—all these had been in vain. Mackenzie called it River Disappointment and set back wearily
along the way he had come, to face at Fort Chipewyan, far
to the south, the recriminations and sidelong glances of
his colleagues, who felt that the whole trip had been not
only fruitless but also disloyal. How could he know that
this river was the key to the development of a fifth of
Canada?

The delta had scarcely changed since Mackenzie's time,
except to creep a little farther into the ocean. This enormous sandpile at the top of the continent is a repository
for the debris of the north. Mud and silt and alluvial rubbish are borne here from thousands of miles away—from
the floor of the Rocky Mountain trench and the slopes of
the Mackenzie Mountains, from the crags of the Rockies,
the canyon walls of the Nahanni, and the chocolate-brown
farms of the Peace River, from the forests of northern
Saskatchewan, and the hard Precambrian crust of the
shield country, from Million Dollar Valley, Wood Buffalo
Park, Uranium City, and the Dismal Lakes. The great
river dumps its silt-choked waters into the ocean at the
rate of half a million cubic feet a second, so that soft sandbars appear in the shallow sea twenty miles north of its
island-studded mouth.

The seacoast loomed out of the horizon, and on its margin there appeared one of those Arctic puzzles that make

the north so fascinating. Here were the odd cone-shaped mounds, a hundred feet or so high, that Eskimos and geologists call *pingoes*. Peculiar to this delta shoreline, they look like miniature volcanoes. They are covered with lake-bottom vegetation, and their core is solid blue ice. They seem to have sprouted from the old lake bottoms like milk squeezing from a frozen bottle—an analogy as near to an explanation as the scientists have been able to come. Side by side with the pingoes on the green-suède tundra lay the patterns of the *polygons,* continuous cracks in the ground forming five- and six-sided figures and caused, it is suspected, by ice lenses drawing the moisture from the soil until it splits like desert clay.

A sandspit poked its slender finger into the ocean almost in the shadow of one of the pingoes. Along its spine, in a hesitant line, ran a little file of buildings. There are no trees this far north, but some of the buildings had been constructed of logs floated for more than a thousand miles down the Mackenzie from the Liard Valley. This was the Eskimo settlement of Tuktoyaktuk, more usually called Tuktuk and, even more usually, plain Tuk. Its English name, Port Brabant, is rarely used.

On the bank a remarkable little woman, spectacled and freckled, with her red hair braided, was waiting to take us in tow. This was Miss Dorothy Robinson, the farthest-north schoolteacher in the country and something of a legend up and down the river. I had expected to meet an older woman, for I had heard of her often, always as "Miss Robinson," and always with a certain awe. She had been teaching day school here for seven years, a capable, efficient, dedicated, no-nonsense variety of schoolma'am, who seemed quite capable of dealing with anyone or anything. She holds a certificate in woodworking, a bronze medallion from the Royal Lifesaving Society, and a medallion and bar from the St. John Ambulance, and is one of the few women in the world to wear the Boy Scout medal. She is a woman, in short, who seems tailored to the country. If this had been the South Seas I should have expected to find her in a Somerset Maugham short story. Her mother, a pleasant, gray-haired lady of aristocratic bearing, was visiting her from Ottawa. "Dorothy," she told me proudly, "was always a great one for the Girl Guides."

Miss Robinson served us reindeer stew in her schoolroom. Then we were off again, flying northwest across the black surface of the Arctic. It looked forbidding, but the Minister of Northern Affairs had insisted on swimming in it during our brief stay at Tuk. It was, he said as he emerged, no colder than the north shore of the St. Lawrence.

On the horizon now we could see the "ice blink"—the odd, silvery glare that is the reflection of the polar cap. Far off in the sea lay the whaleback of Richards Island. Across its smooth naked surface a curious movement was taking place. From our vantage point in the sky there seemed to be a vast swarm of bees clinging to the island in a shuddering cluster. Only when the plane slid down into the sea and we waded through the wet mosses of the shore could we make out what they were—a heaving mass of reindeer, walled off in a long corral built on the rock and muskeg.

There were fifteen hundred of them, a struggling ocean of antlers and snouts. It was roundup time in the Arctic, and on the rails of the corral were perched Eskimo women with their button-eyed babies in their arms, watching as the herders let the animals through in twos and threes, counted and sorted the herd, castrated the young bull calves so they would grow fat, and killed those fawns whose horns had been ripped from their scalps in the melee. The scene was reminiscent of an Alberta roundup, but there were some basic differences. Here the herders and spectators wore parkas instead of blue denims, and the animals had antlers rather than horns. In place of the prairie grasses, lichens grew, dappled with bright patches of yellow daisies and white Arctic cotton and bunches of red crowberries, an Eskimo delicacy that the women preserve for the winter in bags made from the stomachs of whales. I plucked a tiny trailing vine from the wet muskeg. It was a birch tree, and it was perhaps half a century old.

There are now six reindeer herds in the Canadian Arctic. They have been here ever since 1935, when a grizzled Laplander named Andrew Bahr wrecked his health in a memorable and painful trek to bring the originals across the top of the continent from Alaska. The animals were purchased by the Canadian government in the hope that by supplying herds to the Eskimos it could wean them away from the precarious life of the trapper to the more stable existence of the herdsman.

The trek is another Arctic epic. It was expected to occupy eighteen months, but it took six terrible winters, and few of the 3,195 reindeer that started out actually completed the journey. During the first winter, 1929–30, storms so panicked the deer that hundreds broke for home. The Lapps and Eskimos who accompanied the animals spent most of the winter trying to get them across the slippery glare ice of a single river.

The next three winters were among the worst on record in the north. By January 1932 the herd and its herders had been out of contact with civilization for six months and were only three hundred miles from their starting-point. A third of the animals had wandered away. Wolves harried the fringes. Thousands of caribou hurtled past on their annual migration, and the tidal wave threatened to sweep off hundreds from the dwindling herd, for the reindeer is merely a domesticated caribou. One fearful storm cast five hundred animals adrift, and it took six months to round them up again. The thermometer hit seventy below, but the herders could not take shelter: they had to keep up with the herd or lose it.

The following winter was worse. It was so cold the migratory animals didn't appear. There were no caribou, ptarmigan, foxes, seals, or fish. The herd didn't reach the delta until January 1934, and it took another full year to cross it. For eight weeks the thermometer didn't rise above thirty-five below zero. In one forty-eight-below gale the herdsmen had to abandon their charges to save their own lives. The reindeer were soon scattered over fifty miles, and it took more weary weeks to corral them again. The following fall Bahr and his men tried for months to take the animals across the frozen channels, but each time chinook winds swept down and melted the snow to the point where the reindeer lost their footing on the slippery ice. Finally, in February 1935, the herd, cut down to 2,370—most of them new animals born en route—reached its destination. The trek was successful, but Andrew Bahr, the chief herdsman, was a broken man. He had aged ten years in five. He had lost his teeth and his hearing, and he fled the north, never to return.

There are eight thousand descendants of the original herd on the delta today. They are the only source of fresh meat for Aklavik where a meal of reindeerburgers costs one dollar and sixty-five cents. At the moment, some twenty Eskimo families are working with the herds, and one herd is entirely Eskimo-owned. But this particular solution to the problem of diminishing fur harvests is a slow and tedious one. It will take a long time to turn the nomadic Eskimo into a herdsman, or anything else, for that matter—boatbuilder, potato-grower, airport worker, or miner.

It was time to leave the reindeer behind. As we rose from the sea, we had our last view of them—the long, wooden corrals stretching across the whalebacked island, a moving mass of animals imprisoned within them. Once again from the air they looked like a black swarm of bees, with the lonely Arctic all about them, stretching off to the rim of the sky.

Now we began to flit from point to point in the delta.

We stopped briefly at Whitefish Bay, a community of eighty Eskimos, whose main pursuit is hunting the white whales that frequent the coastal waters. A deputation of grizzled old men came down the bank to welcome the Minister and to ask the government for a freezing unit with which they could preserve the whale meat over the lean summer periods when it would otherwise rot. The old joke about selling refrigerators to the Eskimos is not quite so far-fetched as it sounds. The temperature that day was in the high eighties, and the air was pungent with the stench of rotting whale meat.

We flew over another strange northern ghost town—a huddle of black, empty Quonset huts clustered like fat beetles around the tall orange and white spire of a Loran tower more than six hundred feet high. This thin needle, protruding from the pincushion of the muskeg, had been erected by the RCAF in 1949, but it wouldn't work, apparently because of the complicated problems of conductivity caused by the permafrost.

We dipped down into the Napoiak Channel, and here in the maze of ponds and lakes we came upon the continent's northernmost fur farm—a mink ranch operated by a resourceful Aklavik trader.

A dark young girl of about sixteen with a faint trace of Indian blood came out of the woods to greet us.

"Where's your father, Beverley?" somebody asked.

"He went away a week ago," she said laconically. "I'm running the farm here by myself."

She showed us the six hundred mink, each in its own

cage in the forest. Then she took us to her natural freezer where the mink food was stored, a cavern burned thirty-five feet down into the permafrost, so cold at the bottom that it will freeze a load of whitefish solid in twenty-four hours.

"When's your father coming back, Beverley?"

Another shrug. "Maybe in a few days. He don't tell me. He went to Aklavik on business. Be back sometime."

We left her standing alone on the bank with her self-assurance and her six hundred mink, a solitary figure in the great web of the delta. Then we were in the sky again, headed for Aklavik. The world below us was an enormous splintered mirror, reflecting from its thousand fragments the bright rays of the evening sun.

A day or so later we left the delta country behind and flew south in "the land of long shadows and slanting trees," following the natural pathway of the great Mackenzie Valley, toward the little town of Arctic Red River, which lies within fifty miles of the Arctic Circle.

A Technicolor land lay below us, the lakes blood-red with startling chartreuse borders, the ancient dried-up channels and pond bottoms a tawny yellow against the blue-green forest. The red lakes are colored by the action of bacteria that draw iron from the water and oxidize it into rust. The green borders are actually masses of equisetum, the reed-like horsetail that grows so thickly in the hot summers that it often chokes the shallow ponds and channels until they vanish, leaving only a yellow pattern to mark their passing.

And here, lying across this Joseph's coat of yellow, green, and red, was the eerie pattern of the "drunken forests," where spindly spruce trees reel like armies of intoxicated men. This again is the work of the permafrost. The roots, unable to penetrate the soil, run laterally until the trees become top-heavy and begin to list. The Mackenzie Valley is an enormous trough crammed with natural curiosa. Here are beds of burning coal that have been on fire for two centuries. Here is oil seeping from the high banks. Here are sinkholes filled with salt water, puncturing the forest. Here are huge plate-shaped lenses of solid blue ice protruding from the mountainsides.

The Otter settled like a great dragonfly on the cold surface of the river, and there, perched on the bank above us, lay the settlement of Arctic Red River, marking the ancient boundary between the Eskimo and the Indian lands. Northern fur towns are all of a pattern. They are composed of a police compound, a mission compound, and a Hudson's Bay compound. The larger communities also have a Signals compound. The buildings are always identical, each group built to a standard architectural plan, the police buildings red and gray and white, the Bay buildings pink and white, the Signals orange and white, all stretched out in a thin line along the river, or clustered in small groups with strips of forest between them and glued together by a mucilage of Indian huts, log cabins, and tattered tents. To the outsider's eye these little communities are all as alike as Tweedledum and Tweedledee, and bcause of this they give the north a certain unity from Fort Liard to Pond Inlet.

Arctic Red River, clustered in splendid isolation high on the riverbank, is no exception to this rule. There were the same familiar buildings, and there on the hill was the white Gothic tower of the Oblate fathers. As Max Ward taxied the Otter toward the beach, we could see once again the three symbols of the north coming down the trail from the bank above: the two priests in their long wool robes, heavy crucifixes at their waists, the two Mounted Policemen in their scarlet dress tunics and wide hats like figures from a new CinemaScope production, the Hudson's Bay manager in a neat business suit—God, Justice, and Mammon all represented on the shores of the Mackenzie. In this little knot were met the three stages of white encroachment on the north: first the trader, next the church, finally the government. And on the shore, in plastic groups, sat the reason for it all, the young girls giggling softly, the old men impassive as granite. Before the white man came, there were fourteen thousand of these Athapascan peoples, ranging from the Chipewyans on Hudson Bay to the Loucheaux in the northern Yukon. Now there are fewer than five thousand. In a few more years they might have solved the entire native problem by dying out. But now they are on the increase, and this is why cabinet ministers must venture north of the Arctic Circle.

Merv Hardie, the young Liberal Member of Parliament for the five-hundred-thousand-square-mile Mackenzie River district, was bringing one of his constituents forward.

"Come on, Edward," Merv said. "Tell 'em."

Edward Nazon, second chief of the Loucheaux in Arctic Red River, a brown, somber man dressed in shapeless clothing, made little marks on the grass with his toe.

"Well," he said finally, "it's like this." Then he stopped.

"Please, sir," the Minister said. "Please feel free to tell me your problems. Please speak frankly, sir. That is why I have come here."

"Well," the Indian began, "we're having a hard time around this country, you know." Then once again we heard the familiar story. Trapping no longer was enough to support the Indians. Some of them didn't even bother to trap. But there was nothing else they could do. "Look at me," said Edward Nazon. "I got a family of eight. How can I support 'em on fifteen marten? What am I gonna do? I been looking for a job. Where can I get a job?"

They stood around him, the Indians and the young men

from Ottawa in their flannels and tweeds, scratching busily
with stubby pencils on thick memorandum pads: the
young Deputy Minister, a thirty-six-year-old Rhodes scholar, his serious, student's face intent; the man from the
Treasury Board, a quizzical graduate of the London School
of Economics; the assistant deputy, a cheerful, idealistic
Canadien fresh from the cloisters of Laval University, in
Quebec City. There was the problem for the earnest,
scholarly young men to solve. What were men like Edward Nazon to do? The mines don't want to hire them.
Neither do the oil companies, whose helicopters were
fluttering about the Mackenzie Valley, nor the airlines,
building new airstrips at Yellowknife and Fort Smith, nor
the transportation companies, whose tugs were chugging
up and down the river. All these firms, at great cost and
trouble, coping with high turnover and premium wages,
were importing reluctant white workers from the Outside.

They feel they must do this because the natives' background and make-up have not fitted them to work dis-
ciplined hours. Since their first days on the continent, the
Athapascans have roamed the river country like gypsies,
migrating with the caribou by snowshoe or sled or birchbark canoe, living in hastily contrived skin tents, pursuing
the game with spears and flint-tipped arrows. The coming
of the white man turned them into a different kind of
nomad, following the trapline in the winter, drifting toward the settlements in the summer.

This wandering life makes it maddeningly difficult for
the government and mission schools to educate the children. The schools run all year round, but the children
come and go as the parents flit from settlement to forest
and back again. A native child is fortunate to get ninety
days' schooling a year, none of it consecutive. Much of
what is learned is unlearned in the wilderness and must

be learned again. There is no discipline in an Indian family. The children do exactly as they please without remonstrance from the parents.

Watching these people now, as they stood on the grassy slopes of Arctic Red River talking to the men from Ottawa, I was again struck by the melancholy cast of their features, so different from the smiling Eskimos. "A meagre, ugly, ill-made people," Mackenzie called them, and they are certainly a gloomy and morose-appearing race, short and slender of build, with straight black hair, oval faces, high cheekbones, and dark, somber eyes that show traces of the Mongolian fold. This suggests their origins, and so does their harsh, guttural tongue, difficult to grasp because so many words sound alike to the unpracticed ear. The students of language believe that it belongs to the same family of tongues that prevails in China, Tibet, and Siam, and the theory is that these unhappy river people formed the last wave of the invading wanderers who crossed from Asia by the Bering Strait at the dawn of the Christian era.

Now these onetime adventurers are reckoned the least progressive and ambitious of all the North American tribes. What happened to the burst of energy that impelled them to migrate? Probably they dissipated it in the bare struggle for existence that has been their lot for two millennia on the banks of Alexander Mackenzie's unfriendly river. There are no real tribes and no real governing bodies among them. The roving bands are loose and unstable. The only social unit is the family. They have no art, no history, no religion—only a haunting fear of ghosts flitting unseen through the forests.

"We need to work," Edward Nazon was saying, as the young men from Ottawa scribbled away industriously, "but, trouble is, there is no work here."

Indeed, except for the trapline, there is no work anywhere for the Indian, nor will there be until he has adapted himself to the white man's ways. Since the days of Samuel Hearne, white men have had misgivings about the impact of Western civilization upon the northern native. ("I must confess that those who have the least intercourse with the Factories are by far the happiest," Hearne wrote in his journal two centuries ago.) But it is too late now to leave him in isolation. He has been tempted and tainted by the white man's ways until he is neither civilized nor savage, but remains instead a wild, unhappy half-man, plagued by the shortcomings of both races.

By white standards he is a child who lives only for the day. When he gets a job he often vanishes with the first check, which he spends immediately. He does not stock his larder, but buys food enough for only one or two meals at a time. His first purchases, before food, are likely to be yeast and raisins for concocting his potful of brew. He drinks it before it has time to become potent, but none the less it intoxicates him, for he seeks intoxication. His second purchases are almost certain to be tea and tobacco. Only then, if he has more money, will he buy the flour and baking powder which, mixed in a pan with water and lard, make the gluey bannock he devours with his half-cooked fish.

Sometimes he buys no food at all. His money, his goods, the tattered gray tent that is his home winter and summer, even his wife, all these may have been lost to him in the wild gambling parties which, with the brew-ups and the drum dances and the casual sex, are his chief amusements.

The skin drums are his life, for they transport him to a happier world of rhythm. He dances in a circle, hour after hour until dawn, chanting a wordless tune, his feet executing a nimble step that few white men have been able to follow.

He even gambles to the drums; his game is almost a ritual, for every movement of the two teams involved is made to their insistent rhythm. The rules differ up and down the river, but the essentials are the same. The facing teams pass a small object—a short stick or a piece of polished caribou horn—from hand to hand while the drums pound. The opposite side must guess where the object is. In some versions the game operates like musical chairs: the drumming stops suddenly and a designated man on the opposite team must point to where he believes the object is. In other versions the drums never stop, and the pointing and seeking are done in rhythm to them. All night long the drums pound, the players pass the short stick, and onlookers sway to the rhythm and make side bets, and the chanting grows louder and louder as the beat grows more insistent, until the game ends in a frenzy and the gamblers lose their power of speech along with their possessions.

This, then, was the strange foreign world into which the new Minister of Northern Affairs found himself peeping on the banks of the Mackenzie. The pencils continued to scratch as Edward Nazon continued to talk. The sun shone brightly on the Oblate fathers' potato patch and on the tall delphinium running wild among the grasses. Below, the great cold river swept around the bend on its long journey to the Arctic. It was time to move on.

We clambered down the dusty path to the beach again. The old men took up their graven positions on the bank above us, gazing incuriously down upon the scarlet-and-blue aircraft with an unblinking stare. The young girls giggled and jostled one another at the margin of the beach. Then we left the fur country behind, the problems still unsolved, but all noted carefully on thick pads of paper, to be translated eventually into the various memoranda that will shape the future of the north.

2 | Boom Country

The tinsel trail of boom and bust started in Norman Wells on the Mackenzie River with an oil gusher just after World War I. Then it led east across the dark waters of Great Bear Lake to Port Radium and south over the gneisses and granites of Precambrian shield to the gold country of Yellowknife. It was this trail we now followed in the flying Otter. Our only detour was north to Coppermine on the Arctic, the site of some boom town of the future.

Ever since Martin Frobisher brought back fool's gold to the Court of St. James and Samuel Hearne sought copper on the tundra, the north has been thought of as a land of untold riches. This was confirmed beyond man's wildest dreams in 1897 when the world "Klondike" became a synonym for sudden wealth. One hundred thousand stampeders poured north. They trampled over most of the country that was to know later stampedes. They found lead on the south shore of Great Slave Lake and gold on Yellowknife Bay. They saw the cobalt bloom on the high rocks of Great Bear and the oil seeping from the banks near Fort Norman. But none profited because, except for the Yukon's free gold, none of it was worth developing in the days before the airplane.

We had crossed the Arctic Circle and were flying south following the winding furrow of the Mackenzie Valley. This venerable trough has channeled the ancient seas that for all of geological time have spilled across North America in periods of continental immersion. The last great sea was the Cretaceous, a shallow body of water that washed the interior from the Gulf of Mexico to the Arctic. In those reptilian days, ten million years ago, when figs, breadfruit, magnolias, cinnamon, and palm trees flourished in a north then tropic, the continental midriff buckled and warped. Its pelvis tilted to the south, letting in the invading waters of the Gulf of Mexico. Its upper section tilted to the north, and the Arctic swept in. The two seas met and the length of the continent was split by a new ocean three thousand miles long and a thousand miles wide.

When the great seas retreated, they bequeathed a rich heritage. In the steaming swamps that were left in their wake, millions of tiny marine creatures thrived, and then died as the swamps evaporated into plains and valleys. Crushed by the pressure of overlying sediments, their decomposing bodies formed beds of oil and gas which, along with soft coal, are the legacy of the prehistoric past. The tar sands of the Athabasca country in northern Alberta are part of this legacy, and so are the oil pools of Norman Wells, caught between coral reefs just south of the Circle. There is more than a suspicion that petroleum lies in a vast subterranean ocean beneath the moss and the muskeg of the Liard and the Mackenzie; there may even be oil reefs as far north as the Arctic islands where those telltale formations, the salt domes, have been found.

The matted forest, which fledges the fifty thousand feet of sedimentary rock deposited by the prehistoric seas, rolled off below us from the river border to the silent slopes of the Mackenzie Mountains, far to the west. This is the *taiga*, the great Boreal conifer forest that stretches in a thick belt across the continent between the tundra and the southern grasslands and covers almost half of Canada. Ruled across this carpet of trees were the survey lines, hacked out of the underbrush by crews from half a dozen oil companies. We had flown two hundred and fifty miles southeast from Arctic Red River and the oil town of Norman Wells lay just below us.

Here is the only Mackenzie Valley settlement not dependent upon the fur trade, and here is the most northerly oil refinery in the world. Norman Wells, a thousand miles northwest of Edmonton, looks quite different from the other river towns, with its fat silver storage tanks crouching on the banks and its gas-heated homes and bunkhouses painted white and trimmed with lawns and borders of dahlias, phlox, primrose, bright Arctic poppies, and blue delphiniums six feet high.

The Wells is, in effect, a company town. We were welcomed by the resident manager of Imperial Oil Limited, a Canadian subsidiary of Standard of New Jersey, which controls the community. We slept in the modern company hospital, which had no patients at the moment and is more like a small, bright hotel. We drank cocktails and munched canapés with three Standard Oil executives just in from New York, while the buzz of two helicopters flickering about the town drilled steadily into our ears.

The carpeted floors and the pastel walls of the Imperial Oil staff house seemed a world away from the grassy slopes of Arctic Red River; yet Norman Wells does share with the fur towns the same northern pattern of sudden growth and swift decline. A boom built the community in 1920 when Imperial Oil brought in a gusher fifty-one miles north of the old Hudson's Bay post of Fort Norman. (The seepage of oil on the riverbank had been noted a hundred and thirty-one years earlier by Alexander Mackenzie in his diary.) The gusher touched off a stampede. Hundreds of men poured over the mountains from the Yukon and down the river from Alberta on snowshoes, dragging sleds behind them, leaving a trail of dogs' carcasses in their wake, and suffering the usual penalties of famine, scurvy, and exposure that accompanied all the early rushes. As usual, only a handful made money. One resourceful river pilot in Edmonton sold an oil property for a thousand dollars though he hadn't then staked it; then he fought his way down the river through the ice to make good his claim. One trapper made five thousand dollars on oil leases, but was back on his trapline, broke, in three months. A Peace River prospector made twenty-three thousand, spent it in a single riotous winter, and was back at Fort Smith washing dishes the following spring.

Norman was back to slim times almost equally quickly. The oil was there in a vast black ocean beneath the frozen mosses—fifty to one hundred million barrels in the one tapped pool alone—but there was nowhere to use it. In 1925 Imperial capped its two wells, and the boom town became a ghost town. In 1932, when radium and silver began to be mined on Great Bear Lake, the wells were re-opened. But it wasn't until 1942 that the real boom began.

Now unfolded the most bizarre chapter in northern history since the gaudy days of the Klondike madness. The trucks rumbling up the Alaska Highway and the planes winging north along the great staging route needed fuel. The United States and Canada decided to put Norman Wells to use. As a result sixty-one wells went into production, and the fantastic construction of the Canol pipeline was undertaken. At a cost of one hundred and thirty-seven million dollars some three thousand men punched sixteen hundred miles of six-inch pipe through the unmapped mountain country between Norman Wells and White-horse, and then north along the highway to Fairbanks, Alaska.

The implications of this monumental undertaking were not lost on Bechtel-Price-Callahan, the company that built the line. It placed the following sign in its employment office:

THIS IS NO PICNIC

Working and living conditions on this job are as difficult as those encountered on any construction job ever
done in the United States or foreign territory. Men
hired for this job will be required to work and live
under the most extreme conditions imaginable. Temperatures will range from ninety degrees above zero to
seventy degrees below zero. Men will have to fight
swamps, rivers, ice and cold. Mosquitoes, flies and gnats
will not only be annoying but will cause bodily harm.
If you are not prepared to work under these and similar
conditions

DO NOT APPLY

This frank warning was no deterrent. Twenty-five thousand men—soldiers and civilians—poured into the country, and the great silent river suddenly came alive with
boats and barges trundling ten million tons of equipment
and materials north to the job site. So many trucks were
floated down the Mackenzie in two wartime summers—
1942 and 1943—that they had to be stood on end upon the
barges. Negro troops poured through, shivering in the
summer days, though many of them wore two or three
suits of underwear under their uniforms. Shipping was so
badly jammed on the river that thousands waited for a
boat at Fort Smith on the Alberta border for two months,
sleeping in the hotel yard or the corridors of the hospital.

The engineers worked in an impossible land that had
scarcely known the tread of a white man's boots. Only one
man had ever walked over and written about the tor-
mented section of the Mackenzie Mountains that sweeps
down between Norman Wells and Whitehorse. He was

299

Joseph Keele, a government geologist, who had gone in twenty-five years before. The pipeline-builders, who fought muskeg, permafrost, glaciers, and landslides and flash floods, had only Keele's brief description to go on. But through the mountain wall they punched a thousand miles of road, a thousand miles of telephone line, and sixteen hundred miles of pipe.

The Canol was hardly completed before the war was ended and the entire project abandoned. The section of pipeline between Whitehorse and Fairbanks, along the Alaska Highway, is still in use, but the rest has been forsaken. Across the river from the neat little community of Norman Wells lies another northern ghost town—the Canol Camp—a tangle of rotting Nissen huts and warehouses jammed with thousands of spare parts long since obsolete. The pipeline road still winds through the mountains, a ghost highway, its trestles washed away, its right-of-way jammed by slides. Salvage firms have picked clean its bones, stripping away the hundreds of brass valves and power units, the thousands of motors and the miles of pipe. Of the one hundred and thirty-seven million dollars pumped into the venture, the government recovered scarcely one million. As for Norman Wells, it has slipped back to its prewar status. Its oil production has sagged to one fifth of the 1944 figure, for it is still prohibitively expensive to ship petroleum products very far in the north. Norman Wells' closest customer is Port Radium on Great Bear Lake, just two hundred miles to the east. Even over this short haul, all of it by water, the price of light Diesel is doubled. But still the helicopters flit about the sky, and the search for oil goes on up and down the river, against the day when pipelines will be practical and new boom towns dot the Mackenzie Valley.

The following morning we left the oil country behind

and flew east along the Great Bear River, white with rapids, toward Port Radium.

Ahead lay the dark blue expanse of Great Bear Lake, an enormous biological desert, a quarter the size of England, so cold that no plankton lives in its deepest waters, and fish never leave the shoreline. Oil tankers are useless here for the water is so cold that it would thicken the oil inside and it couldn't be pumped. The water never rises more than a few degrees above freezing.

Great Bear is one of a chain of lakes, some huge, some tiny, formed in prehistoric days by the melt water collected in vast sheets at the edge of the receding ice cap. They lie on the edge of the Precambrian shield along the sites of ancient preglacial valleys, which were gouged deeper and broader by the movement of the rock-shod ice sheets. Into these great hollows the melting glaciers spilled their water. Many of the lakes have vanished today, leaving broad stretches of clay behind, but the withered remains of some still exist: the three huge northern lakes, Athabasca, Great Slave, and Great Bear, as well as Lake Winnipeg and the five Great Lakes to the south.

For a hundred and fifty miles we flew east across the navy-blue expanse of Great Bear. Then, on the far shoreline, we saw once again the familiar Precambrian formation that starts here, on the edges of the lakes, and covers two million square miles of Canada, giving a vast section of the north a certain unity; the Labrador country, two thousand miles away, looks very much the same.

There it lay below us, the spine of Canada, a rocky backbone rising from the cold margin of the huge lake and stretching off to the far horizon, lake upon lake, rock upon rock, as desolate and empty-looking as a dead planet in science fiction, its crevices and hollows sparsely plastered with a stone clay or *till* deposited by the sluggish glaciers.

The great shield is at once the blessing and the curse of the north. The wealth lies here. Most of the great mineral discoveries of the past half century have been made not far from its rim—the gold of Great Slave, the uranium of Great Bear and Athabasca, the iron of Ungava—all these and minerals in a host of mines yet undiscovered. But the shield is also the great barrier to the north. It defies roads and railroads as it defies agriculture. It stands as an immense rampart against civilization. No other land in the world is saddled with a bulwark of this mass, and that is one reason why Canada has no real cities in the latitudes of Edinburgh and Copenhagen, Oslo and Stockholm.

We touched down on the chill waters. Steep walls of Precambrian, tinged with blue and pink and gray-greens, towered about us. Clinging to them like barnacles was a series of shops and houses and mine buildings. This was the uranium community of Port Radium on the cliffs of Echo Bay, a vertical town without sidewalks, the buildings joined to one another by catwalks and endless flights of wooden steps.

Bored into this Gibraltar are thirty miles of tunnels, for here, just twenty-eight miles from the Circle and sixty-five miles from the tundra, is the most northerly mine on the continent—the crucible of the atom.

Bill Bennett, the black-browed, bulletheaded boss of Canada's atomic-energy program, had just flown in from Washington when we arrived. We sat down with him in the messhall to a dinner of clear soup, filet mignon, tossed salad, apple pie, and cheese, topped off with brandy, all flown in from Edmonton, a thousand miles away. Here, on the Circle's rim, we were less isolated than many Ontario mining camps eighteen hundred miles to the southeast. Port Radium's season in the sun is so short that the workers get special vitamin pills and ultraviolet treatments each winter to compensate. The climate is such that the lake

stays frozen nine months a year and the miners play base-
ball on its surface until June. Yet the airplane has brought
it so close to civilization that the mail arrives daily along
with fresh meat and vegetables, and men like Bill Bennett
can pop in for dinner straight from a talk with Lewis
Strauss in Washington.

Here, too, on these armored shores, can be traced the
boom-and-bust pattern of the north. Just twenty-five years
earlier, at the height of the stampede to Great Bear Lake,
a respected trader and prospector named D'Arcy Arden
was optimistically predicting to the *Edmonton Journal*
that the lake would support one hundred thousand people
within a generation. Now the generation has arrived and
there are fewer than three hundred workmen in the cliff
dwellings of Echo Bay. Mines, no matter how rich, do not
automatically mean big cities.

The story of the discovery of pitchblende on the shores
of Echo Bay by Gilbert LaBine has become a familiar and
often tangled northern legend. It actually begins a generation before LaBine's day in 1900, when two young northerners, Charles Camsell and his new-found crony, James
MacIntosh Bell, made a three-thousand-mile trip through
the hinterland by snowshoe and canoe.

Both men were destined to be numbered among the
great figures of northern Canada. Bell was a young geologist of twenty-two, just out of Queen's University, who
had gone north with his uncle, the head of the geological
survey of Canada. He was a man of parts, an amateur
painter, who was to marry the sister of Katherine Mans-
field, the story-writer. He had an uncanny knack of being
on the scene of future great mining developments years
ahead of everybody else. Camsell was the adventurous son
of a renowned chief factor of the Hudson's Bay Company
at Fort Simpson. He had been raised in the north, a lean,
spare man with a trace of Indian blood. He had just re-

turned from an abortive attempt to reach the Klondike by way of the Liard, where he had almost starved to death. His career eventually took him to Ottawa, where he became Deputy Minister of Mines.

Now these two young men were skirting the forbidding, oxidized cliffland of Great Bear Lake by canoe, both of them half starved, their feet torn from clambering over jagged rocks, one of their party lost and feared dead. They had pushed south from the unknown Arctic country surrounding the Dismal Lakes, where they had narrowly escaped being murdered by Eskimos, and they were the first men around these shores since the days of the black-robed Abbé Petitot, who had crossed the lake in the 1870's. In his journal the methodical Bell noted the peculiar country through which they paddled—the windy bays, the fiords biting deep into the cliffs, the countless channels, the desolate, bare shores, the high precipices stained with the rainbow hues of various metallic oxides—red, black, pink, white, and green. In the third week of August the party reached the base of the towering cliffs on which Port Radium's buildings are perched today and, with the snow sifting down from the sky and the ice forming on the rough margin of the lake, they pitched camp and made notes about the mottled rocks that rose about them.

The following year Bell published his official report in the *Geological Survey* of 1901. Buried in it was the following sentence:

"In the greenstones east of McTavish Bay occur numerous interrupted stringers of calcspar, containing chalcopyrite, and the steep rocky shores which here present themselves to the lake are often stained with cobalt bloom and copper green."

The report lay tucked away for almost thirty years until Gilbert LaBine, poring through the survey reports from the archives of the Canadian Bureau of Mines, came across it. LaBine was the son of a French-Canadian doctor from the Ottawa Valley, and his whole life had been tied up with mining. At fourteen he had worked in the mines at Cobalt, Ontario. At fifteen he had gone prospecting on his own and soon sold a silver claim for five thousand dollars. LaBine made a successful career of mining, but in 1929 he was down on his luck. His last venture, Eldorado Gold Mines, had been a flop. He was using what little money was left in the treasury in a last-ditch gamble to find a new prospect.

LaBine had already made one trip to Great Bear Lake, searching for the copper that had taken Samuel Hearne halfway across the continent a century and a half before. Alone, he trudged through the Precambrian desertland between the lakeshore and the seacoast, looking for something rich enough to mine. Then when Punch Dickins picked him up and flew him south, LaBine, peering from the cockpit, saw a scene that made his eyes pop. There, on the very lip of the shield at the lake's edge, was "a pattern like an Oriental rug." To LaBine's practiced eye the enormous faulting, the overlays of sedimentary rocks, the greenstones and oxidations, all added up to one thing: mineral wealth. He resolved to return to the edge of the shield the following year to see what he could find.

That winter, searching through the archives in Ottawa for a map, he came upon the Bell report. The boy from Cobalt knew that the presence of cobalt bloom can also mean silver. He was certain that the area Bell described—the steep rocky cliffs and the bright stains—was the same he had spied from the air. But where was it? McTavish Bay, the only identifying point, had six hundred to eight hundred miles of shoreline. Back to the enormous unmapped lake went LaBine the following summer with a partner, Charles St. Paul. The two men, struggling with a sledge loaded with sixteen hundred pounds of provisions, up to their knees in frozen slush half the time, began to inch their way around the shoreline for two hundred miles looking for the lost bay on the edge of the shield.

The glare of sun on snow drove St. Paul to snow-blindness, an affliction that makes the victim feel as if his eyes were full of burning grit. LaBine left his partner in camp and went on alone. Not far away he came upon an island bisected by an open fracture. LaBine put his hand into this rift in the rock and could feel the native silver on the edges. He knew at once that he'd made a spectacular find. Then he raised his eyes from the ground and saw the Eldorado of his dreams. There, just two hundred feet away across the water, rose the cliff with the cobalt bloom upon it. This was the same Echo Bay on which Bell and Camsell had camped and which he himself had seen from the air. He hurried across the slushy ice and began to apply his prospector's pick to the fractures cutting across the face of the rock wall. Before the day was out he had found thirty-eight distinct minerals, including bismuth, cobalt, and a silver vein fifteen feet wide.

One mineral far outweighed the rest. Here, by the most freakish accident in northern mining history, on the shores of the silent fresh-water sea stood one of the few men in Canada who at that time could identify pitchblende, the ore from which radium and uranium are refined. LaBine had been the first prospector in Canada to seek it, thirteen years before. He chopped out a piece of blue-gray rock the size of a plum and recognized it at once. Here was something far richer than silver, copper, or gold, and it was the first time it had been discovered in the Western Hemisphere. Thus began the long chain of events that led to the eventual explosion of the atomic bomb at Hiroshima. The bomb contained uranium that came originally from this very cliff, with its pink and yellow stains, on Echo Bay, Great Bear Lake.

LaBine's strike touched off a new stampede. Prospectors might scoff at the pitchblende and call it "LaBine's coal mine," but the silver was real enough. Once again the boom was on. Men poured north to stake ten thousand claims, so confident of success and prosperity that they envisioned a small city on the banks of Cameron Bay across from the present mine. New strikes sprang up in the bush country all around the lake. Prospectors paid one hundred dollars for a plane seat to fly as many miles. Pat Reid's sleeping-shack at Cameron Bay was jammed with men, women, and children, who paid half a dollar apiece for a spot on the floor next the wall, where it was so cold your hair froze to the logs; a spot next to the stove cost a dollar. Food was at a premium. Gilbert LaBine's elder brother, John, made close to one thousand dollars a week just catching fish.

In the end the bubble burst and Cameron Bay grew to nothing more than a few wooden shacks and a multitude of tents. All the brave plans for it remained paper plans, and they can be seen on paper to this day, a historical curiosity tucked away in a drawer in the offices of the Eldorado Mining and Refining Company at Port Radium. I went up to the office and looked at the city on paper; there it was, the metropolis of the north, neatly surveyed into streets with names like LaBine Avenue and Radium Drive. Now Great Bear Lake supports its single mine, and Cameron Bay is another ghost town on the face of the north.

As for Gilbert LaBine, his mine became government property for good and sufficient reasons during the war. This did not in the least deter him. When the war ended he went out and found another and far bigger uranium mine on the shores of Athabasca Lake, to the south.

But the talk in Port Radium that evening was less of Gilbert LaBine and uranium than it was of Max Ward and the great gold-brick robbery.

"Come on, Max, you know all about it," somebody said. "Let's hear the story."

"Well," the pilot said, "this doesn't make me look too good, but anyway here's how it was:

"I was coming into Yellowknife last month on a routine flight from the Discovery mine, which is about fifty miles north. My freight included two gold bricks, sewed into a canvas bag and put right in the center of the cabin so there wouldn't be any danger of them falling out.

"When we got into Yellowknife, I started helping the passengers off with their luggage. One of them had a real heavy grip. It weighed a hundred and twenty-two pounds, and when I heaved it off I turned to him and said as a joke: 'Say, what you got in that bag, gold bricks?'

"Well, sir, I don't suppose I'll ever live that one down. That's exactly what he did have in the bag as it turned out, though by the time they found out, he was somewhere between Hay River and Edmonton. He'd pulled as slick a job as you'll ever see, and he must have planned it months before.

"What happened was he substituted two phony lead bricks for the two bricks in the plane. You know gold bricks have dull edges and lead bricks sharp edges. He'd taped the edges of the phony bricks to give this effect. He'd made a bag of exactly the same kind of canvas the mine uses, and he'd had it stamped and numbered exactly the way the mine does. Turned out he'd worked six months in the mine just to get all this down pat. He'd bought the lead four months before he pulled the job.

"It was twenty-four hours before they caught on—and only then because of a small error he'd made. You know each brick is numbered. He'd carefully counted the bricks as they left the mine, two at a time. But one day only *one* brick was shipped out and he slipped up. When the numbers didn't jibe on the shipping bills, they got suspicious and after an awful lot of red tape they opened up the bag and found the lead.

"They never have caught him. He left a letter for the paymaster saying he'd forgotten to pick up his pay, but as it was such a small amount, why not send it to some worthy charity? The paymaster looked up the guy's company insurance policy to find out who his beneficiary was."

"And who was it, Max?" someone asked.

"The Vancouver Symphony Orchestra," Max said. "Well, early start tomorrow. I'm going to bed."

The following morning we flew up to the Arctic coast again, to the little Eskimo settlement of Coppermine, one hundred and fifty miles to the northeast.

Our course led across the tundra and along the route of the first prospector ever to search for minerals in the Canadian northwest. Up the twisting Coppermine in 1771, all the way from Fort Prince of Wales on Hudson Bay, had come young Samuel Hearne, aged twenty-six, seeking the source of the rough copper ornaments the Chipewyan Indians brought down to the mouth of the Churchill, explaining that they had found the metal "on the banks of a river far away."

A strange man to be carrying the ensign of the Hudson's Bay Company to the top of the continent, this sensitive and stoic young man whose literary and artistic inclinations far exceeded his desire for commerce, whose vivid journalist's imagination disturbed the scientific accuracy of his reports, whose strong sympathies for the natives were at violent odds with the accepted practices of his day. He was no Mackenzie, stubbornly driving the Indians ever northward for the glory of the fur trade. Indeed, his bloodthirsty guide, Matonabbee, with his eight wives and his predilection for stabbing cuckolded husbands in the stomach, was more the leader of the expedition than he. For it was on the whims of this flamboyant savage that the journey largely depended. In the end Hearne found only a few fragments of copper rather than the rich mines he had half expected to discover on the far Arctic shore. Yet his epic trek across the Barrens stands as the greatest of all pieces of northern exploration, a feat unduplicated to this day.

We were flying over Bloody Falls, where the river knifes through a rocky dike and plunges at breakneck speed over the black volcanic stone. The falls have not changed since that day, "horrible beyond description," when Hearne's Indian companions, their faces daubed with black and crimson, fell like animals upon a group of sleeping Eskimo families and disemboweled them before the horrified young Englishman. One naked eighteen-year-old girl impaled on a spear fell at Hearne's feet and twisted round his ankles, dying and shrieking, and historians have echoed her shrieks and Hearne's tears down through the generations. Fifty years later, when John Franklin happened upon these Bloody Falls, the skulls of the unhappy Eskimos were still there, bleaching in the sunlight. It may well be that the memory of that terrible day, filtering down the decades from mouth to mouth, and the fear it engendered in the cheerful, peaceable natives, laid the groundwork for the murder of two Oblate fathers who ventured into this austere land a century and a half after Hearne. They were stabbed to death by Eskimos who knew only that they, too, were invaders from the south.

The shadow of the Otter drifted now across a terrain as grim in character as it is in history. It is a black land, wrinkled like a prune, with stark ridges of naked basalt forced out of the surrounding rock by volcanic action. The river flows into a false delta immediately below the falls as another reminder that the Arctic sea is shrinking and the land, once weighed down by ice, is rising again.

The whole Arctic coastal tundra from Coppermine to

Pelly Bay, seven hundred miles to the east, presents this same forbidding mien. Is there a fortune hidden somewhere in these tilted ebony scarps? Some prospectors, patiently plodding along the old explorers' routes, believe there is. On the edge of the sea, a hundred miles away, in a weird canyon country of cliffs and waterfalls and basalt ridges, Ernie Boffa, the most famous of the Barren Lands pilots, spotted the bright green stains of copper oxides more than a decade ago. In the same month that we flew into Coppermine, he and his partner (a one-time Middle East fighter pilot named Jake Woolgar) were busily staking the entire area, for here, just as Boffa had guessed, lies an enormous mass of low-grade copper ore. Is this the treasure that Samuel Hearne sought vainly? Boffa thinks so. But is it practical to mine it and export it from this shriveled land on the Arctic's rim? Will another boom town sprout here on these shores, where summer lasts only six weeks? Will the familiar pattern of the stampede repeat itself again, as it has at Norman Wells and Bear Lake and Yellowknife? Until the rock is drilled and the ore is proved, no one can tell.

Coppermine lay below us on the brown seashore baking in the Arctic sun. The town had a strangely groomed look about it, a curiosity explained by the fact that it was expecting the Duke of Edinburgh in just two days. The Eskimos had all been employed raking and sweeping and scavenging, and the whites scrubbing and painting, until the community glistened like a polished apple. But it is a measure of the new interest in the north that within the space of two summer days this little village on the Arctic Ocean could entertain both a Cabinet Minister and a Duke.

In the living-quarters above the new clapboard school, they had already laid out the silver trays and the bone china and the linen covers and the colored toothpicks, all shipped up by the Hudson's Bay Company in preparation for the Duke's visit. Each tray had a little card on it bearing such words as "salted almonds," "stuffed celery," "caviar," and "thin slices salami" as reminders to the caterers. I remarked to the schoolteacher that all this seemed a little out of keeping with life in the Arctic. Wouldn't it be better to give the Duke something more typical of the country?

"Oh, we are," he said. "His Royal Highness is getting Arctic char and roast caribou."

"Then why all the caviar?"

"Why, that's for *us*."

A few minutes later we ourselves sat down to an enormous meal of baked Arctic char, the wonderful fish of the north, richly flavored and textured, with a flesh and a taste resembling salmon. Like so much else in the north—fish, flower, river, and rock—the char, especially in its freshwater phase, is still something of an unknown quantity. Is the species being depleted, like the muskox? Nobody is sure because no scientist has yet charted its mortality rate.

We walked out of the school after the meal and across the dry, brown Arctic grasses and sedges to visit the rest of the settlement, the Anglican and Roman Catholic missions, the weather station, the Hudson's Bay store, the RCMP barracks. In the schoolyard we passed a tremendous granite cube, the size of a small house, which seemed to have erupted from the ground. It had literally been hoisted from its bed by hydraulic action, the water seeping down into crevices, freezing and expanding and slowly raising the huge weight like a barber's chair.

Down near the beach was a skin tent that had been erected for the Duke of Edinburgh so that he might visit a typical Eskimo home. The typical Eskimo and his wife were sitting outside the tent, and when I walked over with my camera the typical Eskimo began to grin cheerfully and chuckle to himself.

His name was Jim Koiakak, he was eighty years old, and he was among the last of the old line of pure-blooded Copper Eskimos. He was and is a man of fierce independence. Until very recently he had declined to accept any assistance for himself. He still refused to cut his hair, but wore it long, according to the old style. His wife Annie (his fourth) had the old blue tattoo marks on her face that bespeak a vanishing tradition. Jim Koiakak refused for years to accept the white man's religion. In 1927 he set up a mock religion of his own, to bedevil the missionaries. In it he gave literal translation to the Christian doctrine of brotherly love, made himself God, and would, for a small fee, perform miracles. In return for a cigarette lighter he promised one woman a long life, but, unluckily, she died the following year, thus undermining Jim Koiakak's new creed. In disgust, he joined the Anglican Church, though his wife remained a Roman Catholic. Here he sat in front of his tent, chuckling and grinning, with his hair over his ears, and his wool hat perched jauntily on his head, and his brown walnut face wreathed in smiles. I thought then, and still think, that it was the merriest face I had even seen. We shook hands several times, the typical Eskimo and I, both of us chuckling and laughing with each other in the summer sun until it was time for me to get back to the plane again and fly south along Samuel Hearne's old route across the tundra.

For land so little traveled, the Coppermine country is rich in history. Back from Bloody Falls, a half century after Hearne, staggered the starving John Franklin on his first overland expedition in 1819. He had been sent by the British government to explore the Arctic coast and it had almost been the death of him. Somewhere beneath us, between Great Bear and Great Slave Lake, lay the site of old Fort Enterprise, where the emaciated explorer, barely able to stay alive by gnawing deerskin and chewing rock lichens, had greeted the walking skeletons of his two associates and heard from their lips a horrible tale of cannibalism—of how their half-crazed French-Iroquois guide had secretly murdered three of the party and fed off their carcasses and of how they had executed him on the spot.

Now, unknown to us, as we dozed in the rear of the Otter, a small drama was being enacted in the cabin forward. Over the radio crackled a distress signal. It came from a pilot searching for Port Radium. He had flown out of Yellowknife that morning with two women passengers—one of them Bill Bennett's wife—but he had lost his bearings. Now he was hopelessly at sea somewhere over the tundra.

Max Ward was finally able to pinpoint his position. He had overshot his destination by two hundred miles and was now over the unpopulated Arctic coastline far to the east of Coppermine. What was he to do? He hadn't enough gas to return to the Port Radium airfield, and his plane was equipped with wheels, which meant he couldn't land on water. The women were growing panicky and there wasn't a landing strip within his reach. He had only one chance: he would have to fly west to Coppermine, where there was a gas cache, and risk landing on the beach. By the time the rest of us learned what was going on, the risk had been taken successfully and the drama on the radio was over.

The land beneath us changed from wrinkled tundra to a filigree of forest, rock, and water. South from Great Bear Lake, all the way to Great Slave, a garland of little lakes and rivers is laid along the rim of the shield. This is an ancient canoe and portage trail, and it was along this wet pathway that the pattern of boom and stampede moved after the radium rush petered out and gold was discovered at Yellowknife Bay.

Yellowknife, on the north arm of Great Slave, was born in the late thirties at the climax of the greatest gold boom in the world's history. Actually there have been two Yellowknife booms, and there is a town to mark each. On a spiny peninsula jutting into the water and joined to the mainland by a narrow isthmus lies the "old town." We were over it now, a picturesque frontier community of hastily constructed frame shacks and log cabins perched among the Precambrian cliffs. This was the original Yellowknife, populated in the wild days of the first stampede. Seaplanes like bright insects were tethered along the shoreline, and we settled down among them. Here I bade good-by to the Minister of Northern Affairs, who, with his party, was flying off to Ottawa, nineteen hundred miles to the southeast. Merv Hardie volunteered to drive me into the new town, a mile or so away.

The new town is a neat and modern village set on gravel flats and populated during the second boom, in 1945. It has very little of the frontier aura about it. It has a hotel with a cocktail bar that retails a Mucker's Special (rye, gin, lemon, and cherry) for a dollar thirty-five. It has a restaurant that sells milk shakes for thirty cents (fifty cents if made with real milk), and a juke box that plays cowboy music for teenagers in mackinaws and blue jeans. It has twelve taxis, eight of them with two-way radios. It has one optimistic resident who owns a television set. It has a newspaper called the *News of the North* and an editor to go with it—an unruly-looking man named Ted Horton, with a shock of black hair and fingers perpetually stained with printer's ink, who writes unruly editorials sounding off against Imperial Oil Limited and Canadian Pacific Airlines for charging too much. It has running water all year round; the pipes are sunk in the sand and warmed each winter so the permafrost won't wreck the system. And it has a hospital, far more modern than can be found in any comparable Outside village, where a hundred babies are delivered each year. This is a remarkable birth rate for a town of just twenty-seven hundred people, especially when five hundred of them are bachelors.

But it was in the old town that I spent my first night in Yellowknife, at a party for the old-timers given by Merv Hardie, whose constituency has the smallest population in Canada and the largest area. A few years ago Merv was just another hardware-store clerk in Yellowknife. Now he's a local figure of considerable importance. When I landed on his doorstep he was staring moodily at a note left him by one of his Indian constituents:

to Hardie

I just drop a few lines to tell you that we got no money now thats why I ask you to help me, since last spring hunt I never work so I got no money now and I want to Build a house for my self here so please help me with the lumber and some stuff for the house if you could do that I'll be glad, my little girl she come out from Hospital last spring and I thought she might catch cold thats why I'm asking you for lumber for the house I ask Indian Agent for the lumber but he said no so what you think of that if you think you will help me please sent me a letter than I'll know I got a kicker but I got no gas if I had some I will hall some log for myself but Indian agent he don't want to help.

Paul Nomba.

Hardie had a pocketful of similar notes. He had been away most of the summer touring the north with the governmental party. Now he was back home and the problems were piling up.

He took me into his living-room, the floor thick with polar-bear skins, and introduced me to a cross-section of the old north:

—A leathery little man named Pete Baker, a veteran of thirty-three years in the north, who had left the olive groves of his native Lebanon after World War I to become a prospector, trapper, and trader and today enjoys the sobriquet of "the Arab of the Arctic";

—A tall high-domed man named Bill McDonald, the most respected prospector in the country, who has a photographic memory and an encyclopedic knowledge of rocks, trees, animals, and plants, whose word is good from Yellowknife to South Africa, and whose advice on any mining property is sought and respected;

—A man as bald as a turkey, with stumps for hands, named Bill Johnson, who has been on every stampede in the north since the days of the Klondike—from Fortymile Creek, Nome, and Fairbanks to Norman Wells, Cameron Bay, and Goldfields—and who blew off his hands while sticking a fuse into a dynamite cap on the shores of Yellowknife Bay;

—A great grizzly bear of a man named Ed de Melt, with a stubbly face and a hairy chest, a trader from Rocher River, who came north fresh from New York in 1918, swamped his boat on the Hay River, lived for two weeks on wild geese and wild onions and landed barefoot on the shores of Great Slave with only a pair of pants, a bedroll, and three dollars in cash. He has seldom worn shoes since and enjoys the enviable reputation of being able to lie supine on the counter of his trading post and pull a can of beans from the shelf with his toes;

—A wiry man with a buckskin face, named Matt Murphy, the oldest of the Barren Land trappers, in from his cabin on Muskox Lake, where no trees grow and where his yearly supply of firewood consists of bundles of thin willow roots tied together into faggots.

"They're always saying I shouldn't go out again," Matt Murphy said to me. "But, I mean, what else is there for me to do? It's my trade, after all. It's what I know. What else would I do? A man has to do what he knows best. They're always writing me and saying: 'Matt, *why* do you do it? Why do you want to live out there on the Barrens?' But I mean, a man has to live, doesn't he? Well, it's a living."

"Listen," Hardie said, interrupting, "Dave Floyd of Associated Airways is going down on a uranium strike tomorrow. Maybe you could hitch a ride with him. How about it, Dave?"

"Okay by me," the pilot said. "We're going down to Thekulthili Lake. That's about a hundred and fifty miles southeast of here. The Giant has a showing there. There ought to be a bit of a rush by the weekend. If you can get down to the Associated wharf by seven tomorrow morning, I'll see there's room for you."

And so, just after seven, I found myself flying across the misty waters of the lake and heading southeast into the sun across the bulwark of the shield. An hour or so later we dropped down upon the north arm of a spidery lake exactly like ten thousand other lakes that speckle the rock country. Like almost all the lakes in this region, Thekulthili points to the northeast—the direction from which came the great ice wall. We taxied in to shore. Here among the little sticks of trees and the ubiquitous bald, polished Precambrian rock were two tents, a couple of canoes, and six men in worn bush jackets who had been sent out by Giant Yellowknife Mines to look for uranium ore. Giant is Yellowknife's largest mine and the fourth largest in Canada. It is owned by Frobisher Ltd., and is part of Thayer Lindsley's great northern mining empire.

"What's new?" a man on the beach shouted. "Any new wars started?"

They had all been traveling and prospecting from lake to lake and river to river, out of contact with the world. Now they had found what they were looking for: the canary-yellow stains of uranium oxide and the blue-gray ore that makes the Geiger counters chatter.

One of them beckoned me a few hundred yards into the bush to show me where the find had been made. The rock had been flayed of its skin of sphagnum moss and there, in a naked streak about twenty feet long and three feet wide, looking rather like a seam of coal, lay the ore—the same coal-like ore that Gilbert LaBine had chipped from the cliffs of Echo Bay a generation before.

This was the best uranium find yet made in the Yellowknife area. But would it mean a mine? Before the week was out, a small stampede to the lake was under way. Two hundred claims were staked. Property changed hands. Optimism rose. But the odds are ten to one that for a generation at least, and perhaps forever, Thekulthili Lake will remain just as I saw it. There are ore bodies on the very edge of Great Slave that in more settled districts would make immediate mines. Nobody bothers about them in the north.

Even Yellowknife's gold was once considered too remote to mine. For more than thirty years before the eventual boom, men had been finding ore in the vicinity of Yellowknife Bay. In 1898 a Klondike prospector found gold at the mouth of the Yellowknife River, but the discovery excited no interest. During the First World War a man named Bruce explored Great Slave Lake and found gold. He is said to have died of grief because he couldn't interest Toronto financiers in the area. In 1926 another prospector actually sunk a shaft on an island near the present townsite and launched a company. But he and his bargeload of machinery were lost in the rapids of the Athabasca River, and the mine was abandoned.

The ubiquitous Dr. MacIntosh Bell, the same man who had seen the cobalt bloom on Great Bear Lake, was on the ground here, too, in 1922 and again in 1928, when he reported finding gold samples at the mouth of the Yellow-knife River. Still nothing happened.

Only after the flurry on Great Bear did mining men turn their attention toward Great Slave Lake. Paddling south from Cameron Bay in September 1934, along the lake-and-river trail, came a small party of prospectors seeking the gold reported by Bell. A storm drove them on the shore about five miles from the present town, and there they found ore. The resulting mine caused a brief rush, but it petered out within a year. Like most prospecting tales, this one had its moments of irony. Two members of the party, wandering through the spruce and poplar, actually staked the richest piece of rock on the lake. They didn't realize what they had and the claims changed hands. But ten years later this became the Giant, Canada's fourth-largest gold mine.

Meanwhile, a company of government geologists was quietly exploring the shores of Yellowknife Bay. Their report recommended the prospecting of three thousand square miles, and another minor stampede occurred. Still Yellowknife hadn't hit the headlines. The great Consolidated Mining and Smelting Company sent its geologists and engineers to the scene and quickly staked the ground that has since become the Con, Yellowknife's oldest producing mine. Here, then, was an odd situation. Both of Yellowknife's major mines, the Giant and the Con—the only ones still in operation today—had been staked. And yet no town had been built and the boom was still to come.

It remained for an English public-school graduate named Tom Payne to touch off the biggest northern gold rush since the Klondike. Payne, a husky bull of a man, had trudged over most of the north from Churchill to Cameron Bay, prospecting, trapping, and working at odd jobs. His last task had been driving tractor for the Ryan brothers, the colorful Irish-American team who handled all the transportation out of Fort Smith, the portage point on the Slave River. The Ryans grubstaked him, and he headed for Yellowknife Bay in a birchbark canoe in the summer of 1936.

This was the beginning of another northern legend. Payne beached his canoe near the mouth of the Yellow-knife River and walked up through the rocks and scrub timber to look over the Consolidated camp. Then he clambered back down toward his own campsite on the shore. On the return trip he sat down, rolled a cigarette, and, as prospectors will, idly chipped away with his pick at some gossan—oxidized rock—and slipped a piece or two into his pocket. Later on, at the lake shore, he panned the loose rock. To his astonishment, good coarse gold rattled around in the bottom of the pan.

Payne immediately rushed back to the spot and covered the telltale signs of his presence with moss so no one would suspect what he'd found. Then he learned to his chagrin that the ground had already been staked. The staker was a well-known Toronto prospector named Murdoch Mosher, who had arrived the year before and left again for the east without realizing what he had. Under Northwest Territories mining law the claims would lapse a year after being recorded—at midnight, September 27— if Mosher abandoned them and did not work the ground. Until then, Payne was helpless.

It was June. Payne sat down and prepared to put in the most anxious and desperate three months any prospector ever spent in the north. He was broke and his food had run out. All he could do was subsist on fish, keep his tracks covered, divert suspicion, and wait it out.

He waited on tenterhooks. The gold he'd found lay directly along a well-worn path leading to the Consolidated ground. As the fateful September midnight approached, it became obvious that other prospectors were going to try to stake the lapsed ground on the chance that gold was there. Payne determined to take no chances. He prepared and marked his stakes in advance. Then, in the pitch dark, as midnight struck, with the snow drifting down from above and the wind blowing gale force, he and an assistant quickly rammed the stakes home. Payne managed to secure four claims, but by then he was a sick and exhausted man. Worn out and emaciated, suffering from scurvy and phlebitis, he was taken out to Edmonton, where he hovered between life and death.

The Consolidated badly wanted to buy Payne's ground, so close to their own. With Payne stricken in hospital, a series of dramatic negotiations took place between William Archibald, the vice-president of the great mining company, and Mickey Ryan, acting for Payne. Both men were storied figures in the north. Ryan was the wiry son of an Irish immigrant from Indiana, a onetime prizefighter and bartender who had come north in 1914 at the age of twenty-two and built up the most lucrative transportation service in the north around the old portage on the Slave River. Archibald was a quiet, unpretentious half-deaf teetotaler, inwardly as tough as whalebone and perfectly capable of learning to fly his own airplane at the age of fifty-three. His mind was a filing cabinet of mining lore, and this had made him something of a legend. It was whispered that he had stood on the site of the Con mine after the briefest of preliminary surveys and said emphatically: "This is the mine; we'll sink a shaft here!" then confidently ordered the milling machinery before the shaft-sinking got under way.

Behind him Archibald had all the bargaining power of Consolidated Mining and Smelting, one of Canada's biggest companies. It owns an immense mountain of lead, zinc, and silver in British Columbia and it is perhaps the largest producer of base metals in the world. Its huge, labyrinthine smelter in the Kootenay Mountains supports a community of 170,000, and its exploration parties are dotted about the hinterland. Indeed, Consolidated's name has become as much a part of the north as that of Canadian Pacific Airlines. Both companies are controlled by the Canadian Pacific Railway, the enormous travel network whose dining-cars and summer resorts are often enough subsidized by the profits of its wealthy offspring.

A stiff financial tug-of-war took place between the shrewd and powerful Archibald and the stubborn, cocky Ryan. Archibald offered the Irishman thirty thousand dollars for Payne's four claims. Ryan turned him down, formed his own company, and started drilling. A year later, in Edmonton, Archibald tried again. He offered Ryan $159,000 for a seventy per cent interest in the company. This was a whopping sum for still unproved ground, but Ryan turned it down, gambling that Consolidated wanted the property badly enough to offer more. He went back to his hotel room and waited all day for Archibald to call. The call came at seven the same evening. Archibald asked him to drop over, ostensibly to discuss a freight contract. The two men talked warily for four hours about freighting. Finally Ryan rose to leave. Archibald remarked casually that it was too bad they hadn't been able to get together on a price for the mine. Ryan agreed noncommittally. At this, Archibald asked him point-blank how much he wanted. Ryan boldly set the figure at half a million dollars for sixty per cent interest. Archibald swallowed hard and assented. This was the biggest sale of its kind in mining history. Nowhere else in the world had such a staggering price been paid for a virtually undeveloped property. Overnight it started the rush that built the town of Yellowknife.

As for Tom Payne, he didn't die after all. He lives in Edmonton today in a mansion on the North Saskatchewan

River. He owns, among other things, a Cadillac, a Ford convertible, and an oil well, not to mention a good chunk of stock in the Rycon mine, which is now part of the Con. Years later, the story goes, someone remarked to Murdoch Mosher, the original staker of the ground, that if he'd held on to it he'd be worth half a million dollars or more. "No, I wouldn't," Mosher replied. "I wouldn't have had the nerve to ask for it."

After the famous sale the shores of Great Slave Lake came alive with prospectors. New finds were made. Other mines came into production. Then war came, mining ceased, and Yellowknife slumped. But when the war ended, the boom began again.

The peak of this new boom came in 1945 when the Giant Yellowknife gold mine came into being on ground that had been staked a decade before. The claims had changed hands more than once. Several companies (including Consolidated) had drilled the rock and found nothing startling. In 1943, on a calculated gamble, Thayer Lindsley's Frobisher company bought the property and hired a shy little geologist, Dr. A. Stewart Dobson, to look it over. He boldly predicted that a vast hoard of ore would be found in the opposite direction from the original stakings. Two years of drilling proved him right.

This was one of a series of incidents that made new headlines for Yellowknife. One company, in a moment of high imagination, flew a prospector all the way to Toronto, called in photographers, and presented him with a bundle of hard cash totaling one hundred thousand dollars for his claims. Not long after, a onetime Saskatchewan dirt farmer discovered a high-grade vein fifty miles to the north that resulted in Yellowknife Discovery mine.

The new boom dwarfed the earlier one. In the first six months of 1945, nine thousand claims were recorded in Yellowknife. The number soon rose to twenty thousand.

There were a hundred companies operating out of the town, and three thousand prospectors in the bush. The Ingraham Hotel beer parlor ran all night and fifty men rolled their sleeping-bags in it because there was no room elsewhere for them. Prices rivaled those of the Klondike days. Nothing sold for less than a dollar. One miner paid $119 to have a keg of nails flown in from Edmonton. By 1948 no fewer than ten mines were ready to mill ore. The future looked rosy and the name Yellowknife was synonymous with "boom."

And yet when I visited the town in the summer of 1954, only two mines were in operation. (A third, Discovery, is fifty miles away.) Giant, the largest, was operating only at half-production. Negus, one of the best-known, had closed down. Akaitcho, with the best potential, had never opened. The bush was empty of men. Hardly a soul was prospecting, save for two groups seeking uranium. A taxi company had failed. The bar in the new Ingraham Hotel was empty. Yellowknife was in a slump.

What had happened? Nothing, really. The gold is still there, but once again it has become too expensive to mine. The cost of everything has doubled since 1939, but the price of gold has been fixed. Here, then, is the final irony. So long as gold stays at this price, the only thing that can save Yellowknife is a world-wide depression. If prices go down or gold goes up, a dozen mines could operate again. Meanwhile, as Jake Woolgar said to me, "A man could find a vein of gold out there in the bush, but he'd have a hard time getting a nickel for it right now." Jake operates Woolgar Grubstakes, a prospecting firm. In 1953 he'd sent eight parties into the bush. In 1954 he had none.

Yellowknife, when I saw it, had settled into a quiet, two-mine town with many of the attributes of a small prairie village and none of the rough, tough atmosphere often associated (usually erroneously) with the north. It had reached the stage where a woman no longer felt she could attend tea parties, as she once did, in slacks and moccasins, but must wear hat, gloves, and high heels. And though, that spring, a bride had gone on her honeymoon by canoe in faded blue denims, her wedding dress was the last word in white lace and her prayer book was trimmed with orchids.

The year before, the Governor-General himself, Vincent Massey, had arrived for a visit expecting to be met at the airport with dog-sleds. To his surprise, he was whisked away in a sleek black limousine, one of three hundred and forty motor vehicles in this town of twenty-eight miles of road.

The townspeople resent the suggestion, sometimes fostered by visiting journalists, that they are creatures out of Robert Service's more flamboyant verses. Ted Horton had an editorial about it in the *News of the North* the week I arrived:

"Residents have had experience with newsmen who came here looking for color, found it, and then blazoned it beyond all reason," he wrote. "There have been those who have come here and gone away to write of us as swashbucklers or as alcoholics or as incipient hermits, but there are no more of that type of person here than there is in Toronto."

He was undoubtedly harking back to the spring of 1951 when an American picture magazine got a hot tip that the year's first boatload of supplies, mostly whisky, would shortly arrive in town. The magazine wired Horton: "Should be exciting and colorful pix of arrival first supplies enthusiasm and frenzy among YK citizens as they break open crates and cases of whisky after long winter of abstinence." They wanted Horton to tell them whether or not they could get a photographer into the town.

Horton replied collect, and at length, explaining conversationally that the photographer could take a scheduled airline flight into Yellowknife any one of six days a week. There would be no whisky boat arriving, but the photographer could relax with a Martini in the cocktail lounge of the Ingraham and study Yellowknife drinking habits by the hour. The magazine replied with a two-word wire: "OOPS SORRY."

On the face of it, Yellowknife, with its golf course, its radio station, and its various fraternal organizations, is a very normal small town indeed. But it cannot escape being a northern town too, with certain northern peculiarities.

The golf course, for instance, is like no other golf course in the world. Merv Hardie and I played a few holes on it one bright afternoon. It is built on Precambrian rock, with hardly a blade of grass for the entire nine holes. Until recently its clubhouse was an aircraft fuselage. The greens consist of oiled sand, and it is a club rule that each player sweep them clear of footprints, using an old doormat on a stick. Golfers make a habit of carrying .22 rifles to snipe at ravens, which are apt to swoop down and make off with the ball.

The radio station CFYK, "The Voice of the Golden North," is one of the most informal in the world. It is run co-operatively by the community. There are no commercials and nobody gets paid. Announcers and program directors include Mounties, housewives, schoolchildren, barbers, and bankers. The studio is in a basement next to a furnace with hot-water pipes overhead. The telephone is on a party line, which means that the announcers have to ask people to stop phoning in requests after ten thirty so other party-liners can get to sleep. There have been some strange programs. One time a telephone operator got her lines crossed and two gossiping housewives came on the air with the whole town eavesdropping. A disc jockey, piping in a local church service, couldn't resist opening the studio microphone and joining with the choir until his wife phoned in and ordered him to stop. Two army signalmen once tuned in on Radio Moscow by short wave and broadcast it over the station. There are similar community-run stations in Dawson, Whitehorse, Aklavik, Hay River, and Churchill, but CFYK is the most ambitious.

The fraternal organizations include the Daughters of the Midnight Sun, a group of fifty or so women who stage fashion shows, operate lending libraries, round up Red Cross blood-donors, and mark the longest and shortest days of the year by an all-feminine party at which they sing in unison that spirited northern lyric "When the Ice Worms Nest Again." The parties have been held in fairly secluded quarters since the night in a local restaurant when two of the Daughters, at the height of the festivities, volunteered to chin themselves on a rafter.

There has even been a bathing-beauty contest in Yellowknife. It has never been repeated, for it was held on a cold spring day when most of the audience wore parkas and the girls in their bathing suits turned so blue with cold that the judges awarded the prize to the only one who arrived fully dressed.

Yellowknife is a town without agriculture. The soil is so sparse that home gardeners, in order to make lawns and flower borders, must scrape meager amounts of glacial till from under poplar trees or haul peat moss from the swamps. Except for a local fishing industry, the town exists almost entirely by its mines. The Con and the Giant bracket the community, one on either side. Scattered through the bush and rocks are the head frames of abandoned mines that have produced nothing or next to nothing or have been closed until the day when gold rises or prices drop. But what the Yellowknife district really needs is something besides gold—uranium, copper, lead, silver, or zinc.

Are these to be found? Are there sites of future boom towns and mines unknown hidden along the horny coastline of Great Slave or out in the corrugated rockland of the interior? It is fairly certain that there are, and, indeed, one such site is already known on the south shore of Great Slave, directly across the lake from Yellowknife, at a place called Pine Point. Here, beyond doubt, lies one of the great lead-zinc ore bodies of the world—perhaps the largest on the continent. The presence of this ore has been known for more than half a century. In the days before the repeating rifle the Indians used to come here to make bullets for their muzzle-loaders. Then in 1898 a group of Klondikers staked the area, believing that gold and silver lay hidden among the lead and zinc sulphides. The usual rush followed from the near-by trading post of Fort Resolution. Men left stealthily by dog team in the dead of night, followed the old forest trail to the ore deposits, rammed home their stakes, and then, disgusted at finding no precious metals, forgot about it.

Since that day half a dozen companies have staked, drilled, scraped, and hacked, sunk shafts, built bunkhouses, trundled in machinery, and spent millions of dollars gambling, negotiating, promoting, and squabbling over the riches of Pine Point. One of the first men on the scene was the remarkable MacIntosh Bell, who visited the area in 1921 on behalf of a group of Boston businessmen. His company started to develop the property, so that by 1929 half a million tons of ore had been proved up and the *Edmonton Journal* was prophesying that "within eighteen months a huge oil-burning smelter will be going full blast on the southeast corner of Great Slave Lake." Once again the familiar optimism came into play as northerners talked of a railway from the Peace River into Great Slave, and a

boom town of thousands. But nothing happened. It was
the old story: the ore was there, but it was too expensive
to mine so far north.

I flew off to Pine Point one morning, bidding good-by
to the gray Precambrian world and crossing the great lake
into a new land—a flat, monotonous country of scrub timber that is really a continuation of the Alberta-Saskatche-
wan prairie. In the heart of this forest mat, a tiny rent was
visible. Here were the faint beginnings of a new town: two
short streets bisected by two short avenues, hacked from
the forest and lined with a neat file of little white bungalows, with bright nasturtium borders and barbered lawns
of velvet green. This was Pine Point, a community cut off
from the world. There is no road leading to it, and no railroad. There isn't even a scheduled air service. But for the
space of a city block Pine Point has the look of suburbia.

It is controlled by Consolidated Mining and Smelting,
which holds about three quarters of the stock of Pine Point
Mines. The remainder, as might be expected, is largely
held by Thayer Lindsley's Frobisher Ltd.

I stayed overnight at Pine Point as a guest of Mr. and
Mrs. Larry Driver, who live in one of the neat bungalows
lining an avenue cut from the forest. A man blindfolded
and dropped into Mrs. Driver's kitchen might easily have
believed himself to be in Toronto or Vancouver. She had a
built-in sink and running water, an electric washing-
machine and refrigerator, a gas stove, and most of the
appliances that go with planned kitchens. In the living-
room there was a new chesterfield suite, a blond coffee-
table, a combination record-player and radio. All these
furnishings were supplied by the company, which operated its own generating system, imported tankfuls of gas,
and favored its executives with most of the amenities of
civilized life. Mrs. Driver had only one complaint: the
Pine Point Ladies' Snowshoe Club, of which she was presi-

dent, had only one other member, the small daughter of Don Douglas, the mine manager.

The following day Douglas and I wandered about the property, talking about the possibilities of Pine Point. The Pine Point ore belt is similar, and perhaps equal in richness, to the great Tri-State ore belt in the United States. The ore bodies run for thirty-six miles in a strip three miles wide. A cautious estimate sets the potential at one hundred and twenty million tons of ore. (It is undoubtedly far greater than this.) The grade is good—about eleven per cent for lead and zinc combined—and much of it can be mined by the relatively inexpensive open-cut process. I remembered what an executive of the Con mine in Yellowknife had said: "This could be the biggest metal discovery on the continent in the past hundred years."

The gold country was full of brave talk about Pine Point, for this forestland holds the key to the development of the north. If the company goes ahead with a mine, it will mean a railroad in from Grimshaw, in the Peace River country—the first into the Northwest Territories. It will probably mean a new power development to supply a smelter at Pine Point. It could mean a town of five or ten thousand. One is actually surveyed now, and the neat little cottages, poking their heads so incongruously out of the wilderness, are the core of it. Once again the familiar predictions can be heard in the north, the same predictions that were made a generation ago about a smelter, a railroad, and a new boom town.

But it may be years before the company decides to develop the vast ore belt on Great Slave Lake. Nobody is sure that, even with this prodigious amount of ore, it will yet be practical to develop it so far north. Don Douglas and I walked past the rotting log cabins and bunkhouses and the discarded machinery and drilling equipment of an earlier generation on Pine Point. Here, cheek by jowl with the neat electrically powered company homes, was another northern ghost town. Here, too, amid a feast of minerals, were the familiar signs of famine.

3 | **River Country**

The old town of Fort Smith was baking in the summer sun and choking in the summer dust when I flew south from Great Slave Lake to pick up a tugboat on the Slave River. Black-braided Indian women, fat and kerchiefed, waddled slowly past the Hudson's Bay compound, their bulky silhouettes in gaudy relief against the backdrop of whitewashed logs. Down on the river, under the high clay banks, the fat little barges were being stacked with cargo for the river ports downstream. Not far away on the shore, old, abandoned stern-wheelers rotted. Squatting along the river line were warehouses stocked with supplies (beer for Yellowknife's tavern, cyanide for Yellowknife's mines). A glossy new Beaver plane, tethered to the beach, was being crammed with buffalo meat to be taken to a group of starving and primitive inland Eskimos, far out on the Barrens. Max Ward's Otter, loaded with live beaver to stock preserves in Saskatchewan, rose from the water and slipped quickly over the horizon.

The Rapids of the Drowned, coursing angrily past the settlement, sang their harsh song. A yellow dog, part husky, scrambled up through the willows, his tongue dripping from his mouth, and sank gratefully into the shade. A ghost of a breeze whispered its way down the river valley and briefly rippled the orange heads of a sea of California poppies behind the schoolhouse. A cabin door creaked open, and the oldest of the old-timers, John LaBine, stood framed in the portal, a pudgy figure in open shirt and shapeless trousers, who chose to live here alone, far from those high towers of finance where his millionaire brothers, Gilbert and Charles, move easily through the fiscal labyrinth of company mergers and stock issues.

Thus Fort Smith in August. It is the capital of the Northwest Territories, an old town, lying just north of the Alberta border, named for Donald Smith, one of the founders of the Canadian Pacific Railway. Its big, square, log buildings cast the shadow of history across it, for they date from an earlier century, when Fort Smith was the anchor point on the famous canoe portage around the rapids of the Slave—a barrier of white water where the river drops one hundred and nine feet in sixteen miles.

Here the past and the present rambled side by side. High above the town came the rasping drone of Associated Airways helicopters. One of them had just returned from a journey through Wood Buffalo Park, the great preserve where twenty thousand bison, the largest herd in existence, enjoy government protection. A mammalogist, leaning from the hovering machine, had been squirting thousands of the animals with yellow paint from a small fireman's pump in order to help chart the animals' migratory habits. Another helicopter pilot had performed an equally valuable service: he had discovered in the park the long-sought nesting grounds of that huge and almost extinct bird, the whooping crane. Other helicopters were back from the Nahanni Valley, to the northwest, where oil companies are now seeking petroleum.

I went into Fort Smith's only hotel (run by the Hudson's Bay Company), and ordered a buffalo steak for dinner. It was tough but palatable. The government markets about a hundred and fifty thousand pounds of meat a year to the Bay, the missions, and the Department of Indian Affairs. By selling buffalo, and reindeer, the government hopes to conserve the ever-dwindling numbers of caribou and moose. There are close to twenty thousand bison in the park now, and it would be quite possible to put a million pounds of meat on the Edmonton market every year, but this has never been done for fear of the outcry that would come from Alberta's beef ranchers.

The key to the development of the north is cheap transportation, and I had come here to the upper river country to find out why it wasn't cheaper. Fort Smith is the key point on the great water highway that flows north for sixteen hundred miles from the end of steel at Fort McMurray, Alberta, to Tuktuk on the Arctic Ocean. From McMurray the freight boats slip north down the Athabasca River to Lake Athabasca and then across the lake and into the Slave River, which runs between Athabasca and Great Slave Lake. Fort Smith is halfway down this river at the head of the long series of rapids that make the Slave impassable for sixteen miles. There are the Grande Rapids and the Boiler Rapids and the Pelican Rapids (so named because pelicans have for centuries nested on the inaccessible island in the center of the boiling water, where no one can disturb them). And finally there are the Rapids of the Drowned.

Around these rapids one of the most famous roads in the northwest pokes its way through the wilderness. Long before the white man's day the Indians were portaging their canoes along a thin trail in the forest. The trail has long since become a road running between Fort Fitzgerald, where one set of boats unloads its cargo, and north to Fort Smith, where a new set reloads it again. Between Edmonton and Fort Smith the freight is handled nine times, which explains why a nickel bottle of soda pop can cost thirty-five cents halfway down the river.

The twenty-five-mile portage road along which the trucks rumble from Fitzgerald to Smith is surely among the most maddening in the world. Anyone traveling it can quickly understand why freight rates are high along the Mackenzie. The road is built on glacial silt. In dry weather it is smothered under three or four inches of dust as fine as talcum powder, which exerts such a pull on the trucks that they must travel in low gear as if climbing a ten per cent grade. As fast as the graders scrape their way to hard bottom, the dust returns. Finally the graders break through into soft sand. When the rains come, the road is transformed into a lacework of potholes. As the rain increases, the dust turns to mud and the road becomes a skein of ruts. Over the years the thoroughfare has been scraped and shaved and gnawed away to a level well below that of the surrounding countryside, so that each spring it is more like a canal. Trucks with a normal life of ten years expire in five under these conditions. In wet weather, when the road is a river of mud, or in dry weather, when it's ankle-deep in dust, it takes a good two and a half hours to drive its twenty-five miles.

Ludicrous as it may sound, there is not one road alone to keep up between Fort Smith and Fort Fitzgerald, but two. One is operated by the Northern Transportation Company for its supply trucks. The other is operated by the Hudson's Bay Company. The twin roads run almost side by side along the river, and both are maintained at heavy expense. Thus far the two companies have not felt able to operate a mutual thoroughfare.

The story of the two roads goes back to the days of Mickey Ryan, the tough little Irishman who turned the ancient portage trail, over which the Red River oxcarts had once rumbled, into a motor road. Mickey, a former boxer, came north in 1914 with his brother Pat, a onetime saloon bouncer and circus blacksmith. The two brothers bought touring cars, got a Hudson's Bay contract, and set about turning the long portage into a motor road. In those days the Hudson's Bay operated common carriers on the river, and almost all the freight shipped into the country came aboard their stern-wheelers. Thus Ryan was able to make a fortune and run his toll road unchallenged until the 1930's, when rival transportation companies came on the scene.

The first brush came with Wop May, the bush pilot, and a partner who had started a transport company in order to move gas to caches along the river. Ryan wanted cash on the barrel to transport one hundred tons of supplies over his portage route at one dollar and seventy-five cents a hundredweight. May and his partner got so angry that they started the country's first airlift and moved the entire shipment over the portage in two old Junkers airplanes.

The second setback presented itself in the person of another stubborn Irish transportation man, named Doyle. Ryan wouldn't let Doyle run a single truck over his road, so Doyle swore he'd build his own. The threat was quite in character. Doyle was an irascible man who occasionally felt that the whole world, animate and inanimate, was against him. Once, at this delicate time, when he couldn't complete a call on the Fort Smith telephone, he slammed down the receiver. "Everybody's buggin' me!" he roared. "Even the goddam telephones!" Whereupon he bulldozed through a tote road next to the Ryans' in sixteen days. The

Ryan brothers tried to stop him by leasing the surrounding land, but they were too late. Doyle's first truckload of supplies got through to Smith from Fitzgerald in six weeks, and the freight rate dropped to thirty-five cents a hundredweight.

Ryan, grown wealthy through his interest in Tom Payne's Yellowknife discovery, has left the country, and so has Doyle, but the two roads still run side by side. The Hudson's Bay bought the Ryan road. The Northern Transportation Company maintains the Doyle road. NTC also operates twenty tugboats and sixty-eight barges over the 2,363 miles of waterways on the Athabasca, Slave, Bear and Mackenzie rivers and on the three great northern lakes.

In point of fact, the bulk of the transportation in the Mackenzie Valley is socialized, though the word is never mentioned. The Northern Transportation Company is government-owned and operated. The company grew out of the original Wop May firm, which Gilbert LaBine purchased in 1936 in order to freight supplies for his radium mine. When the government took over the mine during the war, it got the transportation company as well.

The day following my arrival at Fort Smith, I boarded one of the Northern Transportation tugs, which was heading down the Slave River toward the great lake, then into the Mackenzie and on to the Arctic, 1,623 river miles north of the Alberta border. It is the presence of this great river system, draining one fifth of the land mass of Canada, that has made possible the colonization of the western north. Without it the country would be quite different, for the river and the valley affect climate and growth as much as they affect movement. The district of Keewatin, to the east, is not drained by any great river and, as a result, is a virtually unexplored, unmapped, unknown country harboring only a handful of whites and a few natives. The vast bulk of the population of the north lives along two rivers: the Yukon and the Mackenzie. When comparisons are made between Canada and Russia, people forget that the Russian north has five huge rivers to Canada's two.

And now, with the incense of the poplar in my nostrils, I was following the twists and turns of the great highway that opened the north. For the most part the scenery along the Mackenzie system is neither so lively nor so varied as that of my native Yukon. The banks are generally low and the country flat and featureless. Indeed, if the annual rainfall were only a fraction less, there would be no trees, and this broad basin would be part of the grassy prairie that stops some hundreds of miles to the south.

But if the land is monotonous, its story is not, for history has moved down this river. Before the stubby little tugboats chugged north, the romantic stern-wheelers plied its waters, alive with people and rigged like floating palaces, their white plumes of wood smoke a signal for celebrations at every river town. Before the stern-wheelers, the pointed prows of the trading companies' York boats nosed downstream to return at season's end, gross with furs. Before the York boats, the silent birchbark canoes of the explorers slipped through the dark waters.

This is the river down which a bold and determined young Highlander from the Hebrides came paddling almost two centuries ago, driving himself and driving his Indians, refusing to admit of obstacles, laughing at stories of winged monsters and ghosts and impassable waterfalls, scoffing at predictions that the trip would take so many years that old age would overtake him before its end— paddling, ever paddling, down the great mysterious watercourse that led endlessly north, with each curve hiding the unknown and the river leading God knew where. And others were to follow Mackenzie, leaving their names on forts and campsites, lakes and rivers, until the map became an honor roll of the men who opened the land.

Entire towns and villages, entire mines, entire army camps have moved down the wet highway of the Mackenzie and its tributaries. Yellowknife came down the river. So did Port Radium and Norman Wells. The new town of Aklavik was coming down it now—two hundred and sixty-five thousand board feet of it on the barge ahead of us.

The name of the tug had the ring of the north to it. She was the *Radium Yellowknife,* and the cargo lists of the five barges lashed to her prow read like a northern roll call: sulphur for the leaching plant at Port Radium, whisky for the oilmen at Norman Wells, a tractor for the reindeer station on the delta, speedboats for the Mounties at Arctic Red, fertilizer for the Oblates' potato patch at Good Hope, and—though this was only August—a crate of Christmas parcels for the family of John Gilbey, who runs the experimental farm at Fort Simpson.

The country unrolled past us, vast, empty, mysterious. It was the best month for travel in the north. The flies and mosquitoes were at an end, the temperature was in the mid-seventies, the river was comfortably high, and the skies were speckled with sandhill cranes, whose cries sound like the squeaking of rusty gates. It was pleasant to sit on deck and talk to Captain W. S. Hall, the superintendent of operations for the company—my cabin mate on this voyage—and Captain Brinkie Sveinson, an Icelander from Gimli, Manitoba, who was the master of the *Radium Yellowknife.*

"This is the damnedest kind of operation," Captain Hall was saying. "The trouble is we've got to build boats that will do two different kinds of job. We operate in three big lakes, so we ought to build lake boats; but those same boats have to operate in rivers so swift and shallow that the water—in the Athabasca, for instance—often drops below thirty inches. We've got to drop the weight to get them through, and even then they chew up the sandbars. The result is a compromise, of course.

"Look at the Green Island Rapids. The water was so low there last year the *Radium King* scraped her bottom every time she went through. We had to change her propellers after every trip. And yet these little boats get onto those lakes and what happens? They bob about like corks. To keep the weight down and the draft low we can't put anything heavier than a fourteen-hundred-horsepower engine in any of them. But the wind was so strong in Great Slave last year, as Brinkie here can tell you, that both engines couldn't turn this *Radium Yellowknife* around."

Captain Sveinson nodded in agreement and then began to tell the story of one terrible storm on Great Slave Lake:

"It was when I was skipper on the little old *Radium Express*," he said. "Not the new one—she's a pleasure yacht —but the old one. You had to see that to believe it. Well, we was really into it, tossing and pitching there so bad that the oil heater in the pilothouse ripped loose and smashed up on the floor. Albert, my first mate, he was sick as a dog. There was nothing to hang on to, and there he was, being knocked about from wall to wall and back again. Every once in a while he came past me and I'd grab him and sort of prop him up a bit.

"'Brinkie, kill me and have done with it!' he cries out over the storm.

"'Lie down on the floor, man,' I tell him.

"'But it's thick with oil,' says Albert.

"'What do you care?' I tell him. 'You're going to die anyway.'

"Well, at this point Albert he looks out of the window and shouts that the barge is going.

" 'Get that no-good deckhand and try and make her fast!' I tell him.

" 'He's sick like me,' says Albert.

" 'Well, get him anyways,' I tell him.

"Well, sir, you ought to see Albert. He grabs the hand, he pulls and pushes him onto the barge, he slaps him and he socks him. He props him up and the hand falls down. Albert pulls him up again and he falls down again. He finally did get him onto his feet, but the hand never was much good. But by this time Albert wasn't sick any more and we saved that barge."

There was no storm on Great Slave the following day, when we crossed it. Morning found us alone in an empty world of water, a tiny dot on the slate-gray expanse of the lake, whose unruffled surface stretched off, ocean-like, to the horizon. Once again the silence of the empty land hemmed us in, and the only sounds were the regular chug-chug of the engine and the insistent crackle of the radio set in the wireless room. The company sends out regular weather reports on schedule to its twenty tugboats, and these floating radio stations save it thousands of dollars.

Brinkie Sveinson had his fingers crossed. If the weather held he might be able to navigate the lake without unlashing the five barges from the prow of the tug. In heavy weather the boats cannot push cargo, for the barges up in front begin to buckle and heave and break away, and hours are wasted stringing them out on half a mile of cable behind the vessel.

We were crossing the most ticklish section of the lake: a long stretch of open water off the south shore which every vessel must navigate in order to reach the Mackenzie from the Slave. Here for a hundred miles there is neither shelter nor harbor, and each boat must take its chances with the elements. In the days of the stern-wheelers, vessels often had to wait at the delta of the Slave for as long as seventeen days before they could chance running this gantlet.

"That's because they had to push their barges," Captain Hall explained. "They'd force all the power possible out of the furnaces in order to get across that stretch as fast as possible. You could almost see the cordwood coming out of the stacks. Nowadays we can go out on tow, of course, and don't need to wait at all."

"I had a close one last summer, all the same, just this side of Burnt Island," Captain Sveinson said. "A real bad storm come up and I made a run to get in the lee of the island to wait her out. Well, sir, there was a reef there marked on the charts and there was nothing I could do about it. The wind was blowing so hard the engines wouldn't turn the boat and we were being forced right onto the reef. I just had to let her go and, you know, we went through. There was a gap in that reef nobody ever heard of before and we slipped right over it."

Burnt Island is more an anchorage than a harbor, but it is the only one between the Slave Delta and the start of the Mackenzie River.

"There's an awful lot of stuff gone to the bottom there trying to make that island," Captain Hall said. "I know of one good yacht down under there—a cabin cruiser. And there's an entire bargeload of tractors down there, too, from the old Canol pipeline days. The boat got caught in a big blow and the barge began to take water. She headed for harbor at Burnt Island. As he swung her in, the tractors dribbled off that barge one by one. There's salvage-company divers up there now trying to haul them out."

The lake remained calm. At the mouth of the Hay River there was some swell for a couple of hours—enough to make the cook seasick—but this was the only suggestion of trouble. It took us two days to cross Great Slave, traveling up the curving arm that leads almost due west into the Mackenzie. We reached the start of the great river early in the morning. The lake and the river fused imperceptibly in an island-studded bay; the land, shaggy with conifers, stretched off flatly into the blue haze of summer.

Down the river we chugged, along the braided pathway of islands and channels. The Indian pilot swung the boat back and forth from bank to bank, avoiding the glassy surfaces of the river where the shoals lie and looking for the dark patches that mark the deeper water. Occasionally a white buoy, bobbing out of the river, beckoned the boat into the proper course.

"I went down to the Mississippi last year to have a look at the operation there," Captain Hall was saying. "What a picnic they've got! No guess or by God there, everything marked and labeled. Here we've got sixteen hundred and twenty-three miles of Mackenzie River and only eighteen of them have channel markings."

We were in the Providence Rapids, and the tug was zigzagging across the river to follow the channel.

"When the water's really bad, we've got to take the barges through here one at a time," Captain Hall said. "That uses up a lot of time and helps keep the freight rates up. The Yanks had a lot of trouble here in the Canol days. They didn't know the river, of course, and they lost dozens of barges. It was an almost continual salvage operation."

We passed through the white water and docked at Fort Providence. "Dock" is not the proper word. There are few wharves on the Mackenzie, for the water can rise or drop as much as one hundred and fifty feet in a season. The tug simply nosed into the bank; the deckhands threw some planks over the side and began to unload the freight. The little town sat above us—a carbon copy of all the other toy towns along the river. Not far away was a huddle of wartime buildings, all empty, and the remnants of an airport hacked out of the bush. Like the other towns, Providence had been hit badly by the decline in the fur market. There was no activity except at the river, where a few Indians wandered down to watch the unloading of the boat.

I had decided to travel as far as Fort Simpson, which we reached the following morning. It is the oldest post continuously occupied on the Mackenzie River, and was established in 1804 by the Northwest Company. It has been called the Athens of the North because of its library, to which the chief factor, J. S. Camsell, devoted eighteen years of his life in the last century. There are hundreds of leather-bound volumes here, mainly classical, philosophical, and biographical.

Here is the loveliest setting on the Mackenzie. The river is a mile wide at this point, and you can stand on the bank and look upstream for twelve miles. The town is on an island, perched high above the river not far from the point where the Liard sweeps down from the rolling mountains. Here at Simpson the two streams, one blue, the other yellow, come together and run side by side for one hundred and fifty miles until they finally mingle. Mackenzie noticed the phenomenon when he passed the mouth of this "River of the Mountains," as he called it—and thought it quite an extraordinary sight.

I stood on the bank and watched the little tugboat head out again to mid-river and chug around the bend on the long trip north to the Arctic Ocean. The delays and the storms, the rapids and the portages help explain why, at these ports, round steak worth fifty-eight cents a pound in Edmonton was selling for a dollar five, why beef liver was a dollar and a quarter instead of forty-three cents, why twenty-five cents' worth of tomatoes went for sixty.

The high freight costs explain, too, why the Mackenzie and Liard valleys haven't yet been developed into rich farming areas, as the similar Peace River country to the south has been. There is farmland here, but I met only one farmer. I ran into him on the street in Fort Simpson and he could have been nothing else—a tall, lanky man, with a long, equine face, wearing a pair of loose-fitting blue overalls and a straw hat. His name was Fostner Browning, and his farm was eighty-six miles upriver. He was on his way to the Signal Corps staff house, where I was staying, to sell some potatoes.

"I've been farming up here since 1927," he told me, "and I've never known a crop failure. I've been growing alfalfa for ten years, and I get two cuts off it a year. My big crop is potatoes, but one summer I ripened eighty watermelons. I've got eight kids and I've got thirty-six head of cattle. One winter I had seven calves born, all in sixty-eight-below weather, and they all lived. Some years when things are good I gross four thousand dollars from my farm. But I got a sawmill, too, in case the farm doesn't pay."

On my first evening in Fort Simpson I walked down along the river road and through the poplars to the federal government experimental farm, which had been established seven years before by John Gilbey, a chipper English horticulturist. Here, not far from the older shacks and weed-grown cabins, was a neat house of peeled and polished logs, and a billiard-table lawn bordered by shrubs and perennials.

In spite of a growing-season of only eighty-four frost-free days, Gilbey manages to raise just about everything that thrives on the prairies. Between June and August, lilacs, honeysuckle, and spiræa bloom in his garden along with peonies and delphiniums. Crabapples had wintered successfully the year before, he told me, though the mercury scarcely rose above zero from December to Easter. He had good crops of corn and tomatoes three years out of five, and cucumbers almost every year. Similar conditions exist all down the river almost as far as Fort Good Hope on the Arctic Circle.

Gilbey thinks that agriculture is a useful alternative to the fur trade, but he knows the change-over will be a slow and painful one.

"It's the old story of moving a society from hunting-barter stage to an agricultural," he said as we sat and talked in the big home that he and his assistants had built themselves of peeled logs. "Agriculture is feasible here, but it's hard to make people realize that they will have to use every possible trick to defeat nature. Actually the growing-conditions here aren't much different from what they are at Lethbridge, in southern Alberta. Our big problem isn't the cold or the snow—it's drought. We've got only a twelve-inch precipitation, and that means we've simply got to irrigate."

I walked around his farm the next day and looked at the corn and the tomatoes and the cantaloupes and the long, neat rows of wheat—dozens of varieties all being tested for northern conditions. Gazing at this beautifully manicured land and studying some of the isolated statistics about northern vegetable growth, I could not help being caught up briefly in the same violent optimism newcomers so often feel for northern agriculture. The facts can be so startling—and so deceptive! Horses have thrived north of the sixtieth parallel; winter eggs have been laid by domestic fowl at Fort Providence; green feed has been grown on the edges of the Thelon Game Sanctuary, far out on the tundra; potatoes the size of hen's eggs have been harvested at Aklavik; rhubarb has flourished on the delta; vegetables have matured at Coppermine, and cabbages weighing eight pounds stripped have been harvested at Thunder River—1,277 miles north of the United States border.

Does this mean that the Canadian north is the farmer's

paradise that some enthusiasts have suggested? Hardly. No one knows for certain how much arable alluvial silt lies along the Mackenzie and Liard basins, but an informed guess places it at about a million acres. This sounds like a lot, but it isn't, in a land so vast as the north. Moreover, it has the disadvantage of being scattered in isolated pockets ranging from fifteen-acre patches to fifteen hundred acres. In these areas there's no doubt that mountains of potatoes could be raised, but there is little use farming on a larger scale than the country itself can support. At the moment it simply isn't practical to export a pound of rhubarb from the north, and no one can foresee the day when it will be.

The function of the northern farmer in the future will be to feed himself and his fellows. At the moment this is not being done. The Signals kitchen, where I ate my meals in Fort Simpson, was buying some of its potatoes from Fostner Browning, but the rest were imported all the way from California at great expense. The army must do this because no farmer will contract to supply it all the year round. The mines, the government, and the hospitals all import green foodstuffs from the Outside for the same reason. The north is not yet sufficiently heavily populated for anything else to be feasible. But as the population grows—and the growth will be painfully slow—farming for profit will become more practical along the Mackenzie Valley, and the little tugs that push their barges down the river will not need to bring eggs and tomatoes on the long, tortuous rail, river, lake, and portage route from Edmonton.

4 | Barren Country

I flew back from Fort Simpson to Yellowknife, for I now wanted to fly northeast into the empty land that has haunted all men who come to the north—the treeless tundra that Samuel Hearne named the Barren Grounds. Here, if anywhere, lie all the majesty and mystery of the north, for the stillness of death hangs over these Barrens, and since Hearne's day they have not failed to put men in awe.

The bulk of the tundra country lies between the wooded Mackenzie Valley on the west and Hudson Bay on the east, but the tips of the Yukon, Quebec, and Labrador are also treeless, as are all the Arctic islands. The Arctic desert stretches for a million square miles across the top of Canada, sweeping down from the Mackenzie delta to within a few miles of Churchill in an immense curving diagonal. Barren it looks, but it is not quite so barren as it seems. By the most recent scientific count, the tundra supports seventy-six species of mammal, from the tiny lemming to the lumbering muskox; twenty-two species of bird, from the whistling swan to the snow goose; and four hundred and seventy-four flowering plants and ferns, from the rhubarb-flavored sorrel grass the Eskimos nibble to the white heather, whose tiny stem, no thicker than a man's finger, can be a hundred years old.

I set out from Yellowknife to see the Barrens in Max Ward's new Beaver aircraft, piloted by Harry Taylor, a neat young man who had once flown in the mountains of British Columbia with Russ Baker. Like the Mounties, the missionaries, and the traders, the pilots roam the north like gypsies, giving the country an unexpected homogeneity.

Taylor whisked the Beaver off the lake surface and climbed steeply into the sky, then set its nose over the northeast. The Beaver is perhaps the most remarkable bush plane yet designed. The de Havilland company built it at the end of World War II, and the designers were the country's best-known bush pilots. Before drawing the plans, the company sent careful questionnaires to fifty of them—from the legendary Wop May to the veteran Punch Dickins (who had become de Havilland sales director). The result was a plane that can carry a ton, land on a dime, and fly at eighty below or one hundred and forty above. It has become far more than a bush plane. It's used over the African veldt, the South American jungles, Malayan rubber plantations, and New Zealand sheep farms. The U.S. Army used it in Korea. It is, in short, the answer to a pilot's dream.

We had several stops to make in the Beaver along the edges of the great lake before we reached the Barrens.

We stopped at an abandoned gold mine—one of a dozen or so whose rotting headframes can be seen poking out of the scrub timber in the Yellowknife area—and here we dropped off a small Indian boy and his dog.

We stopped at a prospective gold mine—a bunkhouse and messhall, a dock and some shacks, a few men doing a little development work, and a group of small Indian children playing cowboys and Indians in the woods. All of them wanted to be cowboys.

We stopped at a fishing camp for millionaires run by a Wyoming guide. The millionaires could be seen peering from their tents or sitting idly on the shore in checkered shirts and bush pants, looking like ordinary people. They pay four hundred and fifty dollars a week to fish in waters where the trout are so big and plentiful that anything under thirty pounds is thrown back. The fish stories here are all true, but it is doubtful if anyone believes the declamatory millionaires when they return to Texas and Oklahoma.

By now we had reached the eastern edge of the great lake. Here the flat scenery changed and became more rugged, the cliffs falling sheer a hundred feet or more to the water's edge, the sunken islands emerald green just beneath the surface of the black water, the blue mists enfolding the hills in a tattered embrace. Below us lay Fort Reliance, on the very eastern tip of the lake. It might just as easily have been named Fort Isolation. The only reason for its existence is its position as gateway to the Barrens, the funnel through which trapper, hunter, scientist, and explorer must pass on their way to the tundra.

There are only six permanent residents at Fort Reliance: two Mounties, three signalmen, and a cook, an enormous Dutchman named Pete Kuypers.

"Have you got my beer?" the cook asked, running down along the wet dock as the Beaver edged into the shore.

"Gee, Pete, I forgot it," said Harry Taylor, winking at the others.

"Wait a minute," said the cook, clambering about the baggage. "There's a case!"

"Sorry, Pete," said Taylor; "that's for one of the other boys."

"Oh now, Harry," the cook said, "why would you want to do a thing like that?"

"Maybe you drink too much beer, Pete," Taylor said. "You don't want to spend all your money on beer."

The cook gave Taylor a look of pure astonishment. He

was silent for a moment. Then he began to deliver a short eulogy on beer.

"Look, Harry," he said, "why wouldn't I want to spend my money on beer? Take a look at me. I got no wife. I'm single. I got a good job. Why should I save those little dollar bills? Why should I give 'em all to a bunch of doctors and lawyers? Some men they want women. Some men want a big car. Some want an aeroplane. Me—I just want a bottle beer. I'm as independent as a hog on ice. If I can't get a bottle beer, then I go somewheres else. I take two little bottles and I put 'em in the big 'frige up there. Then, sometime when I'm feeling low, maybe, I open that 'frige door a sliver or so and I see those couple bottles. It gives me a lift to see them there. It makes me feel good. I *like* beer. What else have I got? I work here six months and I make a stake. Then I go into Yellowknife, see two, three friends for a couple weeks. After that it's back into the bush for me for another six months. You know how it is, Harry."

"Okay, Pete," said the pilot with a grin. "There's your beer."

The cook put the beer under his arm and headed back to the Signals compound. Taylor and I walked up to the Mounted Police cabin, where the constable, a Calgary boy who has seen no vessel bigger than a police speedboat, was working away on a full-rigged scale model of the U.S.S. *Constitution*.

"You got to do something to fill in time," the constable said. "I decided to build boats. There's not much to do here. Patrols in the winter—two hundred and eighty miles or so. Three thefts a year ago. Nothing else since. Fishing for the dogs. We take about eighteen thousand pounds of trout a year out of the lake each fall. You get tired of reading. I decided to build boats. There's the first one I built—Captain Bligh's ship, the *Bounty*. Everything works

351

on her. I had to get out an encyclopedia to figure out the rigging. This *Old Ironsides* here is tougher. Come and see the dogs."

We walked outside and were instantly surrounded by half a dozen woolly puppies.

"They'll make a fine team in another year," the Mountie said. "Their mother died, you know, and we brought them up ourselves. We put a finger from a rubber glove on the end of a beer bottle and fed them a proper formula. We sterilized the bottles and burped the puppies over our shoulder just like real babies. We all got quite a kick out of it. It was something to do, you know. There are damn few trappers coming this way now. Jack Knox, one of the real old-timers who used to go out every year on the Barrens, he's gone now. He's had enough. Last time he was lost for eighty-six days out there and the RCAF had to go in for him. He was crowding seventy. He won't go back in again."

"Well," Taylor said, "we ought to be on our way."

"You going out to the muskox camp?" the constable asked.

"We're heading that way."

"How's chances for a lift?"

"Sure, come on," Taylor said.

Again we rose from the waters and headed off toward Artillery Lake and the tundra beyond, where a group of scientists were trying to capture baby muskox alive, for study. On Harry Taylor's big map the country looked like an immense sodden field, speckled by a million lakes and rivers—a reminder that easily half of the Canadian north is fresh water, not land. In the names of these lakes and rivers, hills and mountains, the history and character of the country is written.

Here were names that hinted at stories yet untold: Coldblow Lake and Dogmeat Lake and Hanging Ice Lake,

Starvation Lake and Obstruction Rapids and the Hoarfrost and the Snowdrift rivers.

Here were others given by men roaming a womanless land: Mary Frances Lake and Aileen Lake and Margaret Lake and Helen Falls. And here was the Lake of the Enemy. Who were the enemy and what happened on this lake to give it such a name?

Here were lakes named for the fauna of the country: Wolf Lake and Fox Lake, Ptarmigan Lake and Lynx Lake, Wolverine Lake, Whitefish Lake, and Muskox Lake along with Caribou Narrows and Elk River.

Here were the names of the explorers, the adventurers, and the bush pilots, all graven on the map: Tyrrell Lake, Back River, Hanbury Point, Camsell River, Critchell-Bullock Arm, Douglas Lake, LaBine Point, Lindsley Lake, St. Paul Point, Calder Lake, Breadner Lake, Cruickshank Lake, Wopmay Lake. And here were lakes named for the three Barren Land trappers: D'Aoust Lake, Murphy Lake, and Knox Lake.

Here, mingled with Murky Channel, Red Cliff Island, and Brokenoff Mountain, were the tracks of the *voyageurs:* Nez-Croche River, Lake Sans-Disant, Lake Capot-Blanc, and Lake Tete d'Ours; and with them the tracks of the natives, names harsh with the gutturals of the Athapascan tongue: Sultaza Lake, Nonacho Lake, Kahochella Peninsula, Pekanatui Point, and Nodinka Narrows.

Below us the land stretched off, looking just like the map with the printed names removed, a flat, empty world of lakes. We had left the thick forest belt of the taiga behind us to the south and were flying over the thin sub-Arctic forest, "the land of little sticks" as the Indians call it—the dividing line between taiga and tundra. In the distance we could see the trees thinning out. The poplars vanished first, then the jackpine, then the tamarack. Now we were over the tree line, the natural fence that stretches northwest from James Bay to the tip of the Yukon. Suddenly there was nothing: only an endless rolling desert of brown suède, stippled with the inevitable lakes. For a million square miles the north rolls on like this, and in all this empty land there are only ten thousand humans, almost all of them natives.

The rivers below us looked more like thin lakes, the water in them scarcely moving. Occasionally an unexpected waterfall connected one lake with another, but otherwise the water was stagnant, for there is very little drainage on the tundra. The land has yet to recover from the havoc wrought by the ebb and flow of the ice sheets. The rampaging glaciers threw the ancient drainage pattern completely out of kilter, diking lakes with mounds of rubble, gouging out new rivers, choking up others, and scattering debris from one end of the north to the other until the whole lake-and-river system was topsy-turvy. Now the water sits in shallow hollows, imprisoned by a granite-hard floor of permafrost. There is no more rain here than on any desert, but because of the climate there is little evaporation, either. If the permafrost ever melts, the water will vanish. Then the Barrens will become a gray expanse of desert rock and sand.

This may happen some day, for the north has been slowly and mysteriously warming up. The change has been going on since the turn of the century and has accelerated since 1930. The permafrost line has been creeping north, at the rate of perhaps sixty miles a century, and so has the tree line. The change has been most evident off the once forbidding west coast of Greenland, where cod and halibut are appearing for the first time since the mid-nineteenth century. But the warm-up seems to be general throughout the north. Varieties of animals and fish are being found hundreds of miles farther north than ever before. Eskimo hunters who once caught only the white fox are now beginning to trap the red fox—an animal previously unknown so far north. Moose have ventured beyond the tree line onto the Barrens, and so have the white-tailed deer. The last three decades have been marked by a general recession of glaciers and a rise in air and sea temperatures. There is less Arctic drift ice—a phenomenon that has made shipping far less hazardous. The seasons seem to be changing in length. Forty years ago the annual dog-team patrol along the James Bay shoreline from Moose Factory to Rupert House used to be made in May. Now it must leave a month earlier because the snow vanishes. What is causing the warm-up? Is it permanent or temporary? Will it continue or will a new era of cold begin? No one can say, for the climate itself must be numbered among the northern mysteries.

Below us, in the land of the Snowdrift River, the tundra rolled on, majestic in its monotony. The words of Warburton Pike, a big-game hunter, and one of the earliest of the tundra explorers, came back to me: "There is nothing striking or grand in the scenery, no big mountains or waterfalls, but a monotonous snow-covered waste, without tree or scrub, rarely trodden by the foot of a wandering Indian. A deathly stillness hangs over all, and the oppressive loneliness weighs upon the spectator until he is glad to shout aloud to break the awful spell of solitude." Those words were written more than sixty years ago, but the land is exactly as it was when Pike crossed the tundra. With the exceptions noted, nothing has changed, for this is a land that knows neither erosion by the elements nor encroachment by civilization. The cart tracks left on the tundra of Melville Island by Sir Edward Parry in 1820 were visible to Leopold M'Clintock, who followed his trail thirty-three years later. Hardly a speck of moss had grown over them. It was as if Parry himself were only a few miles away, instead of a generation or more.

The geological history of the north is still graven on the face of the Barrens. The debris left behind by the retreating ice sheet lay strewn across the tundra beneath us. Vast boulder fields, miles across, stretched off in every direction. Cyclopean rocks, dragged to this spot by the glaciers, lay scattered about like lonely colossi. Here was dramatic evidence of the power of moving ice. There are Precambrian boulders weighing several tons on the slopes of the Mackenzie and Rocky Mountains. They have been carried across half the continent, from the shores of Hudson Bay, and hoisted almost four thousand feet by the expanding icecaps.

Moraines of rocky refuse, marking the halts and retreats and jerky readvances of the ice sheets, curved across our line of sight. And then we saw the strangest spectacle of all winding off to the far horizon. It was the bizarre geological formation known as an *esker,* a high ridge of sand and gravel, exactly like a railway embankment, a hundred feet high and a dozen miles or so in length. Some eskers are more than one hundred miles long, and all look uncannily man-made. This one had branches, like a tree, and some of the branches fanned out into hills of pure white sand. The top was flattened by the hoofs of thousands of migrating caribou, who use the eskers as roadways across the Barrens. What caused these snakelike ridges on the tundra? Again, nobody knows for certain, but most scientists believe they are the deposits of sediment made by streams of melt water that flowed in tunnels under the ice in the dying days of the glacial age, when the ice sheets were decaying.

No wonder, then, that the Barrens have always intrigued the human kind. For here is land literally untrodden and here are puzzles yet unsolved. Most of our great Arctic explorers have been haunted by this prehistoric land, though not all of them have understood it. It was across country very like this, though farther to the north, that Franklin and his starving men dragged their heavy sledges, loaded with a fantastic accumulation of bric-a-brac deemed necessary for the subsistence of naval officers, even in tundra conditions: silverware, teakettles, and lightning-conductors, silk handkerchiefs and brass curtain rods, religious books, swords, brushes, button-polishers, and a heavy mahogany writing-desk.

It was across land like this—land, indeed, almost directly below us—that the first white man, Samuel Hearne, came by canoe and moccasin, scratching away in his diary and making his pretty sketches, his imagination fired by the immensity of the Arctic desert, which seemed to have no end. It is a measure of the vastness and forbidding mien of the Barrens that it was a further hundred and twenty years before another white man's moccasins followed in his tracks—those of J. B. Tyrrell, a remarkable geologist who, with his brother, crossed the Barrens by canoe and snowshoe, in 1892 and 1893, his only source of information those same diaries of Hearne's written more than a century before.

No man can fail to be moved by this empty country which has changed not a whit in twenty centuries. Some have been moved to terror by it, some to awe, and some to madness. Some, like John Hornby, have been drunk with the *mystique* of the tundra.

The annals of the north know no more bizarre figure than this wiry, unkempt little Englishman with his matted beard, his long, tangled black locks, and his pinched hawk's face. Hornby was the son of a famous cricketer, a public-school graduate destined for the diplomatic service, but his life was changed when he visited Edmonton in 1903. He became obsessed with the idea of the tundra, and once he visited it, he never left it again except for brief periods—the longest being World War I, during which he won the Military Cross.

Hornby's only desire was to live on the tundra, and his only purpose seemed to be sheer subsistence, for he rarely trapped or hunted or collected scientific information. He thought of the Barrens as his kingdom and he roamed them like an animal, existing in caves or wolf dens and living off the land. His proudest boast was that he could be dropped naked into the heart of the tundra and survive. He shunned the symbols of civilization, and even discarded his dentures on the Barrens. With his single upper incisor he tore at the caribou or wolf meat, which often enough he devoured raw and rotten.

One memorable winter Hornby brought another Englishman north with him, a six-foot two-inch pukka sahib from India, a former cavalry officer named James Critchell-Bullock, who had been invalided to Canada with malaria. The two of them moved far out into the tundra past Artillery Lake, and here they existed for an entire winter, crouched in a cave in an esker, playing chess with hand-whittled men while the wolves howled above the wind across the treeless snows.

One day, so legend has it, Hornby came into Fort Reliance to the police post.

"Bullock is trying to murder me," he told the constable on duty. Then he gave the policeman a sealed letter and vanished again into the Barrens.

The constable read the letter. It was from Bullock. "Hornby is trying to murder me," he had written.

The policeman wearily made a patrol out to the cave, and here he came upon the two half-demented men, wild-eyed, squalid, incredibly filthy, Hornby gnawing on a raw wolf's head, Bullock chewing a caribou's intestine. The policeman shrugged, sighed, and went back to Reliance again. The following spring the two Englishmen emerged alive after walking the entire thousand miles to Hudson Bay.

We were flying over Hornby's country. The caribou were below us, threading their way south in groups of six and seven on their annual trek to the tree line. All through the north I had been hearing the same question, the question that is asked every year at this time: "Where are the caribou? Have you seen the caribou?" For, just as the Mackenzie depends on furs and Yellowknife on gold, the men who roam the Barrens need the caribou. And like the gold and the furs, the caribou are fickle, too. "They are like ghosts," the old Indian saying runs; "they come from nowhere, fill up all the land, then disappear." They may pass the same point several years running. The following year they may not come within a hundred miles of it, so that famine truly follows feast. Why this should be, no one knows, for the coming and going of this naïve, stupid, erratic, and insatiably curious animal is another of the mysteries of the north.

And yet the caribou deserves his place on the back of the Canadian twenty-five-cent piece as much as does the beaver on the Hudson's Bay Company coat of arms. Without the caribou, vast stretches of the Canadian north would be uninhabitable for white men or natives. The caribou has rightly been called a walking department store. The entire animal is edible, from the eyes, which are considered a delicacy, to the half-digested mosses in the stomach, which make a tundra salad. The fur provides blankets, clothing, sleeping-bags, shoes, and upholstery. The scraped skins make kayaks, buckets, tents, drums, and dog harness. The sinews become fish and harpoon lines, drawstrings, thread, and lashing. The bones and antlers are turned into needles, thimbles, arrows, knives, and tools. The marrow and the fat serve as fuel.

When the caribou move, the whole north moves with them. The wolves follow in the wake of the herds, and the white foxes follow the wolves, and the wolverine slinks along behind the white fox, and the ravens fly in croaking flocks overhead. And with them come the Indians, the inland Eskimos and the white trapper. Without the caribou there is nothing, and the Barren Lands are truly barren.

Even as we flew across the tundra, a group of inland Eskimos far to the east at Ennadai Lake were slowly starving because the caribou had not come. They had been existing entirely on flour and water for a month. Only a government plane stocked with provisions saved them from extinction.

We could see the animals now, running in fleet groups of a dozen or more across the worn tundra. Soon, as the caribou moved closer to the trees, the groups would enlarge. The dozens would increase to scores, the scores to hundreds, the hundreds to thousands, and the thousands to hundreds of thousands.

Each August the mysterious movement of the caribou takes place. On the fringes of the Arctic where the herds are grazing—the does together in groups of their own sex, the bucks standing aloof—a shiver of restlessness runs through them and, as if by an unspoken command, every animal begins to follow the call of the blood, south to the tree line. This was what was happening below us now: each animal's nose was pointed the same way—south— and the whole north was moving with them. Soon the land would witness the phenomenon of *la foule*, "the throng"— the caribou moving in thin, endless lines along trails worn four inches deep by constant use, each trail only six inches to a foot wide, and as many as a dozen trails a foot or so apart running parallel to each other. In 1887 a trapper watched just such a line of caribou crossing a frozen lake.

They passed in unbroken stream for fourteen days in a mass packed so tightly that daylight couldn't be seen through the files.

The caribou movement ebbs and flows like a mighty tide. The animals reach the tree line sometime in September. Then, mysteriously, the tide ebbs back to the tundra, so that the animals are scattered all the way from the woods to the Arctic coast. The rutting season comes in late October and lasts for three weeks on the tundra. Then the tide flows back again to the trees, where the caribou winter until the spring, when once again they surge along the familiar trails to the land of the lichen. Why this curious ebb and flow? Is it the flies, maddening them until they flee northward seeking respite? Is it climate driving them toward shelter every fall? Is it diet, making them seek new fields of mosses and lichen? Is it instinct forcing them along ancestral routes? Is it a combination of all these? Or is it some other reason yet undivined? To these questions there is as yet no answer. We are not even sure of the origin of the caribou's name. Does it come from the French *carré bœuf,* meaning "square ox" or from the Algonquin *kalibu,* meaning "scratcher"? (It is the caribou's habit to paw away the snow to reach the mosses beneath.) But one thing is known: like the furs and the minerals, the caribou is a vanishing resource, mined by hunter and trapper and only recently protected in some measure by government regulation. In the old days, when the Eskimo and Indian hunted with bow and arrow, the caribou was on the increase. But the coming of the white man's firearms changed all that. Whalers along the Arctic coast began to consume huge quantities of caribou meat. One ship at Cape Bathurst, in the winter of 1898–9, slaughtered forty thousand pounds. David Thompson, the great explorer and geographer of the North West Company, once saw a single herd of three and a half million animals pass him by. Scientists estimate that by 1900 there were fewer than two million caribou left. The number is now down to three hundred thousand.

The land below us was dotted with caribou, but now a shadow passed over it. Out of the horizon a Barren Lands storm was beginning to blow up, blanketing the country ahead in a dark mist. It soon became apparent that we wouldn't reach the Thelon Game Sanctuary this day. Harry Taylor turned the Beaver about and we flew back to Reliance.

"We'll just have to wait her out, I guess," Harry said as he climbed out of the cabin. "That's one thing about this country. It's a great place for waiting."

And so it is. Nobody rushes in the north, and nobody tries to keep to a set schedule. This is a land of patient men, and the patience breeds a certain optimism. The Eskimo waits for the caribou, and the bush pilot waits for the weather. The trapper waits for furs to come back, the prospector waits for gold to rise. And because the caribou have always come sooner or later, and the weather has always cleared eventually, and the furs and gold have usually risen after a fall, each man waits in hope. Feast always follows famine as surely as famine follows feast.

Gus d'Aoust, the Barren Land trapper, the only one left in this part of the country, was waiting at Fort Reliance when we returned. He was waiting and hoping, too.

"The waiting's the worst this time of year," Gus said. "I'm all itchy to get back onto the Barrens now. I don't much like this sitting."

Gus was fifty-nine years old. He had forgotten his age, but his sister had written a year or so before and reminded him. The tundra had taken its toll of him. His face was lean and drawn from exposure. One eye was gone, and the other weakened by snow-blindness incurred in 1938, the year he first had to eat his dogs on the trail.

In April of that year Gus had stumbled into Reliance from the Barrens after the hardest trip of his life. He had been twenty-seven days on the trail, and the last nine of them had been spent without food or sleep. He was snow-blind. He couldn't face the light or keep his eyes open.

First he'd run out of food. He shot a caribou and ate it raw because there was no wood to build a fire. Then he ran out of shells. He found a caribou slaughtered by the wolves, the meat picked clean from the bones. He cracked the bones and sucked out the marrow. Finally his dogs began to slow down until they came to a dead stop. In a panic he seized an ax and killed two of them. He kept moving, found some timber, and barbecued the dog meat. That kept him alive until he stumbled upon Great Slave Lake and made his way to the police post at Reliance.

None of this had deterred him from a life on the Barrens. Here he was, sixteen years later, preparing to face the tundra once more. His existence is as lonely as a light-keeper's, and far more hazardous. He lives all alone, far from the tree line, slaving from dawn to dark, patrolling his fifty miles of trapline, gathering wood, rustling dog feed, preparing the fur.

At his base camp his home is a log cabin, patched with mud and banked with snow. His furniture is made from peeled birch logs and upholstered in caribou hide. His clothes are caribou hide, too, decorated with the traditional porcupine quills and moosehair rosettes that have been dyed blue with kidney pills bought from the Hudson's Bay Company. Alexander Mackenzie observed the Indians wearing similar decorations when he first entered the north.

Once a week Gus patrols his trapline, depending entirely on his dogs to find the traps buried beneath the shifting snow. As regularly as clockwork the lead dog stops at the trap and Gus removes the fur. On the trapline he lives in caribou-skin tents, warmed by brief fires kindled from roots or wolf fat or caribou marrow.

On Christmas Day he eats his dinner alone—roast caribou thigh, doughnuts, pudding, cakes he has baked himself, and pie made from low-bush cranberries. Then he turns on the Canadian Broadcasting Corporation's famous program, *The Northern Messenger*. Over the ether from Winnipeg, a thousand miles to the south, crackle the brief messages sent out by relatives to men and women in the north, read in flat, unemotional voices by two alternating announcers. The program is heard every Friday night as well as on Christmas Day. The entire north listens in, for it is one of the great bonds that unite the country, a giant party line with ten thousand eavesdroppers. "I've gone through storms and blizzards to get back in time to hear the *Messenger*," Gus d'Aoust told me.

But during the previous winter Gus's radio hadn't worked. For seven months he lived alone, entirely out of touch with the world, without hearing or seeing a single human soul, his only company the five woolly pups he'd raised in a litter. Toward February he ran out of dog feed, for the caribou had not come in quantity. He needs sixty carcasses to keep him going until April, the end of the trapping season, and this winter he'd harvested only thirty-five. With his supplies failing, he headed for Fort Reliance, the wind blowing and the snow whipping around him. White horizon vanished into white sky, and white lake merged with white tundra, so that the whole world seemed all of a piece as if viewed through a dirty milk bottle.

Gus ran out of tobacco, so he smoked his tea. Then he ran out of tea and finally out of food. After six hungry days he looked back at the five half-grown pups he'd raised in his cabin. They were floundering along behind the team in the deep snow, yelping cheerfully. Gus killed them one by one, crying to himself as he did so, fed part to the grown dogs and boiled the ribs for himself. Twenty-six days after he left his cabin he reached Reliance.

He had brought fourteen hundred dollars' worth of fur with him. With one thousand dollars he purchased his next winter's grubstake. The remainder supported him through the summer, and now he was broke again. Gus was looking at Eaton's catalogue when I visited him.

"The women are letting us down," he said, shaking his head. "Not even a wolf trimming, by gosh. It's all this here mouton—this sheared sheep." One year Gus had brought nine thousand dollars' worth of furs out of the Barrens, but he's never done so well again. Now he hasn't the funds to do anything or go anywhere except back to his cabin.

"Don't want to go out anyway." Gus grinned. "I'm scared stiff of the Outside right now. It's ten years since I been out, and I only been to Yellowknife once in the past seven. This is the good life out here. I only wish I could live a hundred and fifty more years so's I could enjoy it."

His eyes lit up as he began to reminisce about the tundra and the future. Surely in the winter to come he would make his stake.

"We're going to get her this year," he said with the heady optimism of his kind. "Yes, sir, we'll make 'er this year. That's why we're going back."

And when he talked, there was no doubt at all that this was the only life that Gus d'Aoust knew or cared about.

The following day, with the skies clear again, we were flying over Gus d'Aoust's country toward the Thelon Game Sanctuary.

Every desert has its oasis, and the deep valley of the Thelon River is the oasis of the Barrens. Out of the harsh, boulder-strewn tundra with its dry brown grasses and glacial rubble, a deep wooded valley loomed up to greet us. Here two rivers, the Thelon and the Hanbury, meet, and here are fat clumps of spruce, wide, grassy meadows, and green copses of willows, all growing on the bottom of an ancient lake.

Here are sand dunes and beaches, white as Waikiki, and here the glossy muskox comes to graze and grow fat on the edges of the round blue lakes. Here in this northern oasis, ironically enough, John Hornby died by inches of starvation. The caribou hadn't come that winter. With him died two young Englishmen whom he had persuaded to come with him into the tundra. The day-by-day diary of one of them, Edgar Christian, who was the last to die, kept almost to the moment of his death, is perhaps the most graphic and detailed description extant of the final stages of starvation. The graves of the three men can be seen along the riverbank, but few men have seen them, for few men, white or native, have entered the Thelon Game Sanctuary.

This great remote preserve has the toughest restrictive laws in the world. No one is allowed within its fifteen thousand square miles without a permit, and permits are next to impossible to obtain. Yet it takes only four police —two at Reliance and two at Baker Lake on the other end of the sanctuary—to guard it from interlopers.

Since 1926, when the sanctuary was established, until very recently, hardly a soul ventured into the Thelon country. Lately the door has opened a crack and a few scientific parties have gained access. For a scientist, a visit to the Thelon is a mouth-watering experience, because the oasis is a scientific oddity. Nowhere else in the world do tundra and tree line merge as they do here. In the Thelon, robins nest alongside Lapland longspurs, and marten and wolverine mingle with muskox, bear, and caribou. Fish lie thickly in the waters. While I was in the Thelon a Harvard scientist caught a two-foot pike using a tomato-can lid as a spoon and a bent nail as a hook. He used no bait.

The Beaver slipped down into a broad valley where the

river widens into marshes. Here, at a point called Grassy Island, we landed. This is the focal point on which the Thelon country's muskox herds are centered and here eight U.S. scientists were camped. They were trying to capture some of the calves alive, a feat never before attempted.

Of all northern creatures, the muskox is the most mysterious. It has been said that its clinical record wouldn't fill three pages. It seems to be part sheep (it has wool, a rudimentary tail, a hairy muzzle, and sheeplike teeth and intestines), and part cow (it thrusts out its tongue to hook grass tufts and has bovine bones). Actually it is neither. It has few living relatives, going back directly to the Pleistocene age. It is, in short, a leftover from a forgotten era.

Where does it live? What are its traveling habits? When are the young born? How many of them reach maturity? Are they on the increase? Why does the muskox inhabit certain islands, like Ellesmere and Melville, and shun others, like Baffin? These are puzzles that still perplex the scientist. What *is* known is that the muskox is one of the world's hardiest animals. It withstands any temperature and subsists easily on dwarf willows and small grasses, which it reaches by pawing away the snow. It weighs around six hundred pounds, and its meat is so much like beef that the muskox today is almost extinct. Whalers slaughtered the animals by the thousand in the second half of the nineteenth century. There may have been a million animals roaming the tundra in 1800. Now the number runs between five and six thousand. Since 1917 the muskox has been protected by law. No one may shoot it.

On the slopes of the Thelon above Grassy Island, in the shelter of a thick stand of spruce trees, we found John Teal, the big, square-jawed anthropologist from Vermont who, with a party of scientists, was trying to capture eight muskox calves.

Teal has spent years tramping around the north and, as an anthropologist, interested in both agriculture and the Arctic, has some intriguing theories about both. He believes that our present-day agriculture is essentially a tropical one, but needn't be. The ancestors of sheep, goats, horses, and cows all came from India, Malaya, and the Near East, and their descendants have never fully adapted themselves to northern conditions. Thus we must create an artificial tropics for them with heat, barns, and feed.

"Why," Teal asked me, "shouldn't we try to domesticate the native animals—such as the reindeer and the muskox? Why shouldn't we turn the ptarmigan into a northern chicken? There are as many as twenty-six varieties or sub-species of the willow ptarmigan in northern Ontario alone. Plant life isn't my department, but the wild grasses and grains that grow in the north are essentially the same as those that the Indians used farther south, and I see no real reason why, eventually, we couldn't domesticate them, too."

Now here he was with his party, ruefully examining the wreckage left by the previous night's storm, which we had seen on the horizon before turning back to Reliance. The rain had come down in blinding sheets, soaking food, tents, clothing, everything—and it was all laid out now, drying in the sun.

Teal told me that he'd come to realize that the only way to find out anything about the muskox was to rear it in captivity where it could be studied. Muskox calves had been studied once before, but the results of that study vanished, and thereby hangs a curious tale. In the days of the Hoover administration the U.S. government was petitioned by Alaska to bring in some muskoxen for study at the University of Alaska. The animals were captured in

Greenland by the only method then known: shooting all the adults and rounding up the calves. The young animals were shipped to Norway, thence to Hackensack, New Jersey, by boat, by train to Seattle, by boat to Anchorage, Alaska, and by train to Fairbanks. Despite this arduous journey the calves survived and were studied for seven or eight years, and even bred successfully. The administration in Washington changed to Democratic, and the muskox program had been launched under Hoover. Teal claimed the Democrats in Alaska saw the Republican muskoxen as dangerous mankillers. At any rate they were all banished to Nunivak Island in the Arctic. A long report was sent to Washington on the results of the study, but Teal has never been able to find it, nor is there any record of it in Fairbanks. The man who wrote it is dead, and our knowledge of the animals' habits is still incomplete.

This explains why Teal and his associates were running wildly about the tundra chasing the unknown animal, whose milk is sweet and nutritious, whose meat is considered finer than beef, and whose wool is as soft as cashmere.

"I started out planning to bring in some middle-aged scientists," Teal told me, "but luckily I settled on younger men, who can run. These muskox don't look like much, but I tell you they skim up these hills like antelope."

Teal and his party had decided the only way to capture the muskox calves alive was to separate the bulls from the herd, drive the animals into the rivers and lakes, chase them in canoes, and capture them in the water. They had already done some fierce paddling without much success, and now the muskoxen had drifted out of the valley and vanished into the tundra. Teal asked Harry Taylor to go off with him to try to find the herd by plane and, if possible, round them up and drive them back toward the river again.

Off they went, scanning the tundra in search of the shaggy animals who, at some distant date, may form one of the great resources of the frozen wasteland above the tree line. The plane was away for two hours and Teal returned empty-handed. He got no muskoxen that day, but Harry Taylor returned a week later, rounded up a herd, and the scientists captured three calves.

We left them on the bank, a little knot of men standing around their equipment, still drying out in the sun. The dark gash of the great sanctuary slashed across the rolling tundra. As we headed back again across the Barrens toward civilization, the muskoxen suddenly appeared below us, black as night, glossy as newly shined shoes, mysterious as ever with their sheep's horns and bull's faces, running like deer across the brown dry land.

And here, almost in its geographical center, I had my last view of the north before returning to the land of traffic lights and parking meters. We were twelve hundred air miles from the tip of Labrador, and twelve hundred air miles from the Alaskan border. The end of steel lay five hundred miles to the south, the Arctic islands five hundred miles to the north. It is a good place to leave the north, with the tundra stretching out on all sides, with the caribou picking their way restlessly toward the trees over the pink rocks and apple-green lichens, with the muskoxen crowding together on the lake's margin, with the green Thelon Valley on one horizon and the gray surface of Great Slave Lake just over the other, with summer at its end and the fog of a new winter already rising from the waters.

If the north has a soul, it is here in this empty land which, harsh though it is, has a beauty that no man who has not lived there a lifetime can really understand. But an old Dogrib Indian put it into words one day when talking with an Oblate priest. There is more than one version of this story, but I like best that quoted by P. G. Downes in his eloquent book about the tundra, *Sleeping Island*.

"Tell me, Father," the Indian asked, "what is the white man's heaven?"

"It is the most beautiful place in the world," the priest replied.

Then the Indian made his memorable reply:

"Tell me, Father, is it like the land of the little trees when the ice has left the lake? Are the great muskoxen there? Are the hills covered with flowers? There, will I see the caribou everywhere I look? Are the lakes blue with the sky of summer? Is every net full of great, fat white-fish? Is there room for me in this land, like our land, the Barrens? Can I camp anywhere and not find that someone else has camped? Can I feel the wind and be like the wind? Father, if your Heaven is not like all these, leave me alone in my land, the land of little sticks."

Postscript

How transitory is northern life! Nothing is permanent. Communities spring up, flourish, and die, all in the space of a generation. Babies are born, grow into childhood, and are trundled off to the south, without a home town to go back to. Port Radium, the mine that produced uranium for the early years of the nuclear age, is worked out. Even the name has vanished; it's now known as Echo Bay. The community of Pine Point, whose birth I recorded in this book, is a ghost town. The railway and the road that I predicted were both built. Production got under way in 1965. Pine Point became the largest open-pit lead-zinc mine in the world. The company described it accurately as a "twenty-year mine." They were out by only a year; it closed in 1986 and the population scattered. Two thousand people once lived in Pine Point; now fewer than a dozen rattle around in another of the north's instant communities.

Yellowknife, on the other hand, has grown and prospered. It has replaced Fort Smith as the territorial capital. And with the price of gold hovering around four hundred dollars an ounce, the two biggest mines – Giant and Con – have found it profitable to reprocess the old tailings, sifting through gravel and slag once thought worthless.

Aklavik, which was supposed to sink into the mud and silt of the Mackenzie Delta, has done no such thing, confounding everybody by growing to a population of more than seven hundred and sixty. Muskrat pelts are fetching more than four dollars apiece as I write this. Tuktoyaktuk has benefited from the oil drilling in the Beaufort Sea; almost a thousand people now inhabit the slender strip that juts out into the Arctic Ocean. And Inuvik, which didn't exist when I first visited the delta, has become a thriving community of three thousand.

It's significant that the tugs that ply the Mackenzie River are now owned by natives. In 1985, the Northern Transportation Company was privatized and sold to the Inuvialuit Development Corporation. And the reindeer herd – there is only one today – was privatized as well. It, too, is owned by a native, William Nasagaluat.

Muskoxen still scamper across the tundra, protected in the inaccessible Thelon Game Sanctuary. The progeny of those that were captured by John Teal and his comrades are to be seen at the campus of the University of Alaska. There they form the nucleus of a small but thriving industry. Their incredibly soft wool – the lightest and the warmest of any – known as quivit, fetches high prices in the form of scarves and vests.

John Teal is dead. So is Fred Carpenter, whom I described as the richest native in the delta. But his descendants are all thriving and doing well. (One is a doctor on Vancouver Island.) Back in the 1960s his youngest daughter, Mary, appeared twice on my television program and became a member of our extended family. She married, raised a family, graduated from university, taught in the inner-city schools of New Jersey and also in Tuktoyaktuk. At this writing she's completing a course in native journalism at the University of Western Ontario and writing a book about her life in the north.

Thus the wheel comes full circle. The little child who romped on the deck of her father's boat while I scribbled away in my notebook is about to launch into her own version of life in the north. What a remarkable book this could be – the first written account by an Inuit woman describing the clash of cultures at the top of the world!

It will, of course, be a far different book from this, and, I suspect, a darker one. Mary Carpenter sees her world from the far side of the looking glass; I saw it from another perspective – the perspective of a stranger, a young traveller moving wide-eyed through an exotic and often exciting realm that to most of us in the south continues to appear as haunting and as mysterious as the jungles of Borneo or the shifting sands of the Kalahari.

INDEX